EurographicSeminars

Tutorials and Perspectives in Computer Graphics

Edited by G. Enderle and D. A. Duce

Methodology of Window Management

Proceedings of an Alvey Workshop at Cosener's House,
Abingdon, UK, April 1985

Edited by
F.R.A. Hopgood D.A. Duce
E.V.C. Fielding K. Robinson
A.S. Williams

With 41 Figures

Springer-Verlag
Berlin Heidelberg New York Tokyo

Eurographic Seminars
Edited by G. Enderle and D. A. Duce
for EUROGRAPHICS –
The European Association for Computer Graphics
P.O. Box 16
CH-1288 Aire-la-Ville

Editors
F. Robert A. Hopgood
David A. Duce
Elizabeth V. C. Fielding
Ken Robinson
Antony S. Williams

Science and Engineering Research Council
Rutherford Appleton Laboratory
Informatics Division
Chilton, Didcot, Oxon, OX11 OQX
United Kingdom

ISBN-13: 978-3-642-70921-0   e-ISBN-13: 978-3-642-70919-7
DOI: 10.1007/978-3-642-70919-7

© 1986 EUROGRAPHICS The European Association for Computer Graphics,
Softcover reprint of the hardcover 1st edition 1986
P.O. Box 16, CH-1288 Aire-la-Ville

Printing: Beltz Offsetdruck, Hemsbach/Bergstr. Bookbinding: J. Schäffer OHG, Grünstadt.
2145/3145-543210

Preface

This volume is a record of the Workshop on Window Management held at the Rutherford Appleton Laboratory's Cosener's House between 29 April and 1 May 1985. The main impetus for the Workshop came from the Alvey Programme's Man-Machine Interface Director who was concerned at the lack of a formal definition of window management and the lack of focus for research activities in this area. Window Management *per se* is not the complete problem in understanding interaction. However, the appearance of bitmap displays from a variety of vendors enabling an operator to work simultaneously with a number of applications on a single display has focussed attention on what the overall architecture for such a system should be and also on what the interfaces to both the application and operator should be.

The format of the Workshop was to spend the first day with presentations from a number of invited speakers. The aim was to get the participants aware of the current state of the art and to highlight the main outstanding issues. The second day consisted of the Workshop participants splitting into three groups and discussing specific issues in depth. Plenary sessions helped to keep the individual groups working on similar lines. The third day concentrated on the individual groups presenting their results and interacting with the other groups to identify main areas of consensus and also a framework for future work.

Part I of this volume gives the background to the Workshop, its scope and goals.

Part II consists of position papers, the invited presentations and an edited version of the discussion following each. The set of speakers covers a significant part of the expertise currently available. This section provided a useful summary of the state-of-the-art for the Workshop and highlighted the issues.

Each participant was asked to identify his major areas of concern prior to the Workshop. These have been condensed and integrated to give a view of the problems prior to the Workshop. Lists of issues were also generated from these contributions and the invited presentations. These formed an initial basis for the Working Group discussions reported in the next part.

Part III concentrates on the work carried out in the Working Groups with particular attention focussed on the Working Group conclusions and questions requiring further study.

Part IV presents the main conclusions of the Workshop and includes an Open List of questions requiring further study. This list indicates the current limits to the understanding achieved at the Workshop. As always, more questions were raised than conclusions reached. This part also includes a bibliography of the area and a glossary of terms used in the book.

The discussion sessions have been heavily edited. The Editors hope that no remarks have been attributed to individuals incorrectly. Copies of the typescript were sent to all participants for comment prior to publication.

The contents of this volume should not be considered as definitive conclusions but as a contribution to the study of methodology in human-computer interaction particularly with respect to single user workstations.

This book should be of interest to anybody with an interest in graphics and interaction in general. Many of the issues discussed have a more general applicability than the particular area under discussion. However, the primary audience is those directly involved in the area of the human factors and design of systems on high-powered single user workstations.

Acknowledgements

The major acknowledgement must be to the cumulative effort of the participants who contributed time and energy to achieve what has been recorded here.

The Organizing Committee was largely responsible for the work prior to the Workshop. Special thanks must be given to the individuals who gave their time.

The main funding source for the Workshop was the Alvey MMI Director who ensured that the right mix of individuals could attend. We are also indebted to a number of organizations who provided significant financial help including Rutherford Appleton Laboratory, Eurographics, SUN Microsystems, Microsoft Corporation and Graphic Software Systems.

The secretariat came from Rutherford Appleton Laboratory's Informatics Division. It worked long hours both during and after the Workshop to ensure an accurate transcript of the workshop in the minimum time. Carol Barnes, Janice Gore and Rita Hollington typed many thousands of keystrokes in the process. Special thanks must be paid to David Duce who organized the secretariat in his quiet and efficient style coping with most catastrophes in his stride; and to Carol Barnes and Janice Gore who worked very long hours typing the drafts of this book.

The Workshop was held at the Cosener's House in Abingdon. Particular thanks are due to the staff there for making us most welcome and coping with our excessive demands in terms of alterations to meal times and accommodation for six computers and a photocopier, in addition to the participants.

Chapter 12 first appeared in the proceedings of the 1985 EUUG Conference in Paris. It is reproduced here by kind permission of the European Unix Systems User Group. Figures 4.1 to 4.7 are reproduced by kind permission of Xerox Corporation.

Unix^{TM} is a trademark of AT&T Bell Laboratories. Ada® is a registered trademark of the U.S. Government (Ada Joint Program Office).

List of Participants

Organizing Committee

Bob Hopgood	Rutherford Appleton Laboratory
William Newman	Independent Consultant
Austin Tate	University of Edinburgh
George Coulouris	Queen Mary College, London
Ken Robinson	Rutherford Appleton Laboratory
Tony Williams	Rutherford Appleton Laboratory

Participants

David Barnes	University of Kent
Peter Bono	Graphic Software Systems
John Butler	Microsoft Corporation
Steve Cook	Queen Mary College, London
Martin Cooper	British Telecom Research Laboratories
Gordon Dougan	Office Workstations Ltd
Arthur Foster	GEC Research Laboratories
James Gosling	SUN Microsystems Inc
Paul ten Hagen	CWI, Amsterdam
Alistair Kilgour	University of Glasgow
Brad Myers	University of Toronto
Colin Prosser	International Computers Ltd
David Rosenthal	Carnegie-Mellon University
David Small	High Level Hardware Ltd
Dominic Sweetman	Whitechapel Computer Works Ltd
Warren Teitelman	SUN Microsystems Inc
Harold Thimbleby	University of York
Mike Underwood	Alvey MMI Directorate
Neil Wiseman	University of Cambridge

Secretariat

David Duce

Note Takers	Secretaries
Tony Cox	Carol Barnes
David Duce	Janice Gore
Liz Fielding	Rita Hollington
Simon Frost	
Duncan Gibson	
Janet Haswell	
Janet Malone	
Mark Martin	
Martin Prime	
Trudy Watson	

Table of Contents

1   Introduction

1.1 BACKGROUND

The Workshop arose from a concern that there was a lack of a definition of window management and a lack of focus for research activities in this area in the UK. The main impetus for the Workshop came from the UK Alvey Directorate's Man-Machine Interface Director. To set the Workshop in context it is appropriate to give a brief overview of the UK Alvey Programme, its origins, aims and current status.

The Alvey Programme grew out of a report produced by a government committee under the chairmanship of John Alvey. The report, entitled 'A Programme for Advanced Information Technology', was published in 1982 [4]. The Alvey Programme can be seen as the UK response to the challenge of the Japanese Fifth Generation initiatives and as a recognition on the part of UK government of the need to invest in Information Technology (IT). The Alvey Report called for support for Information Technology in four main technology areas: Very Large Scale Integration (VLSI), Software Engineering (SE), Intelligent Knowledge Based Systems (IKBS) and Man-Machine Interface (MMI).

The government set up an Alvey Directorate in June 1983 to implement the recommendations of the Report, under the leadership of Brian Oakley. Directors have been appointed for each of the four enabling technology areas and strategy statements have been published for each. A key aspect of the Alvey Programme is that it is a collaborative programme of pre-competitive research. Research projects are carried out by consortia normally involving at least two industrial partners; academic and government research laboratories are included in many of the projects.

Exploitation of research is also a key concern.

Funding for the programme is around £350M over five years. Such funding comes through three government agencies, the Science and Engineering Research Council, the Department of Trade and Industry and the Ministry of Defence; industry itself is expected to contribute 50% of their costs in collaborative projects.

The MMI sector of the Alvey Programme is headed by the MMI Director, Chris Barrow.

The Alvey MMI strategy was published in August 1984 [2]. The MMI programme recognizes the need for research in the MMI area if UK products are to remain competitive in the IT market place. The feeling is that the UK has lost ground in the MMI area over the last decade and that a serious effort is needed to restore the UK position. MMI is seen as playing a vital role in making products from other technology areas usable.

The objectives of the MMI programme are twofold:

(1)   to raise the level of UK user interface design, in terms of innovation and design methodology, so that industry can compete effectively in world markets;

(2)   to improve UK capabilities in pattern analysis, to make possible the use of advanced speech and image techniques in the user interface.

The user interface design objective is being addressed through a broadly-based programme of research in the three closely related areas of user interface design, human factors and design methodology. New techniques for using new workstation architectures and input devices are a component of these activities. Thus there is a lot of interest in using high performance workstations and window management systems. Single user systems are used extensively by the other parts of the Alvey Programme and are a major part of the infrastructure provided through Alvey.

The need for this workshop arose from the recognition that window managers are still at a relatively immature stage and different window managers take very different approaches. Also there appeared to be little consensus on window manager design and no forum in the UK for the discussion of the issues.

Further details of the Alvey Programme are contained in the initial Annual Report [3].

1.2 GOALS OF THE WORKSHOP

The Alvey MMI Director requested that the workshop should address the following requirements.

(1)   Define what should be done in the *short term* particularly to meet the infrastructure needs of researchers in the Alvey Programme. The Alvey Programme has made a substantial investment in Unix systems, and hence window managers under Unix systems need to be addressed.

(2)   Define what needs to be done in the *long term*; it was thought that this might well have implications for the hardware architectures of future workstations, for instance.

(3)   Look at *standardization* issues. Is it timely to embark upon standardization activities, and if so what should be the scope of such activities? Should activities be confined to the UK or take place in a broader arena?

The specific goals of the Workshop were to:

(1)   reach a better understanding of the issues in window managers;

(2)   establish where, if anywhere, there is a consensus;

(3)   identify significant topics for further research;

(4)   produce a written record of the proceedings.

1.3 ORGANIZATION

The Alvey MMI Director asked Bob Hopgood of the UK Science and Engineering Research Council's Rutherford Appleton Laboratory (RAL) to organize the Workshop. The Organizing Committee for the Workshop was:

Bob Hopgood   (Rutherford Appleton Laboratory)
William Newman   (Alvey Software Engineering)
Austin Tate   (Alvey Intelligent Knowledge Based Systems)
George Coulouris (Alvey Man Machine Interface)
Ken Robinson   (Rutherford Appleton Laboratory)
Tony Williams   (Rutherford Appleton Laboratory)

Attendance at the Workshop was by invitation only. At an early stage in planning the Workshop it was realized that there was insufficiently broad experience in the UK of actually building window managers and hence it was felt to be essential to invite some participants from the USA. The participants reflected a wide range of interests, including academic, government and industrial backgrounds. Prior to the Workshop, participants had been told that the aims of the Workshop were to:

(1)   identify issues in the design of the *user interface*, such as interaction styles, methodology needed, target populations and so on;

(2)   identify requirements and problems in the *programming interface*, such as the sharing of tasks between the window manager and the application program, levels of functionality to ensure portability of applications, etc;

(3)   identify constraints and requirements of the underlying *hardware*, including the division of functionality between hardware and software;

(4)   define, as far as possible, requirements for a *standard window manager*, suitable for use on a range of equipment, both to provide a vehicle for research work and also to provide target software for manufacturers to supply and support.

Participants were asked to provide a short (1 page) paper describing their interests, background and the issues in window management that needed to be tackled.

From these papers, lists of issues in the user interface, program interface and architecture areas were extracted and circulated prior to the meeting (see Chapter 14 for more details). Participants also received copies of background material, references [7, 13, 15-17, 19, 20, 34, 39, 42, 44, 47, 51, 58, 64-67] from the bibliography. Thus participants came to the Workshop with at least this background in common.

1.4 STRUCTURE OF THE WORKSHOP

The structure of the Workshop followed the same pattern as the historic workshops at Seillac, France, on Methodology of Computer Graphics [25] and Methodology of Interaction [26]. A number of the participants had in fact been involved in these workshops.

The first day was given over to invited presentations from seven speakers. These were intended to set the scene, both in terms of historical perspective and current research activities.

After the invited presentations, the Workshop split into three Working Groups, initially focussing on the Application Program Interface (API), User Interface (UI) and Architecture of Window Managers respectively. The Working Groups were intended to meet in parallel sessions during the second day, with plenary sessions at the middle and end of the day for reporting back. It was envisaged that some regrouping and redirection might be necessary in the light of progress made and indeed, as recorded in Part III of this book, this turned out to be the case. The format for discussing issues in the Working Groups derives from work in the standards area surrounding GKS and other graphics standards.

The third day was set aside for preparation of Working Group reports and formulation of conclusions. It is in the nature of a workshop that it is unwise to make too rigid plans in advance for the end of the workshop and in the event further Working Groups were formed which met on the final day and there was a lengthy plenary session to discuss the progress made and formulate conclusions. The issues lists presented in section 14.5 formed the basis for the Working Group discussions.

The invited presentations form Chapters 2-8 of this book and all but Chapters 3 and 5 were produced from transcripts of the presentations. Presenters were given the opportunity to correct these before publication. Chapters 9 to 13 are papers submitted by participants which were not actually presented, but were circulated as additional background material. Colin Prosser had originally intended to present the paper in Chapter 10, but at the last minute decided instead to address the issue of introducing window managers to Unix systems, because he felt that the issues raised in Chapter 10 would be better addressed by the Working Groups. His actual presentation forms Chapter 2 of this book. It is worth noting that although the paper is written with Unix operating systems in mind, the issues raised apply much more generally than to Unix systems alone, and turned out to be topics around which a lot of discussion centred.

1.5 DEMONSTRATIONS

Throughout the Workshop SUN, PERQ and Whitechapel MG-1 systems were available for participants to explore their respective window managers. The SUN system ran both SunWindows and Andrew; the PERQ ran the PNX window manager, while the Whitechapel ran their new window manager.

1.6 TERMINOLOGY

A number of terms are used in different ways by different authors and speakers in this volume. For example, the term *user* can mean the *applications programmer* or it can mean the *workstation operator*.

Terminology within window managers is also a major problem in that each system seems to have its own terminology at present. Towards the end of the Workshop a Task Group was set up to look, *inter alia*, at this issue.

In this volume, the authors' and speakers' own terminology has been used, no attempt has been made to incorporate a consistent terminology. It was felt that since terminology was an issue at the Workshop it would have been entirely wrong to factor in a *post hoc* rationalization of terminology.

A glossary of the more important terms is presented in Chapter 25.

Part II

2 Introducing Windows to Unix: User Expectations

Colin Prosser

2.1 INTRODUCTION

This talk is aimed at giving a general overview of the main issues to do with window managers without going into details. My position paper (see Chapter 10) raises many other issues, but my view was that these are probably best discussed in the Working Groups.

The focus is on introducing windows to Unix environments because of the interest of the Alvey Programme in the problem of window managers under Unix systems. Considering windowing in Unix systems does, however, force a wider context on windowing issues, and other or future operating systems should not be forgotten.

2.2 USER EXPECTATIONS

When introducing windows to Unix environments we are trying to provide the user with good facilities. What will the user expect? Considering windowing in Unix systems from this point of view, five key expectations may be discerned:

(1) **Compatibility.**

The benefits of the windowing system should apply to existing (not just new) applications.

The windowing system must provide an environment in which existing applications and commands continue to work unchanged. But it must do more than just that; it must also provide the means for enhancing those programs. There seem to be two methods of doing this. One way is through a better shell facility where a graphical interface provides general-purpose text-oriented command manipulation. Another way is to take an existing command or application and build a specialized graphical interface around it. The former approach is being investigated at RAL. The latter approach has been applied successfully, for example, by Office Workstations Limited who have produced a graphically oriented higher level debugger (called 'hld') based around 'sdb' running on PNX.

(2)   **Intercommunication.**

Windows enable several separate contexts to be presented in one overall context. It seems natural to allow operations to apply across the separate contexts as well as within contexts.

This leads to the idea of being able to select from the output of an application running in one window and to supply this as input to an application running in another window. This concept is often called *cut and paste* between windows. A simple example might be to run 'ls' to obtain a directory listing in one window and to use this output to provide a filename as input to a program running in a different window. On systems known to the author, this sort of operation can only be applied to limited kinds of objects and frequently only to text.

(3)   **Portability.**

There is an expectation of software portability among Unix systems. Similar considerations apply to applications using windowing facilities.

How are we to achieve portability? We have to look at the problem in terms of variants of the same system as well as in terms of quite different systems. The SPY editor (see section 3.3.1) was quite difficult to port to different Unix systems. Why? What makes it easy, generally, to port things between versions of Unix systems? A standard programming interface is important in resolving this difficulty. We must tackle the issue of standards for windowing systems. Can we take GKS [28] as a basis for building or should we start again? There will be problems if we try to address too large a goal - look at CORE [24]. So should we go for a minimal system? These are some of the alternatives to be considered.

(4)   **Distributed Systems.**

With networks of (possibly mixed) systems, use of windowing systems should apply elegantly network-wide.

With networks, such as the Newcastle Connection on PERQs, we are confronted with a whole new set of problems. For example, PERQ PNX uses a window special file to associate a name in the filestore with a window, and the Newcastle Connection allows transparent access over the network. However, if you try to archive a window special file on a PERQ using a VAX archiver over the network, it may not work quite as expected if the VAX archiving system does not have any knowledge of that type of special file. We must account for applications not knowing about windows. As another example, what should happen if I perform a remote login from a PERQ to a SUN? What does it mean? What window system applies to that login session: the one on the PERQ or the one on the SUN? Issues such as these have yet to be tackled.

(5)   **Graphical Toolkit.**

The programmer needs tools to assist effective exploitation of windowing capabilities, both to create new applications and to modify existing software. The notion of tools includes examples to follow which provide guidelines for good design.

What graphical primitives should the system support in libraries and as system calls to provide a graphical toolkit? To give an idea of the richness of the toolkit I am contemplating, I would consider that most existing windowing packages for Unix systems, including PERQ PNX, are, at present, relatively bare of tools. That is not to say that high quality applications cannot be built with today's windowing systems. However, experience shows that it can take considerable effort. It would be difficult for the unskilled user to write, for example, SPY without any assistance. What is a graphical toolkit and what support is required from the operating system? What guidelines can we provide to encourage good design?

2.3 DISCUSSION

Chairman - Bob Hopgood

Rosenthal: On point (2), there are two systems on the SUN next door that allow this: SunWindows and Andrew.

Prosser: I would be interested to see what you have done.

Hopgood: They should be more general than that. What does it mean to pass a picture to a text processing program?

Williams: Or worse still, spreadsheets with complete expressions. Are we moving the bitmap or the representation of the expressions?

Hopgood: There is a whole problem in specifying what you are passing.

Prosser: We could pass structured display files with type tags, but we must extend the model of window management defined in Tony Williams' paper (see Chapter 3) as it does not cope with it at the moment.

Hopgood: Was your reference to GKS in point (3) meant to be provocative?

Prosser: If you like. GKS just does not address window management problems.

Rosenthal: On point (4), we have done this on our system. It allows uniform access to all windows on our 4.2. We have even tried running it over SNA.

Prosser: You have assumed an application program interface and a network standard that the other system must support also. Can we agree on it? There are many different solutions. Yours is one, but is it for everyone? There are many people who would prefer a solution within an ISO standards context.

Rosenthal: Anything with an 8-bit byte stream is enough.

Teitelman: Also missing from the list is the graceful migration between applications written for displays with varying resolutions and from colour to black and white. That is an issue: device independence.

Myers: I am disturbed that there is no one here to represent other than the general purpose window manager interface we all know, namely a specific interface like the Macintosh. Its user interface is set.

Teitelman: A general purpose window manager should allow you to emulate the Macintosh, or have good reason why not.

Prosser: You still land up with conflicts for somebody who has a context editor for his work, Macintosh-style, and some other applications bought in from different companies using a different user interface.

Rosenthal: The big Macintosh book lists all the routines you can call and tells you what they will look like on the screen. It is difficult to see how you can take these routines and produce a different interface. You could provide a virtual Macintosh with a window or some other system but to provide the set of routines to do something different would be difficult.

            Another issue is that standards take too long to produce. A *de facto* standard window manager which is freely distributed and widely used may be the only way to achieve consensus on the interfaces and capabilities of window managers.

Bono: I also do not see any user expectations about performance issues in the list. When building a product there must be performance requirements. Is there nothing we can say, or do people have an implicit model: "as fast as possible"? We should talk a little about performance.

Williams: Some feedback techniques do not work if the window manager's performance is too slow. Some machines do not move bits fast enough.

Bono: There are also size performance issues, as on small machines. There are tradeoffs between precalculation for a faster user interface versus keeping raw data. There is a lot of practical experience that needs to be documented.

Prosser: Yes, I think performance is important to get slick user interfaces, but we cannot enforce them on everyone. There are cost tradeoffs when building a machine. Some people can live with the degraded performance sometimes and therefore you may tailor your user interface in that direction.

Bono: You are looking for a single answer. There may not be one. It is an issue. There is lots of experience in this room and we may be able to categorize things.

Myers: There are representatives of 60% of the world's window managers here and they have virtually identical appearance. Their differences are listable. Is this because they are based on two systems from PARC or because there are, say, only seven ways to write a window manager?

Hopgood: They all look different to me, although I agree they all have square things on the screen!

Rosenthal: They are all the same. The difference in application programming level between a tiling and an overlapping window manager is very small.

3   A Comparison of Some Window Managers

Tony Williams

ABSTRACT

An architectural model of a window manager is presented. Some commercially available window managers are compared in relation to this model. Specific attention is given to the window managers supplied by SUN, APOLLO, and ICL (PERQ PNX).

3.1 INTRODUCTION

The Science and Engineering Research Council has adopted a coordinated plan to ensure that the UK academic community makes the best use of the resources available to it, especially its limited manpower. The Council has therefore decided on a policy of creating a common hardware and software base to act as a nucleus for future developments in single user workstation practice. Initially, the common software base is Pascal and Fortran-77, running under a Unix operating system, and using the GKS graphics package. The common hardware base consists of ICL PERQ and SUN workstations, linked locally by Cambridge Ring or Ethernet, and nationally by an X25 wide area network. The Common Base group at RAL is responsible for coordination, support, and software development for the Common Base Policy.

This paper was prepared for the Alvey-sponsored Workshop on window management. It is deliberately contentious at times, with a view to instigating discussion and clarification. The information on window managers has been extracted from the suppliers' manuals, augmented by RAL experiences in using the systems. In some cases this experience is limited, and the information given here may be incorrect, and is certainly incomplete. This paper should not therefore be regarded as definitive.

Commentary on some other window managers has been added subsequent to the Workshop, derived from presentations and discussions there. These are the Whitechapel MG-1 window manager, Sapphire (PERQ Accent), and the Andrew system developed for SUN workstations at Carnegie-Mellon University's (CMU) Information Technology Centre (ITC) in collaboration with IBM.

A conceptual model of window management is presented, and some commercially available window managers compared in relation to this model. Specific attention is given to the SunWindows system, the APOLLO display manager, and the ICL PERQ PNX window manager. Specific references are not given, but a bibliography of papers of interest is included in Chapter 24.

The comparison is made in the light of two rather different goals, which, broadly speaking, characterize two classes of window manager to be found today. One function of a window manager is to provide a means by which a user can switch attention between multiple independent tasks at will. This corresponds to the *single window per session* model. The other is to provide support for complex applications which wish to use multiple display windows to support a powerful and flexible dialogue. This corresponds to the *many windows per session* model. This is typified by systems such as Smalltalk-80 or Interlisp-D. Our goal in the Common Base group is to combine these two facilities, providing the protection required to run mutually ignorant applications, while allowing for the level of integration of facilities offered by such systems as Star, both within and between applications (where achievable). The term adopted for this is the Integrated Open System.

3.2 A MODEL OF WINDOW MANAGEMENT

This model of window management is presented with the intention of identifying the architecture and components of a conceptual window manager. The model is generated partly by abstraction from some existing window managers, and partly from a personal viewpoint.

The purposes of the model are to provide a context for comparison of window managers with widely differing functionality, and to provide a *strawman* model for discussion at the Workshop.

The model is described in terms of the concepts supported by the model, the components of the model, and the architecture.

3.2.1 Concepts Supported by the Model

This section is primarily intended to define the terms used in this paper: terminology differs considerably according to subject area, for example, the terms *window* and *viewport* have quite specific meanings in the area of graphics standards, but are used differently in other areas. Along with these concepts, some issues are listed, which highlight differences between window managers, and interfaces to other components of system software.

● *Window*: a context for display and interaction; normally associated with a visibly distinct portion of the display surface. Issues are: the attributes possessed by a window; mechanisms for window creation and destruction; mechanisms for altering the attributes of a window.

● *Imaging model*: the set of graphic primitives, and the protocol for their display. Issues are: support for multiple levels, as in GKS; the degree of device independence; support for multiple graphics packages (eg GKS, GINO etc); whether the visible appearance of the image is fully defined by the imaging model.

● *Input model*: the set of input primitives and modes, and associated protocol. Issues are: asynchronous versus synchronous communication; dialogue determination; queue management; virtual device emulation (as in GKS); filtering and software generation of input events.

● *Pane*: an independently accessible part of a window, with a defined geometric relationship to the other panes of the window. (Sometimes called a subwindow.) The main issue is whether these should be supported by the window manager, or some higher layer. Confounding considerations are facilities such as allowing a separate cursor pattern for each pane, allowing different processes to request input from different panes etc.

● *Bitmap*: a component of implementation of a window; variously called a *pixrect*, or a *panel*.

● *TTY emulator*: a mechanism for character stream interaction, provided as a means of communicating with applications written for character terminals; a gateway to history.

● *Task*: an application system, which is a client of the window manager.

● *Window descriptor*: a bundle of attributes of a window.

● *Sharing*: mechanisms to enable many-to-many communication, between tasks and display, and input devices and tasks. Issues are: the degree of transparency of this sharing; and arbitration of control between user and tasks.

● *Protection*: mechanisms to restrict communication, and ensure correct behaviour of tasks with respect to the required transparency of sharing.

● *Naming*: methods of identifying entities such as client applications or windows, and communicating the identity. Both public names (cf Unix filenames) and private names (cf Unix file descriptors) are needed.

● *Mapping*: mechanisms to implement sharing and protection. Issues covered here include those related to redrawing of windows following movement, or resizing.

- *Grouping*: manipulation of a collection of objects as a single entity, such as the set of windows associated with a single task. Grouping and subwindowing might be seen as different ways of achieving the same effect.

Icons are deliberately omitted from this list. All of the systems studied which support icons do so differently in terms of visual presentation, application interface, and implementation. There does not appear to be a consensus about the conceptual function of icons, nor an adequate framework for comparison. The only common characteristic is that they are small!

3.2.2 Components of the Model

The components described here do not necessarily refer to specific software components. They are identified for purposes of exposition.

WMS   the window management service; provided via a notional software interface to client application programs.

WMI   the window manager interface: a client application which manipulates windows on behalf of the human user.

GTK   a graphics library and toolkit. This is task-dependent, and provides higher levels of interface, such as menu functions, form filling, and property sheet editing, as well as the normal functions of a graphics package such as GKS.

TTY   notional subsystem implementing TTY emulation.

PTY   channel for character stream communication between task and TTY emulation subsystem, providing a notional software interface to each side.

APP   application task; may comprise one or more processes.

Display   notional visible display surface(s).

Input Devices   notional set of physical input devices, including keyboard(s) and mice.

3.2.3 Architecture

Figure 3.1 shows the above components in schematic form, with the connections between them. The boundaries between components are intended to signify information hiding. For example, the WMS is the only part of the system which has information about the position and rank of all of the windows. Connections represent use of a service provided through a well-defined interface.

The comparison given below attempts to show how the different systems implement windows, by discussing the placement of functionality relative to the components of this model. The issues which need to be resolved to convert this model into a specification for a window manager are:

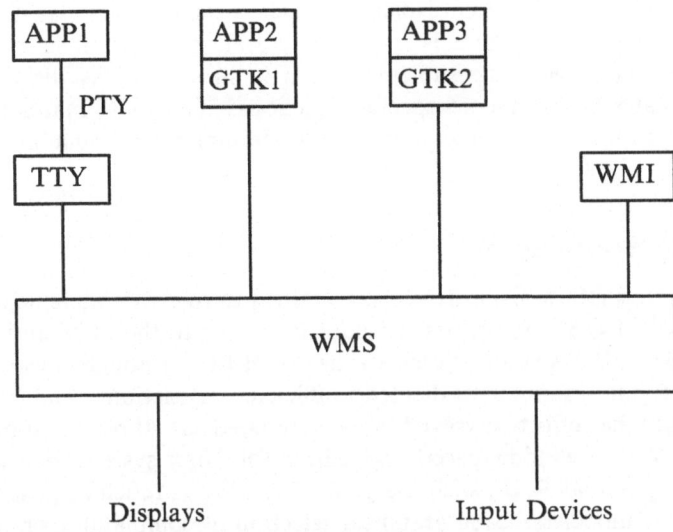

Figure 3.1 Architectural Model

- where window bitmaps are stored, or which components are responsible for generating them;

- what kind of window hierarchy and taxonomy is supported;

- how updates to window contents and layout are reflected in updates to the screen;

- how input events are handled and distributed, and how feedback is provided;

- where address space boundaries exist, communication mechanisms between components of the model, and the nature of the information communicated.

These issues need to be considered in the light of the performance implications, the configurability and extensibility of the window manager, and concerns of portability and device independence both of client applications and the window manager itself.

3.3 COMPARISON OF WINDOW MANAGERS

This section provides a comparison of some window managers, in relation to the model described above. They are compared in terms of support for the concepts outlined above, and the placement of responsibilities and services within the implementation. The segmentation of the implementation by address space boundaries is discussed, as this has effects on sharing, protection, and performance. The detailed comparison is in terms of the overall architecture, and the interface provided to application programs, but some comparative observations are made concerning the user interface. Occasional points will be noted to illustrate inconsistencies and other minor oddities of particular implementations.

Information on the APOLLO display manager is rather sparse, as it is distributed over several manuals, and there is no architectural overview. It is not possible to determine how the underlying implementation is structured, as the only available information relates to the use of specific functions. The SUN manuals provide an abundance of information at the user and programmer level, but no architectural overview was available.

3.3.1 The SPY Screen Editor

Much of the information given here was obtained during the implementation of the SPY editor on PERQ PNX, and its subsequent porting to the SUN and Whitechapel MG-1 machines. SPY was not ported to the APOLLO, although it was hoped to do so. Study of the manuals indicated sufficient restrictions and programming difficulties that the effort involved was estimated at three man-months as a minimum. SPY is a window-based text editor for Unix systems developed by the Common Base group at RAL, with the goal of making as much as possible visible to the user. SPY is modeless, using graphical selection of command operands, after the style of the Smalltalk editor, and editing commands are almost exclusively invoked using the mouse, with a mixture of fixed, pull-down, and pop-up menus. Uniform ways of cancelling actions before completion are provided, as is a single-level *undo* facility (which will also undo global changes). The keyboard is used for input of new text, but backspace, delete word, and delete line commands are supported on control keys for compatibility with the Unix terminal emulator. It supports concurrent editing of multiple files, with each shown in a subwindow. The user moves between files and performs copy and move functions on arbitrary blocks of text simply by moving the mouse appropriately, using a postfix command syntax. Unix regular expression searches and substitution are provided. All text, including filenames and search/replace patterns, is edited in the same way with the full set of commands available.

The more unusual characteristics of SPY which are of interest here relate to the questions of feedback and dynamic display. Techniques of press-feedback-release-action are used, which are by now common in window-based systems. As in Smalltalk, the range of the selection is highlighted during the draw-through action by the user. Continuous rate-controlled scrolling is supported. During scrolling and editing, SPY provides many graphical representations, dynamically updated in the inner loop of the interaction techniques. Such displays show the visible portion of the file relative to the whole, the position of the selection, the current line number, and the position of markers (as in James Gosling's Emacs). Space allocated to subwindows is reapportioned by dragging title bars, which may slide over each other, or nudge others along. Given the high speed of RasterOp provided by PERQ PNX, these techniques lead to a comfortable, fast, and effective user interface, by showing the effect of an action to the user before the action is completed.

SPY is therefore a demanding test of the ability of window managers to support highly interactive applications. Some minor points arose during the SPY development, and are worth noting:

● the ability to change window size was added to PERQ PNX after the first version of SPY was in use, and SPY was modified to respond appropriately without inordinate effort;

● when ported to the SUN and MG-1 approximately 10% of the source of SPY was window manager dependent, with the most difficult problems being related to the handling of input;

● the MG-1 window manager was not available during the porting exercise, but a software interface to the display was provided which is largely equivalent to that provided for a window;

● the performance characteristics (discussed in the comparison below) severely impact the effectiveness of some interaction techniques.

3.3.2 User Interface Considerations

Window managers affect the user interface both in the functions provided for manipulating windows, and in the constraining effect they place on applications.

All of the window managers provide functions to create, destroy, reposition and resize windows, and to adjust the depth order (ie move to top or bottom), but use differing techniques for their invocation. The APOLLO display manager provides many commands, which may be typed to a special window, or bound (by profile) to function keys or mouse button transitions. The current cursor position is used by those functions requiring coordinates. PERQ PNX and SunWindows provide pop-up menus for these functions. SunWindows creates windows in a default position and size, which is usually obscuring the window the user was last working in. PERQ PNX prompts the user for a rectangle defining the window. As an anachronism, PERQ PNX maintains a *window manager window* to which the user may type commands to invoke the functions. This is also used for error messages, and a confirmation ("type y or n") which is required when terminating the window manager. (This means that the user cannot terminate the window manager if the keyboard is broken.) Both PERQ PNX and SunWindows provide accelerators, which do not require menu selection, for the pop and move functions. In addition, PERQ PNX interprets the pop function as a push to the back if the window was previously entirely exposed. Sapphire provides several techniques for the same function: pop-up menu for novices, accelerated forms using differing mouse buttons in the title bar, and control key sequences for experts. The MG-1 uses window controls on the window borders, in the style of Macintosh, but requires the user to type a command to the shell to create a new window. The latter means that if all windows are busy, the user cannot create another, which seems to lose much of the benefit. The Andrew window manager is a tiling manager: windows do not overlap. Window position and size are initially determined by the window manager, but the user may adjust the boundaries. Windows are only created by invoking programs.

Keyboard input is directed to the window containing the cursor position on both the SUN and APOLLO, but is directed to the currently selected window on PERQ PNX, which leads to frequent errors, especially since newly created windows are not selected by default. PERQ PNX requires the user to select a window by clicking a mouse button before he can communicate with the application owning the window. Such activities as *cut-and-paste* between windows therefore require an extra click, and cannot be achieved through a dragging action. This constrains the ways in which applications can use multiple windows and provide efficient interaction techniques. When the cursor moves out of a window, mouse input is directed to the window manager until a window is again selected. The appearance is therefore asymmetric, and leads to phenomena such as *falling out* of windows, causing difficulty. The benefit is that any point on the window may be identified for functions such as move or pop, rather than only the border being usable. Sapphire and the MG-1 require the user to select a window for keyboard input, known as the *listener*. Mouse events are directed to the window containing the mouse position. Andrew allows the user to specify through a preference file whether keyboard input should follow the mouse, or require a select action.

We have seen no mouse-driven interactive programs which run within a window on the APOLLO: the demonstration programs all work by temporarily taking over the entire display. Pads (the APOLLO equivalent of a terminal window) are keyboard-driven, although the cursor position may be moved using the mouse. The cursor normally resides on a character cell, and the shape is changed to a blinking rectangle of that size shortly after the mouse stops moving. It would appear that writing an interactive program which will coexist with others is very difficult to achieve. Very recently, APOLLO have demonstrated a Dialog Manager, which provides the kind of user interface discussed here. This indicates that the problems are not insurmountable, but quantification of the effort needed is not available.

The systems studied have differing performance characteristics. SPY was developed on PERQ PNX, which has a very high speed RasterOp function, enabling smooth dragging actions. The APOLLO DN550 has equivalent performance to PERQ PNX, but other factors prevented the port. When SPY was ported to the SUN and MG-1, actions such as dragging subwindow title bars became unsuitable as the response time increased sufficiently to interfere with the user's hand-eye coordination. (It should be noted that beta-test versions of the MG-1 hardware and software were used, and the performance is expected to improve considerably with time.) Sapphire and Andrew use a low bandwidth communication path from clients to the window bitmap, and therefore dynamic feedback cannot be implemented by clients; only that supplied by the window manager itself is sufficiently fast. The performance characteristics also show in the visible speed with which menus appear, but this does not significantly degrade the interface. Andrew has some experimental mechanisms by which applications can download procedures to perform application-specific echoing, but this is at the expense of sacrificing protection.

A second point about dynamic feedback is that if redrawing is performed directly on the display bitmap, the flicker becomes very disturbing. It is preferable to assemble the picture in an off-screen bitmap, and copy it to the screen, so the user sees the updates apparently instantaneously. This phenomenon might well modify implementors' perceptions of the performance tradeoffs. An alternative is of course to double-buffer the display, and switch buffers during vertical retrace, but this entails severe difficulties in synchronizing between multiple applications.

3.3.3 Windows and Window Descriptors

The SunWindows system supports three layers: the Pixrect layer providing low level pixel manipulation functions, the Window layer providing a hierarchy of overlapping windows, and the SunTools layer, providing for the interactive creation of applications and associated windows. The SunTools layer requires that applications conform to a particular style of control structure, and supplies many of the functions of a *User Interface Management System (UIMS)*. Windows are linked in a hierarchical structure, overlapping their parent and older siblings. Windows are constrained to lie within the bounds of the screen, or the parent window in the hierarchy. Different classes of subwindow are provided, to support text, graphics, option forms, and the like. Overall, the window system provides a rich and perhaps over-complex set of functions.

The APOLLO display manager provides character stream interaction via *pads* (see below), and allows application programs temporarily to take over the display space associated with a pad to perform graphical output and input. Arbitration between competing applications is achieved through explicit acquisition and release of the display and input devices. Windows are created on command from the user, in which case a command interpreter is invoked, or on request from an application, in which case there appear to be some limitations on the functionality.

The PERQ PNX window manager provides the abstraction of a virtual display and associated input devices for each window. Applications may update window images without concern for interference with others. A separate application process performs the functions of creation, deletion, moving, ranking, and resizing windows on command from the user. When a window is created on request by the user, a command interpreter is invoked (the Unix shell), to which further commands can be given to invoke other applications. PERQ PNX provides a kind of special file, which contains the attributes of a window which will be created when an application opens the file. Facilities are provided for creating these special files. This is the only way of creating windows from application programs. A further complication arises, in that one of the stored attributes determines whether multiple opens of the same window special file each create a new window, or share the same one. Windows may be partially off-screen.

Andrew provides a non-occluded rectangular portion of the display, but the client requests for resources (eg size, number of colours) are treated as hints by the window manager. It is normal for the window manager to request that the client redraw the window contents as a result of rearranging the windows. Sapphire and the MG-1 support retained windows, where the client is unaware of redraw activity.

3.3.4 Imaging Model

All of these systems provide a number of functions to construct images, including BitBlt or RasterOp, line drawing, text drawing and the like. These may be performed on the display, in windows, or in bitmaps in off-screen memory. SunWindows additionally supports a variety of functions such as replicated texturing, and stencil functions. APOLLO supports a large number of functions typical of graphics packages, including polygonal area filling. These primitives are invoked by calling library procedures or system calls. On the SUN and APOLLO, the display frame buffer is mapped into the application address space, and the library functions directly modify the bitmap, requiring processes to lock out each other explicitly to avoid interference with the cursor image. On PERQ PNX, the window bitmap is held in the kernel address space, and is modified by the kernel when the system call is invoked. The cursor image is held in a separate bitmap, and does not interfere with graphical output.

All systems assume the characteristics of a memory mapped raster display. SunWindows and APOLLO place the details of device access (control registers etc) in the client address space, in a library. Here too is the knowledge of the number of bits per pixel. PERQ PNX, MG-1, and Sapphire place these details in protected server processes, or in the Unix kernel, but the client is aware that the display only supports one bit per pixel. Andrew provides a set of output primitives, and the client knows nothing of the bitmap characteristics. All systems use device coordinates, but libraries are provided (such as GKS) to perform world coordinate transformations.

3.3.5 Input Model

SunWindows provides an event queue, with events triggered on change of state of input devices (including mouse position and elapsed time). Events may be triggered when the mouse enters or leaves a window. SunWindows reports only the change of state of the device in the event record, which allows applications to lose track of the complete state of the devices, and get out of step. The SUN supports a three-button mouse with the buttons separately encoded, and either an ASCII-encoded keyboard, or a completely unencoded keyboard with each key state separately detectable. SUN provide the 'select' system call to determine if input is available on any of a set of file descriptors.

The APOLLO supports a three-button mouse, and an encoded keyboard. Events are enabled in a similar manner to the SUN, but it is not clear if they are queued, or only monitored when applications request input (cf GKS REQUEST mode input). Locator events may be enabled, provided the display has been acquired (which prevents other applications from accessing the display), but the application is responsible for tracking the cursor to follow the mouse.

PERQ PNX provides full support for the GKS input modes (SAMPLE, REQUEST, EVENT), with a three- or four-button mouse, and an ASCII-encoded keyboard. Events may be triggered by mouse movement, button press or release, key depression on the keyboard, or elapsed time, but time is only counted while the window is selected (see below). The complete state of the input devices is reported with each event, including the mouse position in three different coordinate systems. Applications may request that a Unix signal be sent when an input event occurs, so that they need not poll. When the size of a window is changed, a signal is sent to the process(es), but an event is not generated, so that synchronous processing is made harder. A level of indirection is maintained, so that physical mouse buttons are mapped to *virtual* (I hesitate to say logical) buttons.

The MG-1 provides an event queue containing information about physical key and button transitions, with mouse coordinates and a timestamp attached. The client may specify which classes of action are to cause an event to be queued. Andrew encodes mouse events as a virtual keyboard character, and the client then reads the associated mouse data. Sapphire translates keyboard and mouse events into abstract events, through a client-supplied table, but this is insufficient to support menus and pick devices completely, and feedback is not supported.

In all cases, emulation of logical input devices such as pick and choice devices is left to higher levels of software, although some library functions are provided to support menus.

3.3.6 Panes

SunWindows supports subwindowing through its hierarchical structure of windows. The APOLLO allows pads to be divided into panes, but leaves subdivision of graphical windows to higher levels of graphics packages. PERQ PNX provides no support for subwindowing, leaving it to applications or graphics packages. All systems provide support for application-defined clipping rectangles, which helps in implementing subwindowing as a higher layer.

The MG-1 supports windows constructed from a number of panels, each with its own bitmap containing the image. Some panels in a window are used by the window manager for the border controls, and the others are used by the client for image display, scrolling controls etc. Similarly, Sapphire constructs windows from a number of viewports, which may be separately addressed by clients.

3.3.7 Bitmaps

All of these systems provide support for bitmaps to generate and store off-screen images. PERQ PNX provides a complete bitmap for each window, and another for the screen, although terminal emulator windows are optimized, and only the characters are stored (see TTY emulation below). These bitmaps are stored in the kernel address space. Off-screen bitmaps may be allocated in the application address space. PERQ PNX requires a file descriptor for an open window to be specified for graphical output, even if both the source and destination are memory bitmaps.

Also, RasterOps cannot be performed between windows, as only one such file descriptor is given.

The APOLLO requires the application to acquire the display prior to graphical output. If the window is partly obscured, the window may be brought to the front automatically, or the application may be suspended until it is unobscured, or a list of visible rectangles may be determined (at the application's option). It is the application's responsibility to clip its output to the visible region.

SunWindows maintains a single bitmap for the display, as does Andrew, although clients may request off-screen bitmaps. The MG-1 provides a bitmap for each panel, stored in the application's address space. Sapphire and the BLIT (Teletype 5620) subdivide windows according to the overlap conditions, and provide a bitmap for each portion, stored in the server address space.

3.3.8 TTY Emulation

The APOLLO provides for a stream interface through pads, which are transcript files which the user may edit to supply keyboard input to applications. Support for cursor-addressable virtual terminals must be done by applications needing them, using *raw mode* for the keyboard input.

SunWindows provides for virtual terminals through the SunTools layer. A separate process acts as the terminal emulator, allowing programs written for VDU terminals to run unchanged. The same technique is used by Andrew.

PERQ PNX provides limited terminal emulation in the Unix kernel. The same file descriptor is used for both character stream I/O and graphical I/O. This causes some confusion when graphical programs and terminal I/O interfere with each other, and complicates the problems of modalities in the input system. For example, terminal input is normally line buffered, and this determines the triggering of keyboard events when enabled for graphical input. The keyboard characters are stored in a separate queue, although events in the graphical input queue indicate that a key has been pressed. This potentially allows time ordering of events to be lost.

Sapphire provides a centralized typescript service which provides terminal emulation for clients. The MG-1 provides a default (VT100) emulator in the Genix kernel, but implementors may provide additional emulators as user processes.

3.3.9 Sharing and Mapping

In the SUN and APOLLO systems, the screen is shared among competing applications by explicit locking by application programs. In the case of SunWindows, this is performed automatically by the graphics library. On the APOLLO, the application must explicitly acquire the display. SUN provide a means of batching updates, to avoid costly locking calls for each primitive. Andrew serializes remote procedure calls by processing each message from any client to completion.

SUN and APOLLO require the client application to redraw portions of their windows which become unobscured (called *damage repair*) or are read back (called *fixup*, eg for scrolling). SunWindows optionally provides for bitmaps to hold obscured portions of windows, but the support is incomplete in that they are not automatically updated when the window size is changed. Normally, graphical output is clipped to the visible portions of windows, and the remainder is discarded. Severe asynchrony problems can arise when redraw requests occur during client computation or display update.

PERQ PNX transparently updates the screen from the window bitmaps. Functions are provided to suppress this update to improve performance of batch updates, and these can also be used to suppress update of the screen until a complete image has been drawn, to eliminate distracting flicker. Display damage repair is performed totally transparently by the window manager, and fixups are not needed as the window bitmap is used for these functions.

PERQ PNX input events are directed to the currently selected window (specified by the user by pressing a button while pointing at the window), but mouse events may be directed to the window manager interface process, leaving the keyboard connected to the window. In order for the mouse to be connected to a window, the application must enable graphical input, and the user must subsequently select the window. When the mouse leaves the window, mouse events revert to the window manager interface process. Reentering the window does not reselect it automatically.

At the SunTools layer, control is retained by the tool library functions, making it difficult for an application to wait for either user activity or some other external event (eg network activity). SUN input events are directed to windows according to the set of event types enabled, and the window(s) containing the mouse position at the time the event was triggered. Event types may be enabled differently at different levels of the window hierarchy.

On the SUN, interactive creation of windows (eg to invoke a new task) is performed on the user's behalf by the Tool Manager. Each tool has a subsidiary process which responds to input events on the window borders to provide for moving, resizing, and ranking of windows.

3.3.10 Protection

PERQ PNX provides complete protection between windows. Output is always clipped to the window bitmap, and windows can only be read by applications which have a file descriptor for them, or for the entire screen (which may be protected). The window manager interface process uses a private interface to the kernel to perform the window manipulation functions. These are not available to applications, which protects the user from rogue programs, but prevents applications from providing aids to the user (such as popping a relevant window to the top when appropriate).

SunWindows and the APOLLO rely on good behaviour on the part of the graphics libraries and applications, which is to remain within their windows and avoid interfering with each other. The entire screen may be read as normal memory. Even if the application clips to its own window boundary, it may read back portions of another's window which overlaps it. Tools may perform window manipulation functions such as popping to the top.

Andrew, Sapphire, and the MG-1 are fully protected. The MG-1 permits a client to specify the listener, provided it has access to the current listener.

Protection of the window manipulation functions (pop, move etc) is achieved in PERQ PNX, Andrew, and the MG-1 by restricting access to the software interface for these (ie by restricting functionality). SunWindows and the APOLLO are unprotected in this respect.

3.3.11 Naming

SUN, MG-1, and PERQ PNX use Unix file descriptors to access windows, which are private to the owner and its children. They also provide global names of special files, which may be opened by unrelated processes. Client tasks are identified by their process identifier, and process group identifier.

The APOLLO provides a window number. It is not clear how this can be used by other processes. Sapphire and Andrew use IPC (*Inter Process Communication*) ports and sockets respectively to identify windows.

3.3.12 Grouping

None of the systems provide support for grouping of windows so that they can be manipulated together (eg brought to the front).

3.4 ARCHITECTURE, ADDRESS SPACES AND COMMUNICATIONS

The SUN system places most of the functionality in the application address space, and uses system calls for locking. Unix signals are sent to the application to indicate the need for damage repair etc.

PERQ PNX places almost all of the functionality in the Unix kernel, including the terminal emulator but not the window manager interface process. System calls are used by the application to perform graphical output, and signals are sent to the application to indicate when a window size has changed. Clients may request that a signal be sent when an input event occurs, but size change signals can only be sent asynchronously.

Figures 3.2 to **3.5** show the architectural characteristics of these systems in relation to the model shown in **Figure 3.1**. There is no figure showing the APOLLO architecture, as insufficient information is available.

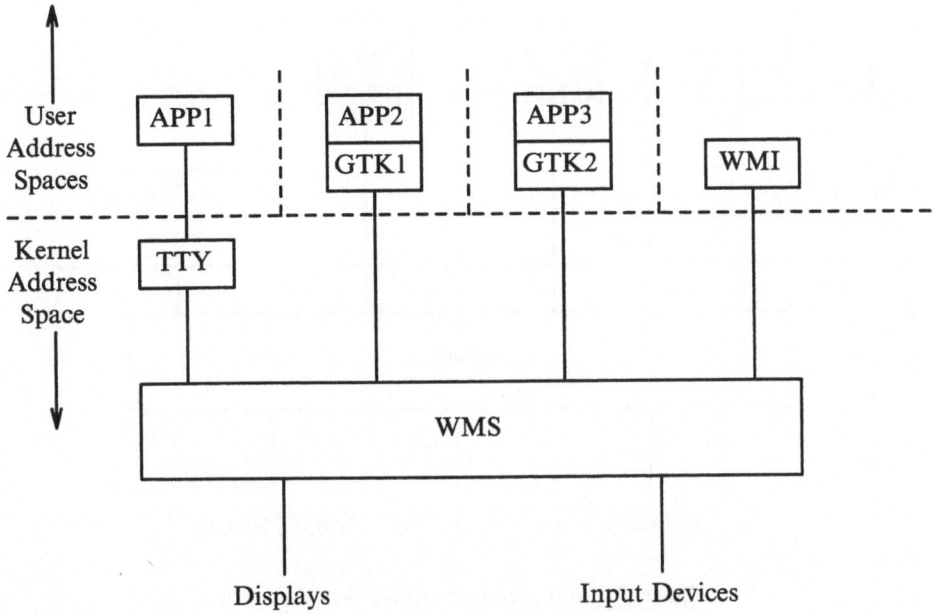

Figure 3.2 PERQ PNX Architecture

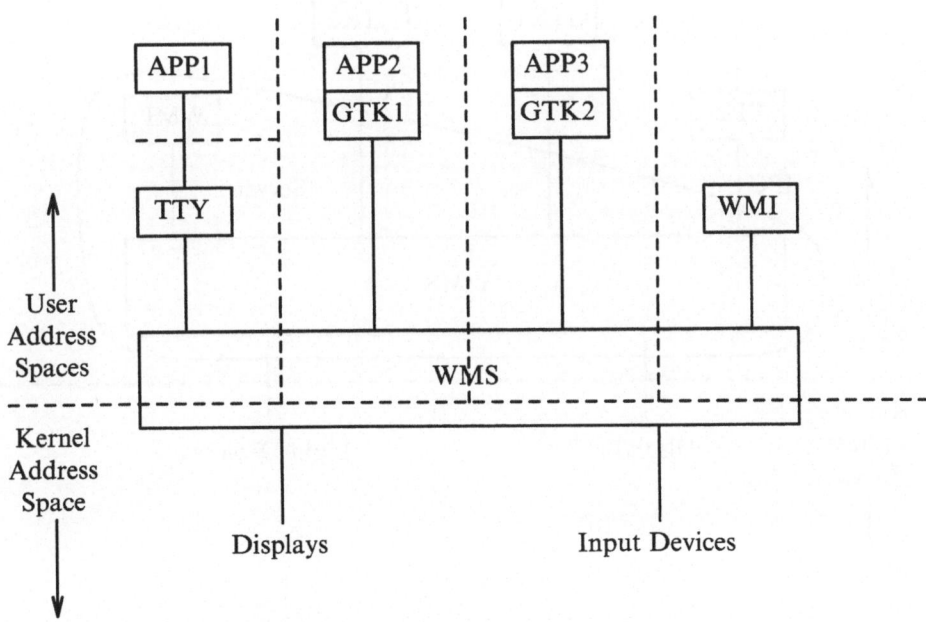

Figure 3.3 SunWindows Architecture

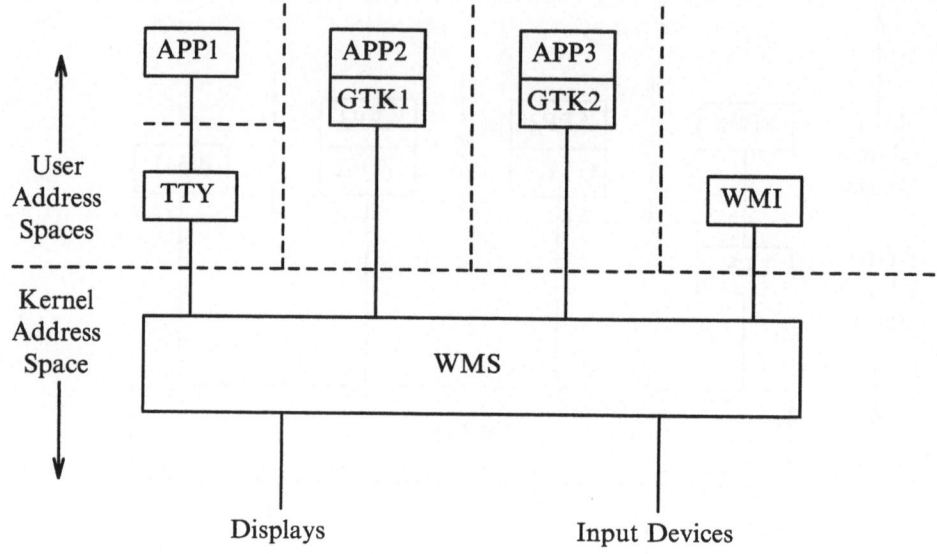

Figure 3.4 Whitechapel MG-1 Architecture

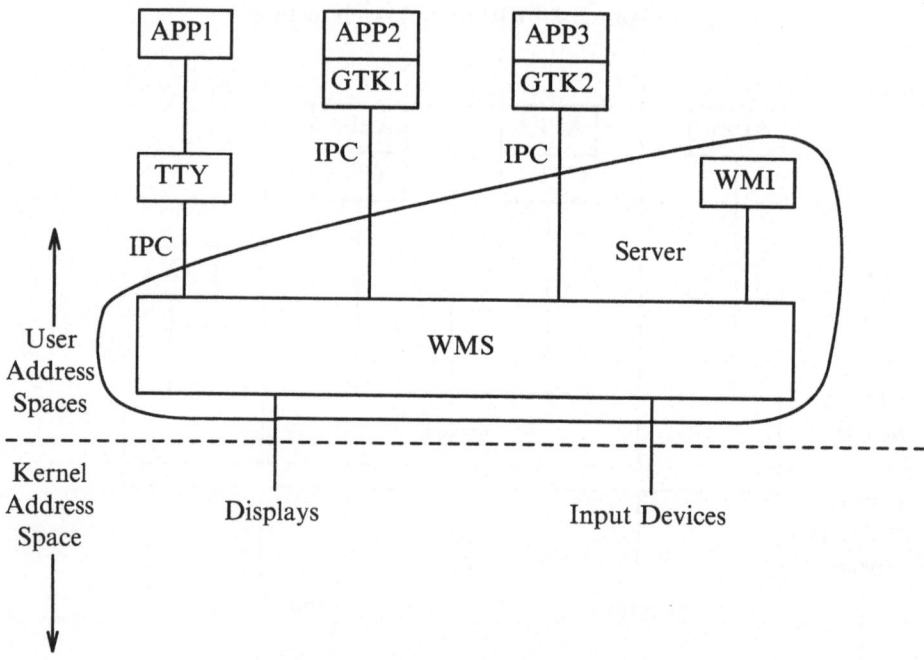

Figure 3.5 Andrew Architecture

Communication between applications and the kernel occur by system call and signals. PTY channels are implemented as pseudo-devices in the Unix kernel, and appear as normal terminals to the application. Sapphire uses asynchronous message-based IPC for communication between processes. Andrew uses stream-based IPC, and batches messages to improve throughput. Messages requiring a reply cause the client to wait until the stream has been processed, and the reply received. Normally, all messages are buffered until such a reply is required, which corresponds to the GKS deferral mode BNIL (Before Next Interaction Locally).

3.5 OTHER SYSTEMS

Sapphire and the BLIT are closer to the PERQ PNX window manager than the others, in that the virtual display abstraction is maintained, but they only store the hidden rectangles, not the entire window.

Systems such as Interlisp-D and Smalltalk are rather different, in that they only support a single address space. Communication between application and window manager is by procedure call, and can go both ways. The window manager can store pointers to application data and procedures to perform damage repair and fixups, with no performance penalty. This makes the boundaries between application, graphics package, and window manager much more tenuous, and cannot reasonably work with a multilanguage, multiple address space system. Additionally, the entire system is tied to the particular programming language and paradigms supported. The Macintosh goes further than this in not supporting multiprocessing. MS-Windows follows the *process per window* model by providing each process with a virtual display, accessed through a *standard* set of graphics primitives. Window management follows the tiling paradigm rather than the overlapping window paradigm.

3.6 SUMMARY

We have found that it is possible to port highly interactive programs among quite different window managers. As a result, we have reached conclusions on a number of issues:

(1) Simplicity of the application program interface is a blessing. Richness at the expense of simplicity is a disadvantage. Complex clipping or damage repair mechanisms are particularly problematic.

(2) Good performance in communication between the application and the window is necessary to provide application-dependent and dynamic feedback.

(3) Uniformity in manipulating images in the window and in hidden buffers is essential.

(4) Optimization of common cases such as text drawing must provide complete support, if the benefit is not to be entirely lost.

(5)   The greatest area of difficulty is in the handling of input. This is where the largest differences arise, and consensus is most lacking. In particular, applications which will coexist with others require assistance from the window manager in knowing the complete state of the input devices.

(6)   A rich toolkit would ease the application programmer's task, but it is hard to build one suitable for a wide range of applications.

Some issues which have not been tackled, and therefore not yet resolved are:

•   *Device independence for colour images*: bitmap representations can abstract out details of device control, but issues concerning number of colours arise.

•   *Portability of data representations*: items such as images and fonts will be a significant concern in the near future.

Finally, the main concern to be tackled is that of enabling multiwindow applications to coexist with others in a harmonious fashion. Providing equivalent facilities to the user in moving information within and between applications at a level more abstract than the display representations will require definition of new protocols. Providing the same degree of extensibility (to the user) in a graphical interface as that common in textual interfaces represents a challenging research project. The current generation of window managers appears to provide insufficient functionality to undertake these tasks, and some impose substantial restrictions.

3.7 ACKNOWLEDGEMENTS

I would like to thank my colleagues in the Common Base group and in the Informatics Division of RAL for their assistance in preparing this presentation, their work with window managers and interactive applications, and the implementation of SPY. Particular credit is owed to Mark Martin for his work in porting SPY to some of the systems discussed in this paper, and his analysis of the problems. I am grateful to William Newman and the Workshop Organizing Committee for their comments on a draft of this paper.

3.8 DISCUSSION

Chairman - Bob Hopgood

Teitelman: You said the APOLLO system was all keyboard-driven with the cursor being moved by arrow keys. Is that because they are trying to stay compatible with machines that don't have mice?

Williams: For a long time, the mouse was an option on the APOLLO system. The implication is, therefore, that all the user interface software has to work without a mouse.

Teitelman: One of the things we ought to discuss is whether or not we want that as an option or whether we should insist on some kind of pointing device.

Williams: Agreed. That is one of the ground rule issues that you have to sort out. Our own view at RAL is that you have got to have a mouse - you may be able to survive without a keyboard but you can't survive without a mouse.

Teitelman: In relation to input and signalling changes, could you define synchronous and asynchronous?

Williams: Synchronous input is where input is only delivered to the application when it has issued a read call. Asynchronous input is where the window manager notifies the application via a software interrupt.

Teitelman: If several events occur, there may be different time lapses in their execution so that the order in which the events occur is not preserved.

Williams: No, the order is always preserved.

Teitelman: One reason why the user might want synchronous events for window changes is where you delete a window and immediately start typing. The user wants to know that the keystrokes are being interpreted in the context of the window already being gone even though the window manager might not have actually finished removing it from the display.

Williams: That is the separate issue of synchrony with the user. Type ahead is one obvious area, mouse-button ahead is another. Depending on the time lag, it becomes more or less workable. In SPY, we do not allow mouse ahead because it gets too confusing. You press a button, nothing happens so you press it three more times. Eventually, the pop-up menu comes up, the next press is interpreted as a menu hit you did not want, the menu goes away, the next press brings it back and the user sits there totally confused!

Teitelman: But the user usually doesn't have trouble with type ahead.

Williams: If it is not echoed quickly, you still have trouble. At one stage in SPY, you could type ahead and the echo would lag further and further behind. We put a lot of effort into making it echo the keystrokes fast enough to be as near as possible fully synchronous with the user.

The issue I was really referring to was the question of synchronization with the application program. If you issue a command and it is some task, such as rewrite the filestore, that takes two minutes, what happens if the user changes the size of the window? If you are not careful, the application gets hit with a signal to rewrite the window in the middle of its filestore code and doesn't know what to do with it. The paradigm has to be to take the signal, remember it and, when you come back to the main processing loop, take the corrective action.

4   Ten Years of Window Systems - A Retrospective View

Warren Teitelman

4.1 INTRODUCTION

Both James Gosling and I currently work for SUN and the reason for my wanting to talk before he does is that I am talking about the past and James is talking about the future. I have been connected with eight window systems as a user, or as an implementor, or by being in the same building! I have been asked to give a historical view and my talk looks at window systems over ten years and features: the Smalltalk, DLisp (Interlisp), Interlisp-D, Tajo (Mesa Development Environment), Docs (Cedar), Viewers (Cedar), SunWindows and SunDew systems.

The talk focuses on key ideas, where they came from, how they are connected and how they evolved. Firstly, I make the disclaimer that these are my personal recollections and there are bound to be some mistakes although I did spend some time talking to people on the telephone about when things did happen.

The first system of interest is Smalltalk from Xerox PARC.

4.2 SMALLTALK

I was at the meeting where Dan Ingalls came up with the good idea of windows in Smalltalk. The ideas in the Smalltalk window system have propagated rapidly and most of the groups at Xerox PARC have used others' good ideas in their own environments.

Smalltalk had the first real window system. It used *overlapping windows*. In the early system you could only interact with the window that was on top, like a desktop. This simplifies the window system, but many people felt it was disadvantageous and this was subsequently corrected in later versions.

Smalltalk was the first system to use a *cut and paste*, modeless editor. *Modeless editing* was originally introduced in the Gypsy text editor at PARC, but Gypsy was not a full window system. Bravo [35] had the first display editor that had exposure at PARC. It was a fancy modal text and format editor. It had text insertion mode and command mode and it was easy to forget that you were in insertion mode and to insert commands into text, and conversely to delete a document accidentally when in command mode. Cut and paste eliminated modes. Anything typed is text directed at an insertion point which can be moved with the mouse. Insertion is a form of pasting, and cutting is a form of moving so two simple commands form the basic model which is very attractive. The Laurel message system included a text editor that allowed two ways of operating: modal and modeless, but gradually users all moved to modeless operation.

Smalltalk-76 [26, 27] was developed on the Alto, a 16-bit machine with 64 Kbytes of memory. A lot of concern went into fitting the system onto this small machine with its small virtual address space and it proved to be good for prototyping only.

Smalltalk-80 [21] was designed with the Dorado in mind. This was a real system with large virtual memory, dynamic storage and garbage collection and Ethernet communications.

Slides from Smalltalk systems showed:

- an early A4 picture of a nut and bolt (**Figure 4.1**);

- a clock (from a 1983 system): a system is shown to be maturing when clocks and games appear;

- *multipane windows*, *pop-up menus* (**Figure 4.1**);

- a Smalltalk browser (**Figure 4.1**).

The Smalltalk language has methods and submethods for inheritance and subclassing which is something we intended to do in Interlisp and Cedar but never got round to doing.

4.3 DLISP

I wrote DLisp [60] which was first presented in 1977 at MIT. This system was a hybrid implementation involving the Alto and MAXC (PDP-10).

The Lisp part of the system communicated with a server running on the Alto which handled communications with the screen. The server could do things such as put up rectangular areas on the screen, but had no knowledge of windows as all the window information was in the Lisp. Communication between the Alto and Lisp was by packets over Ethernet. The idea of using this architecture belongs to Bob

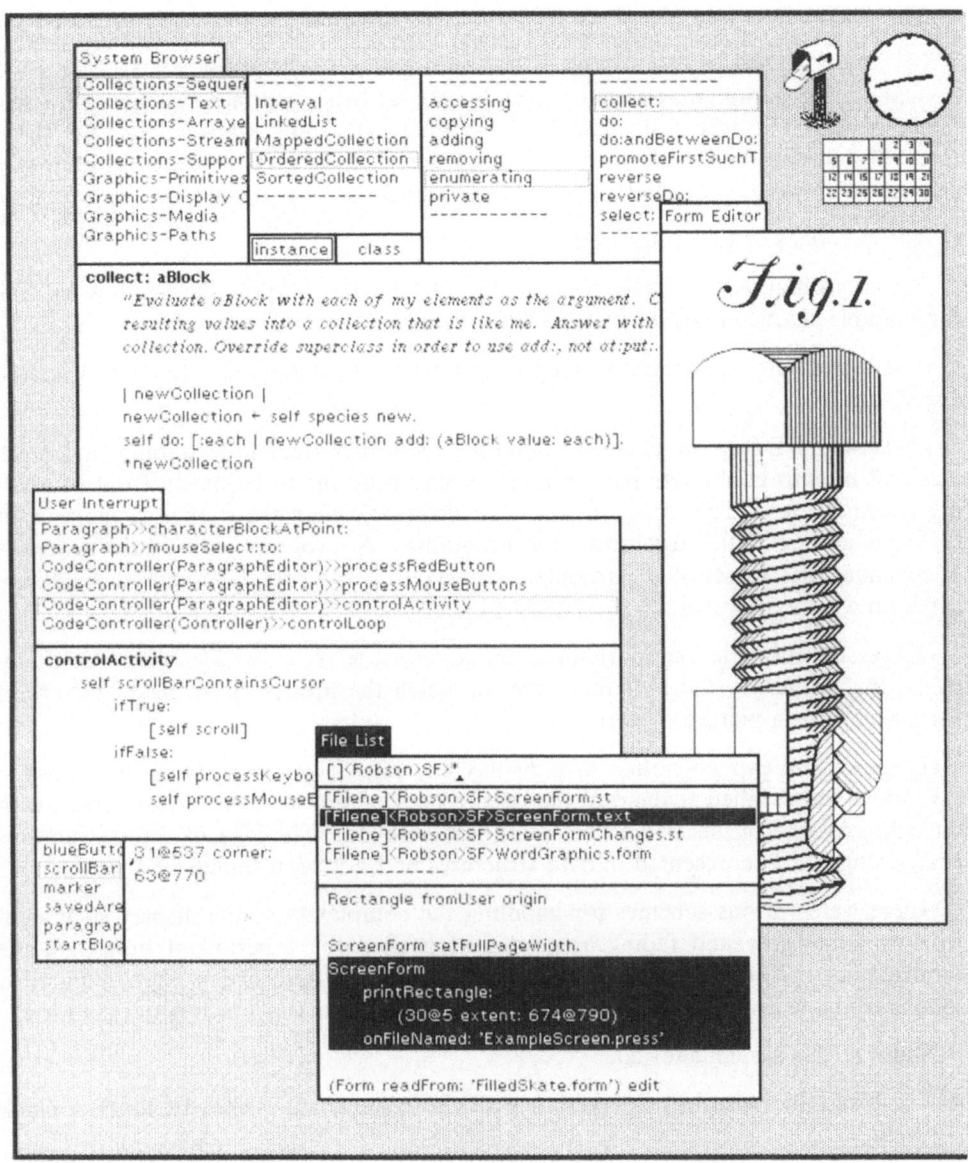

Figure 4.1

Sproull. The system worked amazingly well although the user interface had to be tailored to the limitations of the machine. For example, you could not drag images, nor could cursors be changed in response to moving in and out of areas.

Most of the user interface was concerned with timeout. A special character in the input stream signalled a mouse event and there was a special event when there was no activity.

The system was completed in 1977 but was not heavily used. It provided the starting point for Interlisp-D.

The editing paradigm was not cut-and-paste and the interface was awkward and menu-driven. The editor allowed textual editing with some knowledge of list structure. The system had built-in document classes such as text, desktop, window and canvas which were predefined. These classes could not be extended.

The key ideas of the system are described below.

Partially obscured windows were treated in the same way as the window on top, for example characters could be typed into them.

This system provided the first support for use of *multiple fonts*. (Smalltalk used a single font.)

Windows in DLisp were *defined descriptively* rather than procedurally (a Lispish idea). Programs could also pass in a set of specifications to be put in front of existing specifications. This made it easy for users to tailor their own systems, as it involved editing data structures, not programs. A program could also search a specification list to see if a particular specification was present. This idea did not catch on widely, however.

The system provided support for multiple views, ie *recursive windows*. An example of this is the *Morton Salt Box* label in which the product label has a picture of itself which has a picture of itself etc.

There was no explicit notion of a display context. If you positioned the mouse in a window and scrolled it then all the occurrences of the window on the screen with their appropriate offsets had to be found and scrolled. The idea of transformations and scaling being represented in data structures had not been thought of yet.

There were various schemes for handling the complexity of the display such as: a window going grey and fading away if not touched for a period of time; and the arrangement of *related windows into desktops*. The latter scheme then required a tool to navigate around desktops. The later idea of icons is a much better solution.

Slides of this system showed:

● a standard typescript interacting with the system, with different fonts, a clock etc;

● a menu of menus, rather than a stack of menus;

● an error occurrence, when an appropriate menu comes up showing, for example, the call stack;

● a mail system for the first time integrated in a graphics environment.

Both Smalltalk and this system are single address space systems so the problem of referring to a data structure in another address space does not arise.

In DLisp there was the notion of commands referring to the current window, and the currently active window had a distinguishing pattern in its name stripe.

4.4 INTERLISP-D

The Interlisp-D [12] system that was implemented on the Dorado initially included DLisp but the DLisp code eventually disappeared.   Interlisp-D also runs on the Dandelion.

Interlisp-D was a real system with about 1000 users and was influenced by Smalltalk: it was an object-oriented system.   There were 20 classes of objects that could be displayed and users could add their own objects.

Initially there were no multiple processes or monitors although you could switch between tasks via the caller - callee relationship.   Later, as a result of the influence of Cedar/Tajo, multiple processes and monitors were added.   This involved finding and fixing all the places in the code where the system accessed global resources.   There is no preemptive scheduling in the system (yet).

Retained (or cached) windows were added, initially for speeding up performance, for example with menus, but later retained windows were found useful for hiding from the programmer the fact that his window was not on top.

The text editor in this system was modeless.   It also allowed a mixture of a markup (bitmap editor) style interface with text.

4.5 TAJO (MESA DEVELOPMENT ENVIRONMENT)

At the same time as PARC was working on Cedar, work was going on in Systems Development Division of Xerox on developing a graphically-oriented Mesa development system called Tajo [41, 55, 68].   Tajo was begun in 1977 and was used by Cedar implementors between 1980 and 1982.

In Cedar they took Mesa and added storage management, atoms and lists to it. The Systems Development Division were unwilling to incorporate these changes.

Tajo was a multiple process, integrated, interactive program development environment with *scroll bars*, *subwindows*, pop-up menus etc.   It used a 3 button scheme for scrolling with the mouse.

The key ideas of Tajo are described below.

Tajo was the first system to use the notion of two states of a window: *open* and *closed (iconic)*.   Initially a closed window was represented by a small labelled rectangle on the right of the screen.   As it was difficult to determine the contents, pictorial representations were used very shortly afterwards.

The other interesting thing about Tajo was the control structure used.   In the traditional approach the program believes it is in control of its environment and it controls interactions with the user.   The order in which user input is requested (sequentially), is driven by the convenience of the implementor of the tool, not that of the user. In the Tajo approach, the program passes in a procedure and specifies to the window manager an event or events of interest and the procedure is called under window manager control when a specified event occurs. The user is in control: Tajo interacts with the user until the user indicates "do it", when Tajo *notifies* the appropriate tool that some user action intended for it has taken place. The tool obtains its parameters by means of system-managed forms. The user could walk his way through a tool and then leave things to the window manager, with the program just extracting the data. The problem is that programs have to be written in this way - they say you have to "turn your programs inside out" as compared to conventional structure. SUN is addressing the issue of this programming style.

Slides on Tajo showed:

- an example of a control panel showing rudimentary icons;

- buttons used to activate processes; the application program does not worry about placements, it is just called;

- mail system.

Tajo was fairly widely used and was a development environment for the Star. It is still in use.

Tajo was the first system to use *static menus*. It was found that pop-up menus were good for new users, but that the same interface that is easy to learn is not necessarily good for experienced users. The user has to wait for a menu to come up and then has to scan it visually for the relevant entry. A static menu is already there and the user can *mouse-button ahead* in a reflexive way.

A Tajo user could also edit what he wanted into a static menu and the system would search the pop-up menu for that string and call the associated procedure.

Tajo influenced both Viewers and SunWindows.

4.6 THE DOCS SYSTEM (CEDAR)

Docs was developed in 1980 and 1981 but had serious performance problems and was not completed. It was influenced by DLisp and was the first system to use the Cedar Graphics Model which was a prerunner of the Adobe Imaging Model [69] (a data structure with all the scaling, transformation etc information).

The system had the same idea as DLisp of using data description for windows and documents, but there seemed to be a preference for procedural window interfaces at the time.

The key ideas of the system were as follows:

- the system provided support for *scaling and rotation* (via Cedar Graphics);

- there were retained windows;

- Docs was object-oriented and had support for subclassing;
- the separation of a window from the object being displayed in the window (this was not the case in Viewers):

  - the ideas of documents, document classes (string, file, window, drawer, stream) and viewboxes which have home and target documents;
  - that a document has a procedure for presenting itself in a viewbox;
  - the notion of viewboxes existing in a document, and of viewing a document, which has the potential for recursion.

4.7 VIEWERS (CEDAR)

The current window system in Cedar is based on the Viewers Window Package [40, 65]. Its design and implementation began in 1981 and the system had its first users in May 1982. Its influence can be seen in Microsoft's MS-Windows. It was decided to sacrifice some flexibility for performance and robustness. Consequently Viewers had less functionality but better performance than Docs, came up quickly, and worked well.

Viewers is a notification-oriented system, as a result of the influence of Tajo, and is also object-oriented with a number of objects in the system.

Whiteboards in the system are a spatial way of presenting objects and were influenced by Smalltalk browsers. Neither Cedar nor Viewers support subclassing. As a result, it is necessary to duplicate and edit code to provide an object which may be only slightly different from an existing object. Subclassing was supposed to be provided but just did not get implemented.

The key ideas in Viewers are detailed below.

This was the first *tiling window manager* that I know of. This makes for faster mouse hit detection. I was originally from an environment of overlapping windows but found that I preferred using a tiling window manager. There are conflicting views on this however. You can *mouse ahead* but some discipline must be involved in doing this. Predictability is important from the user point of view but Cedar went too far in not allowing overlapping windows and thus also not allowing pop-up menus. I think it is a good idea to allow transitory windows in overlapping mode. The SUN allows overlapping windows but it is surprising how many people take the trouble to tile.

Another novel idea is the *TIP (Terminal Interface Package)*, which provides for the separation of the function of the system from the particular user interface used to invoke that function. By changing a data structure, a new interface can be obtained. The user can tailor the interface. Although sensible defaults are provided, the fact that the user can change things makes agreement on the interface less of an issue. Not everyone will want to spend the time tailoring a system and a complaint about Unix software is that it has not aged sufficiently for sensible defaults to be provided.

The flexibility of the system is shown by an example of how events associated with mouse buttons can be changed in the TIP to obtain a new user interface. This idea has been retro-fitted to Tajo and is planned for James Gosling's new system, SunDew.

Slides on this system show:

●   richer icons (**Figure 4.2**) - this raises again the question of what you should be able to do with icons, eg type at them, delete them etc;

●   the built-in notion of the screen being divided into two columns (**Figure 4.3**);

●   typical screen configurations showing the use of multiple fonts and (**Figure 4.4**, **Figure 4.5**) the notion of text being *organized as a tree structure* which enables the user to specify the depth to which he wants to go and also allows nodes to be moved around;

●   an example of a more sophisticated tool: an icon editor, with a user interface defined by a TIP table (**Figure 4.6**);

●   a scanned image clipped to the outlines of characters defined by splines which reveals the strength of the graphical underpinning of the system (**Figure 4.7**).

The shortfalls of the system are that there is no support for subclassing; that viewers can only be specified via programs and not data; and that there is no separate notion of a viewer and an object being viewed.

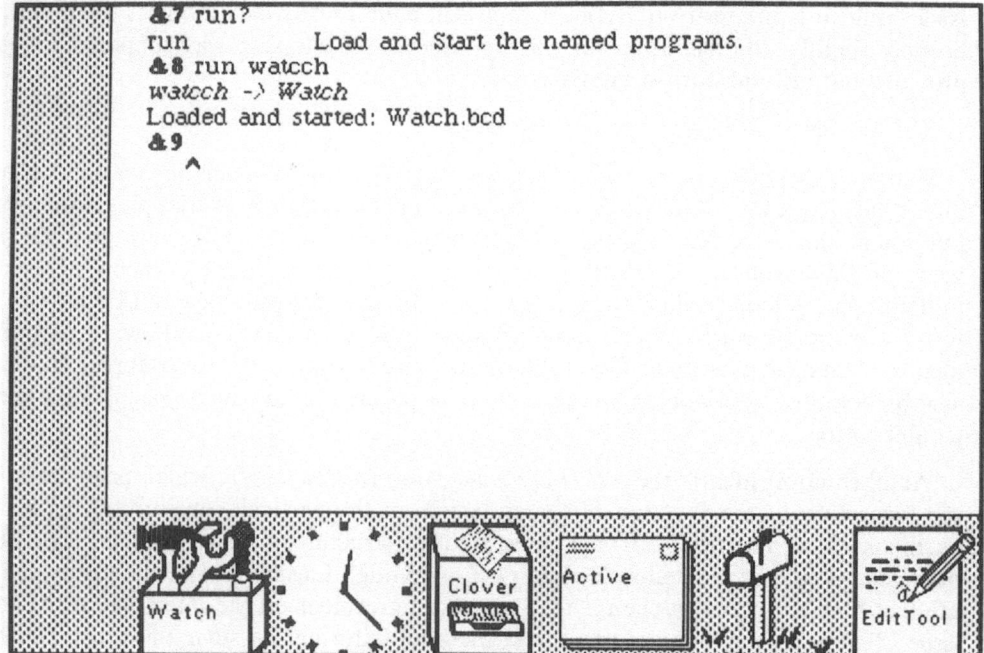

Figure 4.2

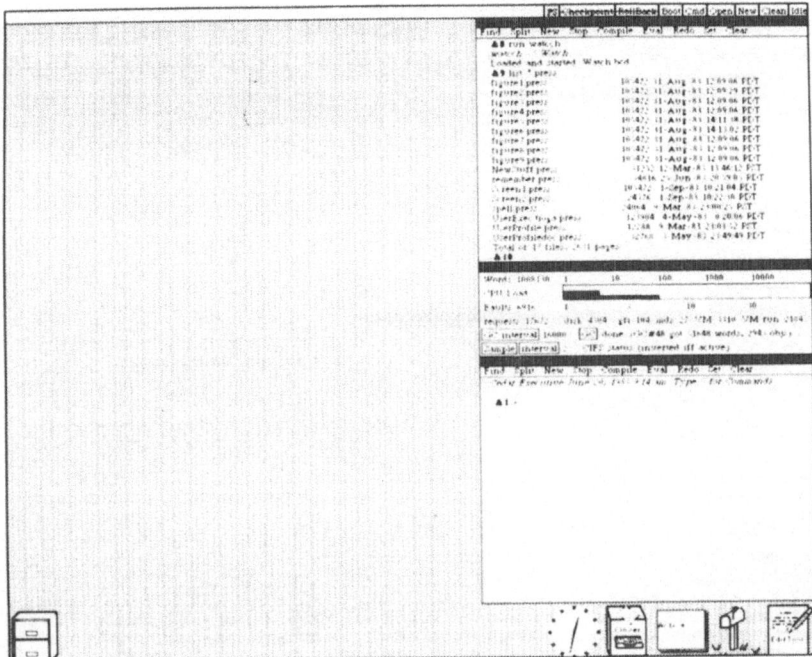

Figure 4.3

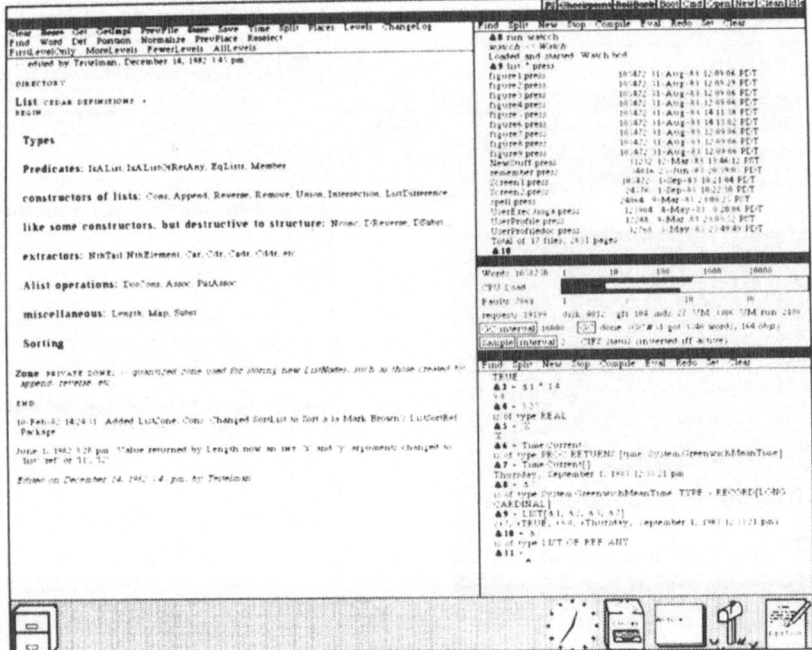

Figure 4.4

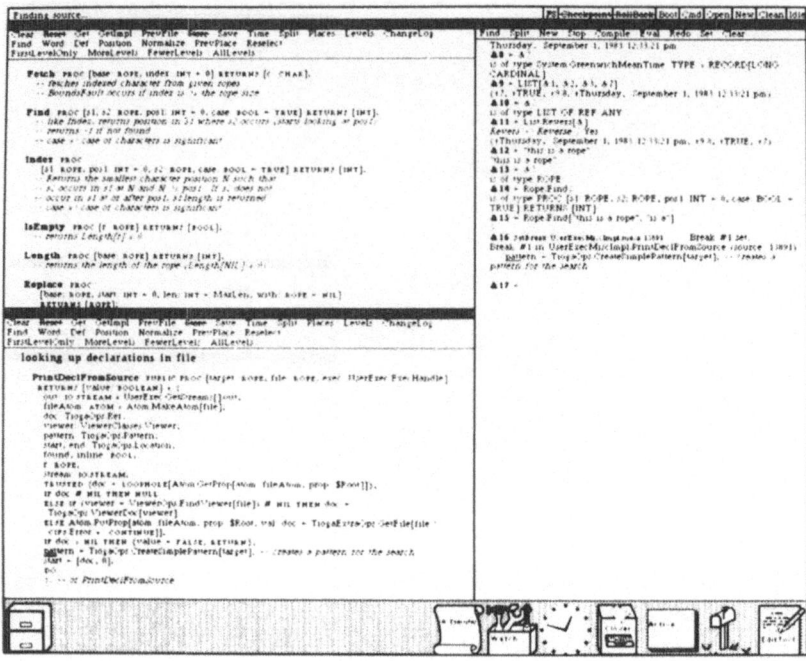

Figure 4.5

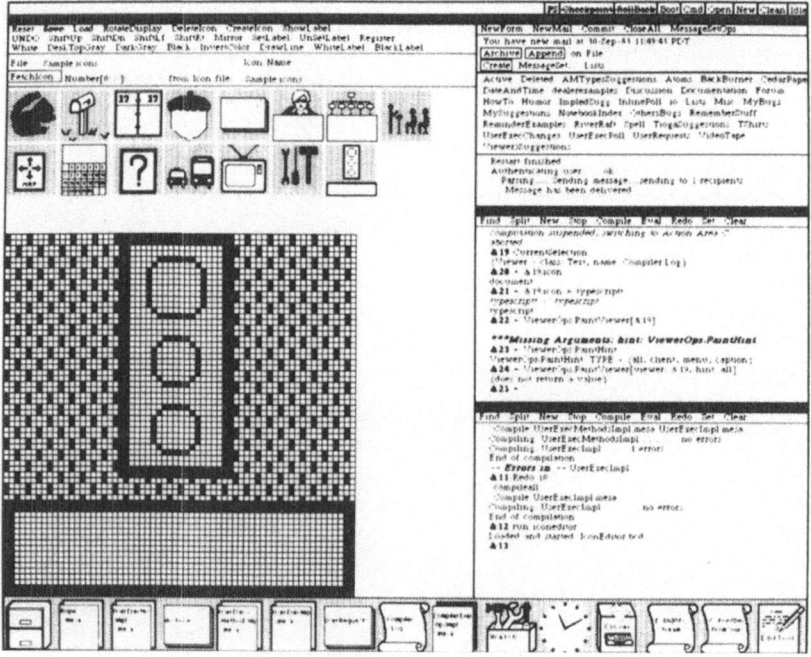

Figure 4.6

Figure 4.7

4.8 SUNWINDOWS

SunWindows [61, 62] is an attempt to bring windows to a Unix system. It has synchronization problems of a *multiprocess environment* that I find objectionable. The problems are aggravated by multiple address spaces, which means that the protocols with which you are communicating have to be worried about.

There are three ways to partition the function of window management:

(1)   in the same address space as the client process - this requires replication of the window system library in each application and makes large demands on disc space;

(2)   outside the address space of the client in the kernel of the operating system;

(3)   outside the address space of the client in a server process - this requires remote procedure call support, which has not been available in Unix systems until recently.

SunWindows uses the first two. The disadvantages of this are: inadequate debugging tools, coupled with the fact that you need to program the window manager in a different style if it resides in the kernel; bugs in the window system threaten the integrity of the entire system; no parallel development of applications and user interface is possible; and there is a large body of code in wired-down memory.

Examples from SunWindows are:

- a graphical interface to the Unix formatting utility 'indent', which is a format program allowing different styles;

- different options for scrollbars, buttons and bars - the move is towards libraries that users can build on in the Unix spirit;

- an icon editor which has graphical images, a preview area etc;

- a tool for manipulating full-screen crosshairs.

I believe that the system must provide hooks for users to do what they want. The window system cannot legislate on taste.

Finally, the last system to be considered is SunDew.

4.9 SUNDEW

SunDew (see Chapter 5) is an *extensible distributed window system*. The window manager is in a user process. In it applications communicate with the window system via programs written in PostScript. James Gosling will discuss this system.

4.10 DISCUSSION

Chairman - George Coulouris

Myers: It might be worth mentioning that the current system on BLIT uses many of the same ideas as DLisp.

Teitelman: Yes, that is another case where you have a separation of the window management function from the application program. The good ideas in that area came from Bob Sproull.

Williams: You mentioned TIP, does that deal with dragging and pointing actions?

Teitelman: One of the pseudo-events that it recognized was mouse-move so you could put into your TIP table that every time the mouse moves I want the following event to be generated in which case you would continually get mouse-move events. If you did not have that event in the TIP table, you would not see those events. You could even specify how often you wanted it depending on whether you were interested in just the final end point or the whole trajectory.

Williams: Did it achieve it by sending events to the application?

Teitelman: Yes, and the system was fast enough so that it all worked.

5 SunDew - A Distributed and Extensible Window System

James Gosling

5.1 INTRODUCTION

SunDew is a distributed, extensible window system that is currently being developed at SUN. It has arisen out of an effort to step back and examine various window system issues without the usual product development constraints. It should really be viewed as speculative research into the *right* way to build a window system. We started out by looking at a number of window systems and clients of window systems, and came up with a set of goals. From those goals, and a little bit of inspiration, we came up with a design.

5.2 GOALS

A clean programmer interface: simple things should be simple to do, and hard things, such as changing the shape of the cursor, should not require taking pliers to the internals of the beast. There should be a smooth slope from what is needed to do easy things, up to what is needed to do hard things. This implies a conceptual organization of coordinated, independent components that can be layered. This also enables being able to improve or replace various parts of the system with minimal impact on the other components or clients.

Similarly, the program interface probably should be procedural, rather than simply exposing a data structure that the client then interrogates or modifies. This is important for portability, as well as hiding implementation details, thereby making it easier for subsequent changes or enhancements not to render existing code incompatible.

Retained windows: a clean programmer interface should completely hide window damage from the programmer. His model of a window should be just that it is a surface on which he can write, and that it persists. All overlap issues should be completely hidden from the client. I believe that the amount of extra storage required to maintain the hidden bitmaps on a black and white display is negligible - based on the observation that people generally do not stack windows very deeply. The situation is somewhat different with colour, but there are games to be played. Retained windows is one way of hiding window damage, but we do not want to commit to a particular solution to this problem at this time.

Flexibility: users need to attach devices, change menu behaviours and generally modify almost all components of the system. For example, the menu package ought to be independent of the particular format or contents of the menu, thereby allowing the user to develop his own idioms without having to reimplement the entire system.

Part of flexibility is device independence: SUN provides a spectrum of display devices to which clients need consistent and transparent interfaces. This leads directly to portability, which we also need to achieve.

Users should be able to make various tradeoffs differently than in the standard system, because of either particular hardware or performance requirements. For example, if the system provides retained windows because we believe that the cost in terms of memory usage is worth the performance improvements, a user should be able to make this tradeoff differently, for example if he has less memory.

This extreme flexibility might appear to be at odds with having a clean, simple, well-abstracted programmer interface, but we do not believe that it is.

Remote access to windows: in the kind of distributed networked environment that SUN promotes, it is natural to want to be able to access windows on another machine as naturally as the NFS promises to support accessing remote files. We believe that this will fall out of any reasonably designed system.

Powerful graphical primitives: the primitives that the Macintosh provides should be considered as a lower bound. Curves and colour need to be well integrated. Attention should also be paid to what CGI [30], GKS [28], CORE [24] and PHIGS [6] need. A consequence of an emphasis on power and flexibility is the ability to emulate other window systems, eg it would be very valuable to be able to provide an emulation of the Macintosh toolbox.

Exploit the hardware: in particular, none of the systems mentioned above deal well with colour. In the future, colour is going to play an even larger part in display design. One can view black and white as a temporary technological stopgap, just as happened with television. Besides, SUN makes some pretty good colour displays, so the window system should exploit them. One implication of this is that the font file format must completely hide the details of the representation of characters, since we might eventually want to support antialiased text, and even illuminated monastic typefaces.

Perform well: the performance of the current window system should be considered as the minimum acceptable level. Performance in the common cases is especially critical. The new system should perform faster than the current system on such common operations as repainting and scrolling of text.

5.3 DESIGN SKETCH

The work on a language called PostScript [1] by John Warnock and Charles Geschke at Adobe Systems provided a key inspiration for a path to a solution that meets these goals. PostScript is a Forth-like language, but has data types such as integers, reals, canvases, dictionaries and arrays.

Inter process communication is usually accomplished by sending messages from one process to another via some communication medium. They usually contain a stream of commands and parameters. One can view these streams of commands as a program in a very simple language. What happens if this simple language is extended to being Turing-equivalent? Now, programs do not communicate by sending messages back and forth, they communicate by sending programs which are elaborated by the receiver. This has interesting implications on data compression, performance and flexibility.

What Warnock and Geschke were trying to do was communicate with a printer. They transmit programs in the PostScript language to the printer which are elaborated by a processor in the printer, and this elaboration causes an image to appear on the page. The ability to define a function allows the extension and alteration of the capabilities of the printer.

This idea has very powerful implications within the context of window systems: it provides a graceful way to make the system much more flexible, and it provides some interesting solutions to performance and synchronization problems. SunDew contains a complete implementation of PostScript. The messages that client programs send to SunDew are really PostScript programs.

Two pieces of work were done at SUN which provide other key components of the solution to the imaging problems. One is Vaughan Pratt's Conix [53], a package for quickly manipulating curve bounded regions, and the other is Craig Taylor's Pixscene [63], a package for performing graphics operations in overlapped layers of bitmaps.

Out of these goals and pieces grew a design, which will be sketched here. The window system is considered in four parts. The imaging model, window management, user interaction, and client interaction. The imaging model refers to the capabilities of the graphic system - the manipulation of the contents of a window. Window management refers to the manipulation of windows as objects themselves. User interaction refers to the way a user at a workstation will interact with the window system: how keystrokes and mouse actions will be handled. Client interaction refers to the way in which clients (programs) will interact with the window system: how programs make requests to the window system.

What is usually thought of as the *user interface* of the window system is explicitly outside the design of the window system. *User interface* includes such things as how menu title bars are drawn and what the desktop background looks like and whether or not the user can stretch a window by clicking the left button in the upper right hand corner of the window outline. All these issues are addressed by implementing appropriate procedures in the PostScript.

5.3.1 Imaging

Imaging is based on the stencil/paint model, essentially as it appears in Cedar Graphics [65] and PostScript. A stencil is an outline specified by an infinitely thin boundary that is piecewise composed of spline curves in a non-integer coordinate space and which may be self-intersecting. Paint is some pure colour or texture - even another image - that may be applied to the drawing surface. Paint is always passed through a stencil before being applied to the drawing surface, just like silkscreening. This is the *total* model: lines and characters can be defined using stencils. Lines are done as narrow stencils - underneath it all, it is not really done this way: special cases are exploited wherever possible.

One can think of a stencil as a clipping region. Stencils may be composed by union, intersection and difference to create new stencils.

The Macintosh graphics system, QuickDraw [18], can be easily cast in this framework: their GrafPort is simply a paint box, and all of the shapes that can be drawn are subsets of the capabilities of stencils. Many other 2D standards fit in easily as well, and the extension of the model to 3D is relatively straightforward.

Vaughan Pratt's work on conic splines presents us with an opportunity actually to realize this model and achieve good performance.

Almost all imaging functions are provided not by the window manager but by PostScript processes. For example, if one wanted rounded rather than square corners on a menu package, this could be done by modifying a PostScript procedure. Scope rules determine whether modifications are global or local.

5.3.2 Window Management

Pixscene [63] makes windows cheap and easy to create. If a client wants to create a window quickly as a pop-up, the window system will handle it. It very efficiently makes sure that each window is always complete: overlap is not visible to the client.

Even though windows behave as though the image is retained, clients will have to deal with requests to redraw from the window system. This will generally only happen when a window is stretched, in which case the client probably has no use for the old image, anyway.

Pixscene is based on a shape algebra package. The ability, provided by Conix, to do algebra very rapidly on curves should make non-rectangular windows perform well.

5.3.3 User Interaction - Input

The key word in the design of the user interaction facilities is *flexibility*. Almost anything done by the window system preempts a decision about user interaction that a client might want to decide differently. The window system therefore defines almost nothing concrete. It is just a loose collection of facilities bound together by the extension mechanism.

Each possible input action is an *event*. Events are a general notion that includes buttons going up and down (where buttons can be on keyboards, mice, tablets, or whatever else) and locator motion.

Events are distinguished by where they occur, what happened, and to what. The objects spoken about here are physical, they are the things that a person can manipulate. An example of an event is the 'E' key going down while window 3 is current. This might trigger the transmission of the ASCII code for 'E' to the process that created the window. These bindings between events and actions are very loose, they are easy to change.

The actions to be executed when an event occurs can be specified in a general way, via PostScript. The triggering of an action by the striking of the 'E' key in the previous example invokes a PostScript routine which is responsible for deciding what to do with it. It can do something as simple as sending it in a message to a Unix process, or as complicated as inserting it into a locally maintained document. PostScript procedures control much more than just the interpretation of keystrokes: they can be involved in cursor tracking, constructing the borders around windows, doing window layout, and implementing menus.

Synchronization of input events: we believe that it is necessary to synchronize input events within a user process, and to a certain extent across user processes. For example, the user ought to be able to invoke an operation that causes a window on top to disappear, then begin typing, and be confident about the identity of the recipient of the keystrokes. By having a centralized arbitration point, many of these problems disappear.

5.3.4 Client Interaction

Client interaction with the window system can be broken down into three layers: messages that get passed between the window system and the client, the programs that are contained in the messages, and a procedural interface to program construction. This is one of the key unique points about this window system: clients send *programs* to the window system whose elaboration causes graphic operations to appear. The client program does not send graphic operations directly. There is, of course, a procedural interface to program construction that blurs the distinction.

This approach allows the client to redefine the protocol to compress messages passed to the window system. For example, if the client wishes to draw a grid it can download a procedure which iteratively draws the lines, generating their coordinates as a function of the loop index. This is a substantial compression over transmitting a large set of lines, even if the grid is drawn only once. There are other performance advantages: message-passing interactions are relatively slow and downloading a procedure that will respond locally eliminates this overhead. For example, if a client program needs rubber band lines, then rather than have the window system send a message to it each time the mouse moves, it can download a procedure that will track the mouse locally.

There are a number of features of PostScript that make it attractive. It is very simple, and it is complete. Its simplicity makes it fast to translate and interpret - this can almost be done as quickly as packets can be disassembled in a more traditional IPC environment. Adobe did a very good job of designing a set of primitives and data structures that fit together well. Its chief drawback is that it can be hard for people to understand; the postfix notation is well-suited to consumption and generation by programs, but humans find it obscure.

It is important to think about the client programmer's model of what the window system does. We expect there to be two levels of model. The first completely hides the existence of PostScript with a veneer of procedure calls that construct and transmit fragments of PostScript programs. The second exposes PostScript. Beyond a certain level of functionality, learning PostScript is inevitable: it can be pushed off by making the veneer more comprehensive, but this just makes the eventual leap harder.

In order to give a flavour of PostScript, a small example is given in conclusion.

A PostScript Example

The PostScript code to generate the figure shown in **Figure 5.1** is:

```
clippath  pathbbox  newpath
2 div exch 2 div exch  translate
250  250  scale 90  rotate
25 (0 .9  moveto 0 0 1 90    -90  arc
          0 0 .9 -90 90  arcn  fill
          .88 .88  scale 22.5  rotate) repeat
```

The first three lines set up the environment, centre the image and set up the transformation matrix. Then the coordinate system is changed by scaling down .88 in both directions and rotating 22.5. This is repeated 25 times.

Figure 5.1

5.4 DISCUSSION

Chairman - George Coulouris

Williams: What is the scope of the devices you are considering? I don't suppose you intend running the window manager on a graph plotter.

Gosling: The crudest display we are willing to accept is 1 bit per pixel black and white but we also support 8 or 24 bits per pixel colour or 4 bits per pixel black and white.

Williams: Essentially bitmap raster devices.

Gosling: Right - although when you get to greyscale devices, things stop behaving in a model that is comfortably compatible with RasterOp. You have got to be able to deal with antialiasing, such things as subpixel positioning begin to make sense. It makes sense to draw a character midway between two pixels because you can use antialiasing to shift the character over by subpixel amounts.

Bono: When you use the word PostScript, do you mean literally that PostScript is in some way your virtual machine instruction set? It has not been extended or generalized?

Gosling: It has been extended. It is a superset. We are committed to implementing everything in the PostScript telephone book that makes sense. They have a few commands that are particular to their storage allocation and to the fact that they are going to a printer and these are not implemented. We have imported some things that are peculiar to a display and a small number of incompatible changes to the language have been made which we spent a long time talking to the people at Adobe about to make sure that was reasonable. In particular, we added garbage collection and lightweight processes. There are very tiny ways in which the semantics of PostScript's memory allocation strategy shows through in the printer version because they have a quick and dirty storage allocation mechanism and that wasn't really useful in this system.

Bono: The virtual machine was not virtual enough.

Gosling: Right. When we made the generalization to multiple processes, their storage allocation mechanism just completely broke and so we had to use garbage collection instead and that necessitated some small semantic changes but they are not things you are likely to see. All of the important things such as how you specify a curve, whether you can render an image rotated 37 degrees, all of that is there or intended to be there.

Hopgood: How do you handle input?

Gosling: Input is also handled completely within PostScript. There are data objects which can provide you with connections to the input devices and what comes along are streams of events and these events can be sent to PostScript processes. A PostScript process can register its interest in an event and specify which canvas (a data object on which a client can draw) and what the region within the canvas is (and that region is specified by a path which is one of these arbitrarily curve-bounded regions) so you can grab events that just cover one circle, for example. In the registration of interest is the event that you are interested in and also a magic tag which is passed in and not interpreted by PostScript, but can be used by the application that handles the event. So you can have processes all over the place handling input events for different windows. There are strong synchronization guarantees for the delivery of events even among multiple processes. There is nothing at all specified about what the protocol is that the client program sees. The idea being that these PostScript processes are responsible for providing whatever the application wants to see. So one set of protocol conversion procedures that you can provide are ones that simply emulate the keyboard and all you will ever get is keyboard events and you will never see the mouse. Quite often mouse events can be handled within PostScript processes for things like moving a window.

Sweetman: How do windows relate to canvases?

Gosling: I did not use the word window because its overloaded with all kinds of semantics. Does it have a border? All that a canvas is, is a thing on which you can draw. It is not even rectangular.

Sweetman: Do you see canvases on your display?

Gosling: Yes you can. A canvas is a thing on which you can draw. It might be visible on some display and it might not. If it is visible, you can specify its position in a $2\frac{1}{2}$D coordinate system. It is opaque but you can get a transparent effect if you want something to show through a window, by cutting a hole in the window.

Williams: You say clients have to accept redraw commands. Is there any indication as to how soon they are supposed to do them?

Gosling: The client can ignore the request if it wants. The screen image will look a little funny. Or it can wait half an hour - it does not affect the integrity of the screen. It will affect the integrity of its window but nothing else because all the canvases are maintained in apparent isolation from each other.

Williams: Will the visual image just contain what was there before?

Gosling: You can do that, if you wish. For most applications it does not make any sense to retain the old bitmaps so you might as well just blow them away and replace them by whatever is most convenient - which is probably what was there before. There are some times when you would like to retain the old bits - that is there as an option. I really want to make it difficult for people to exercise that option as it is a very tasteless thing to do in general.

Bono: I hope I am not being overly opaque about this but it seems like I have a sense of déjà vu in that it's a lot better way of doing what people did with display lists, where you sent things down to Vector Generals or whatever. They were little programs and there was some grouping structure but everything is done so much nicer now in the sense of having complete programs and a better set of primitives etc. Am I missing something from the model or is that really what is going on?

Gosling: One of the things that tended to characterize all the display list languages was that they tended to be tailored very much towards what the hardware could do. PostScript tries to stand back and say "I don't want to know what the hardware can do, I want to know what makes sense for the user".

Bono: What I would like people to do when they do look at standards, instead of ignoring them, is to look at, for example, the CGI work; this is a set of functions which some people claim is a good instruction set (forget the syntax for the moment, just look at the functionality). We would like to get some comment on whether it is a good set of functions and that is what you should be looking at rather than ignore the standards. All of this could be fitted in a standards context if we get it right.

Gosling: One could easily use the CGI graphics model for this instead.

Teitelman: The innovation here is not that we are using PostScript. The reason we chose PostScript is due to a lot of historical connections and proximity to the people who are doing it.

The interesting thing is that all these processes look as though they are executing in one of those old single address environments. It is a single user process that James has been able to implement lightweight processes in. You don't have lightweight processes in Unix systems, which you really need to implement realistic user interfaces.

Gosling: There is really nothing new here. It's just putting it together in a different way.

Rosenthal: It is worth bringing out a number of points about this style of window manager. There are some real limitations, though I think this is the way we should go.

(1)   Some help from the kernel is needed. This is easy in 4.2 which has a sensible IPC. It could be done in System V through shared resources etc.

(2)   A reliable signal mechanism is essential. The window manager has to stay up. It is the only routine for talking to the system and hence must stay alive. We have 100 systems running and only experience 1 - 2 crashes per week. This is good by Unix standards!

(3)   Applications cannot read pixels back - this is just too slow.

(4)   There **must** be a way to make the client think it has a real terminal, such as the 4.2BSD PTY device, otherwise all old programs misbehave.

(5)   There must be a mechanism for downloading application code into the window manager process, for example, rubber band line mouse tracking is done by a user level process.

(6)   There must be off-screen space in the window manager.

Examples of systems built in this way are:

BLIT [50];
Andrew (CMU)(see Chapter 13);
VGTS (Stanford) [36];
X (MIT).

The BLIT system is successful - people wrote programs for it. I believe it is the only successful window manager for a Unix system.

Myers: Maybe that is because BLIT doesn't run a Unix operating system.

Rosenthal: Overall, it is a Unix software environment.

Williams: We should bear in mind that Rob Pike says that to do anything sensible
                using the BLIT, you need to write two processes which communicate:
                one running in the Unix host and one running in the BLIT, and this
                must be harder to do than, say, writing two programs which don't com-
                municate.

6   Issues in Window Management Design and Implementation

Brad Myers

6.1 INTRODUCTION

Sapphire (the Screen Allocation Package Providing Helpful Icons and Rectangular Environments) is a very powerful window management system running on the PERQ personal workstation. Design for the system started early in 1982 and it has been a product of PERQ Systems Corporation since mid-1983. A description of the user interface for Sapphire is given in [44] while some experiments to judge the effectiveness of the progress bars is given in [43]. This paper will concentrate on the design decisions that were made during the development, how such design decisions interact and, finally, the issues that need to be addressed by future designers of window management systems.

The term *window* will be used in this paper for the rectangular environment manipulated by the window manager. Window is a term that causes confusion due to its use in graphics with a different meaning. The same applies to *viewport* which more closely approximates to an area of the screen in graphics. It is probably necessary at some stage to come up with a different term.

Adjectives associated with windows that also cause confusion are *active* and *current*. Most window managers are used on computer systems with a single keyboard and mouse with multiple windows displayed on the screen. Many systems connect the keyboard to one window at a time and that window is called the active or current window. However, all the windows are current as they are being displayed. In some window managers, including Sapphire, output can be sent to multiple windows concurrently, no window is more active than another. Consequently, I will use the term *listener* to define that window which is currently associated with input coming from the keyboard. Under certain circumstances in Sapphire, input from the mouse will be associated with the listener irrespective of whether the mouse coordinates are within the listener's window boundary or not. Later, it will be necessary to consider the problems that arise when multiple input devices are provided.

Sapphire is a much more complete window management system than most. The options available at the application program interface are the minimal set that provides the necessary functionality. On the other hand, the user interface provides a high degree of functionality based on the view that the window manager should provide more information and control to the user than most of the earlier systems. Consequently, this paper will concentrate on those aspects of the system associated with the user interface.

6.2 USER INTERFACE

6.2.1 Sapphire Icons

A major design goal for Sapphire was that the window manager should provide more information to the user than just the output displayed in the rectangular window. Sapphire, like many window managers, adopts the covered window paradigm which allows windows to overlap on the screen. Windows can be thought of as pieces of paper on a desk. A window may be on top of another window just as one piece of paper may be on top of another piece of paper. Commands must be provided to allow the user to bring certain windows to the top and to specify which window is the listener. Even with these commands, it is sometimes difficult to manage a large number of windows. The screen gets cluttered and finding a desired window is difficult. Some systems (SUN, Macintosh) have defined an *icon* as a little picture, often at the bottom of the screen, to represent the window. The window can be shrunk until only its icon is visible. Unfortunately, the icons contain very little information and this limits their usefulness.

Icons in Sapphire differ in that they provide a great deal of status information. The 64×64 square icon contains the following eight pieces of status information as shown in **Figure 6.1**:

(a)   *Error indicator*: a small bug appears in the top left of the icon to indicate an error has occurred.

(b)   *Keyboard*: a keyboard appears at the middle top of the icon to indicate that the process is waiting for input.

(c)   *Exclamation mark*: this is reserved for specific application-defined attention signals.

(d)   *Process name*: the application program may optionally replace this with some other useful names.

(e)   *First progress bar*: this is used by the application program to indicate what percentage of the current task has been completed. This progress bar is repeated underneath the title of the window itself. A random sequence of vertical lines changing in position is used when an application program is unable to identify how much of the task is complete. The changing random image at least indicates that the application is still executing.

(f)   *Second progress bar*: this is used to indicate how much of the entire job has been completed. For example, it might indicate how much of a command file had been processed if this was how the application program had been started.

(g)   *Off-screen indicator*: three dots at the bottom of the icon indicate that the window has been moved off-screen.

The border of the icon is shaded grey if the associated window is the listener.

The main reason behind Sapphire icons is the view that a user running many tasks at the same time gets confused or does not remember what the various tasks are doing. He needs some aids to control and monitor the different processes. Of these, the progress bar is the most important in that it tells the user whether the task is running, how long it has been since it started, and approximately how long it has still to run. A formal experiment [43] demonstrated that users preferred systems with progress bars. Novices felt better about the system since they knew that the command had been accepted and the task was progressing successfully. Experienced users had sufficient information to allow them to estimate completion times and, therefore, to plan their time more effectively.

Icons provide a good example of how one design decision affects another so that there is much less freedom in designing a system than is apparent when you start. For example, it was decided early on that the icons always provide useful information and so should always be on the screen even when the window is visible. The alternative paradigm of the icon as another representation of the window, with one or other appearing but not both, was rejected as this could lead to the position where the window was on the screen but covered and the icon off-screen. Consequently, no status information would be available to the user.

With a Sapphire icon, you have the problem of deciding whether commands such as 'move' (reposition the item at a different position either on or off the screen) when applied to an icon is referring to the icon or the window associated with it. Is the command applied to the icon or effectively sent through it and applied to the associated window? One solution would be to duplicate all the commands so that you had both 'move icon' and 'move window' commands. Rather than do this in Sapphire, the decision was taken to group all the icons together in a single window. Commands such as 'move' then only apply to windows. The decision to associate icons with windows rather than have only one or the other on the screen led to the decision to group the icons in a window.

The icon window behaves much like other windows so that the icons as a group can be moved around or removed altogether if the user does not like icons. The icon window can be covered by other windows. Its size and position can be

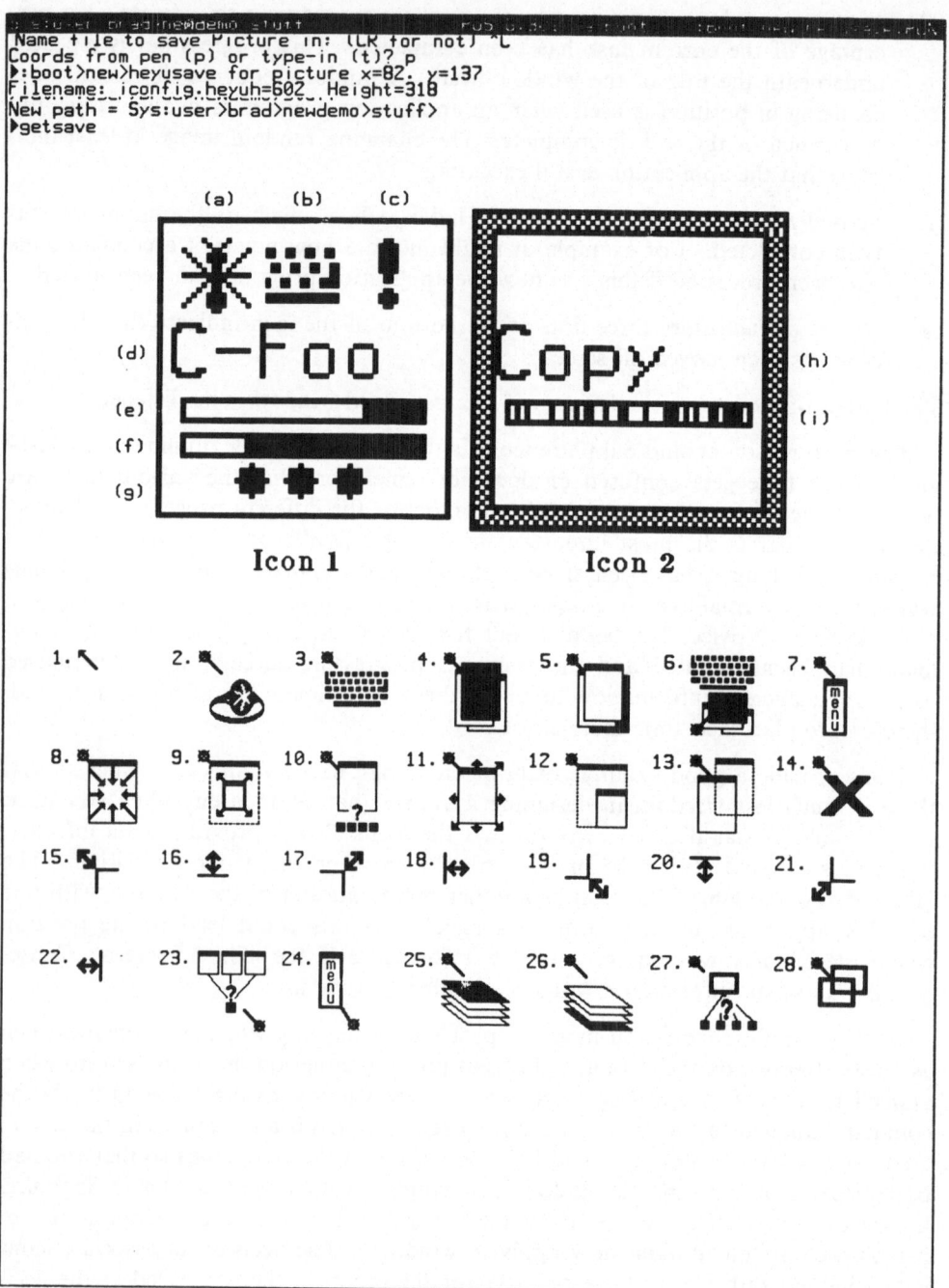

Figure 6.1

changed. The icons in the icon window are not rearranged except on user command. When a window is deleted, the icon is removed but the hole is not filled until another window is created. Thus users can remember which icons go with which window by position.

6.2.2 User Control

To provide more user control in Sapphire, each function provides three different interfaces to the user:

(1)   pop-up menu;

(2)   direct pointing device button press;

(3)   keyboard.

Sapphire has a conventional pop-up menu interface and all commands can be initiated in this way. A button press causes the menu to appear. The user picks an item from the menu and the menu disappears, restoring the picture that was underneath. Advantages of pop-up menus include the fact that they do not take up screen space and novices do not have to remember all the commands before they can get started. With a system such as Sapphire with a rich set of commands, the size of the pop-up menu can get very long and users find that it takes a long time to select a command.

The Sapphire accelerators provide a faster interface to these functions. The goal is to make the most common window manager commands very easy to specify, for example, with a single button press or keyboard key being sufficient. The title line of a window is divided into three sections with the left and right sections having the same effect. The puck has three buttons so that the two areas and three buttons give six commands that can be initiated by a single button press. Sapphire sets these six commands to the most commonly used ones. The actual assignment of commands to these six alternatives can be changed by the user.

Sapphire also provides a keyboard interface to the commands. As there is a large number of commands, a special prefix key is used which effectively sets the system in Window Management Mode and the next key press indicates the command to be obeyed. This facility was provided primarily for people who preferred not to use a pointing device. We were surprised to find that many users preferred to use the keyboard mode of input. However, it should not be surprising if you analyse the alternatives using the keystroke model. This is especially true for commands not available on the title lines.

One problem with keyboard input is that it turns the system into a modal one and people then become confused as to which mode they are in. Sapphire attempts to alleviate the problem by having the cursor picture change depending on the mode. Also, the cursor picture shows what command will be given, allowing users to abort commands *before* they are executed.

6.2.3 Issues

The experience with Sapphire has raised a number of design issues with respect to window management systems which can be categorized approximately as:

(1)   user adaptation;

(2)   integration with User Interface Management System (UIMS);

(3)   interference between application and window management models;

(4)   differences in window management models.

Particular users may have a mode of working which is desirable for them but which may not be generally applicable. For example, some users may like the top and listener commands to be distinct. The first makes a window uncovered and the second selects a particular window for accepting input. Other users find this quite confusing. They expect that when they bring a window to the top it is the one that is listening to them. The system must allow the users to tailor the user interface and this might be implemented with a User Interface Management System.

How does the User Interface Management System relate to the window manager? To tailor the window manager requires a UIMS. However, UIMSs require window management type functions. Real questions arise as to whether you integrate the two and, if not, which do you implement first?

Another issue is the interference between the user interface of the window manager and the user interface of the application running under the window manager. No matter how simple the user interface of the window manager is, it needs to specify functions such as which window is the listener, and commands such as top and move. For example, Sapphire requires a button press to change the listener while other systems just require the cursor to be moved into a window for that window to become the listener. Thus, in Sapphire you require an explicit press to change the listener and moving outside the window does not change things. The Sapphire window manager model is, therefore, one where presses are important events and movements are of less significance.

Compare this with applications where movement is the main operation. Many applications use pop-up menus where movement is important as it changes the highlighted menu item. In a Bravo-style editor, moving the cursor may well cause the cursor picture to change. We may thus have an application where movement is the dominant operation running under a window manager where button presses are the dominant operation or vice versa. In such cases, the user is likely to get confused.

A related question is whether commands to the window manager get passed to the application. For example, should a command to change the listener also get sent to the application for information? If it gets sent through and the application is not expecting it, that will cause problems. If it is never sent through, the user may do something expecting the application to respond and it does not. Interlisp-D allows the application to choose whether it gets told. However, this is equally confusing as that also can lead to inconsistent and confusing responses.

Finally, there is the point that all window managers are different. If you walk up to a random window manager having used another, you really do not know what to do. Thus, you can have portable applications which cannot be used because the window manager between the user and the application is completely different.

6.3 INPUT

An important problem is how input from the user is dealt with and passed to the application program. On the output side there are still many issues but it is basically a choice between several options all of which we know how to implement. On the input side, we really do not know the right thing to do nor do we have an adequate model of what we are trying to achieve. There are really only two choices - polling and queuing - for the input model and the third question is the complication caused by multiple input devices.

6.3.1 Polling

If polling is used as the input model, either the application program or some other process must sit in a tight loop asking all the relevant devices if they have any input. This works reasonably well in an environment where there is a single process. However, as soon as you have multiple processes it is not very efficient as you can use up a lot of processor cycles and lose characters and events.

6.3.2 Queuing

Queuing presents a number of problems due to the lag between the time the event occurs and the time it is interpreted. Existing operating systems queue keyboard input. Certain errors require the input buffer to be cleared and the lack of synchronization makes it difficult to know to what point you should clear out the buffer. A similar problem occurs with pop-up menus when you queue up the button presses. The user hits a button to select a particular menu item, nothing happens immediately so he hits it again. Meanwhile the system acts on the first button hit and then acts on the second button hit in the environment after the first button hit has been accepted. Consequently, the user gets totally confused.

In many systems, specific events such as 'abort' cannot or should not be queued. The user does not want it to happen later. He may be trying to close down the system now or stop output going to a printer. To handle such events, you need an entirely separate mechanism.

Type ahead is also a problem in non-homogenous systems. On a loaded system, different things may happen if the command is interpreted immediately by whatever is currently running rather than waiting until it reaches the front of the event queue. This occurs frequently in Unix systems with a program like Emacs. The Unix shell interprets everything immediately while a program like Emacs requires the Unix kernel to stop interpreting the characters and give them to it direct. Consequently, you have to learn not to type ahead when using Emacs. As we go to more sophisticated shells and more sophisticated applications, such problems are likely to arise even more.

6.3.3 Multiple Windows

A separate problem occurs when interfacing different processes to the same set of windows. If you think of the windows as corresponding to different terminals, they obviously need to have different queues and characters go separately to each window. However, when you have multiple windows for the same program, do you want one queue for all the windows so that you can keep the events synchronized or do you have separate queues for each window but timestamp the information so that you know which event came first?

A related issue when a program is using several windows is how you identify the listener. Two windows may be cooperating and input sent to one is passed by the application to the other for execution. The listener has to be specified as the first window yet the user sees the input being acted upon by the second and he gets a very confused model of the system. The problem is even worse if windows are divided into subwindows as the user may not even be aware of the subdivision.

6.3.4 Multiple Input Devices

While the window manager only has to deal with a single keyboard and pointing device, it is relatively easy to define the listener as a single window and allow both input devices to move as a group from one window to another. In the future, people are likely to realize that they have two hands, two feet, ears and eyes. Speech I/O, foot pedals etc will mean that the user has a variety of input devices from which to choose.

In such an environment, it is not clear that it is sensible to move all the input devices from one window to another as the listener changes. Some devices may only be used with certain windows in which case you require to move some devices with the listener while leaving others pointing at the old listener. The problems are: how do you specify which devices are attached to which window, and how do you let the user know?

6.4 IMPLEMENTATION

6.4.1 Picture Updating

Sapphire allows windows to overlap and that immediately raises the question whether you allow updates to the parts of the windows that are covered. Sapphire allows this and there are several ways in which it can be done depending on what you are optimizing for. The main issue is how to deal with refresh when a window becomes uncovered.

(1) *Speed*: the fastest way to refresh the picture is to have the complete picture off-screen and RasterOp it back on to the screen when it becomes visible. The disadvantage is that it takes a lot of memory for the off-screen images of windows.

(2) *Memory*: the application is asked to refresh the parts of the screen that become visible. The application probably has a much more concise way of representing the data held in the window. Usually, the application knows what it has displayed in the window. There are very few programs that cannot refresh the picture. After all, they generated it in the first place.

A compromise between the two solutions above is to save only those sections of the windows that are covered. This avoids having two copies, one off-screen and one on, of the information on the screen that is not covered.

Sapphire provides both of the choices. The application can choose to do the update or request Sapphire to save off-screen those parts of windows that are covered. This is done at the time the window is created. Sapphire also provides a third alternative which allows the application to specify neither. In this case, the screen is blank when the window is uncovered.

Interlisp uses a different scheme whereby a window saves the picture which is underneath it. This is very useful with pop-up menus which then appear and disappear very quickly. Sapphire also provides this facility calling such windows *courteous*. Thus windows in Sapphire either remember what is in them or what they are hiding.

Our experience has been that trying to provide both courteous and normal windows does not work very well. If you have windows that have off-screen memory and courteous windows overlapping each other, and you move one of the windows to the top, there is no order in which you can update the windows that will be correct. They all have to be updated first or you have to use separate buffers into which you move information temporarily.

6.4.2 Rectangle Lists

To identify what parts of windows are covered so that graphics can be clipped appropriately, most systems keep a rectangle list with individual items marked as covered or not. On a graphic operation, the window manager goes through and updates the covered portions in off-screen memory and the uncovered portions on the screen. Sapphire has such a list.

Deciding the order in which the rectangles are processed is analogous to the problem of shifting elements in an array. In that case, you either shift the elements from the top of the array first or the bottom depending on whether you are moving elements up the array or down. In the case of moving rectangles, the order in which RasterOps occur is different depending on whether you are moving the rectangle up and to the right, up and to the left, down and to the left or down and to the right. There are four different orderings in which the three subparts of the rectangle are moved. An example of moving the rectangle up and right is shown in **Figure 6.2**.

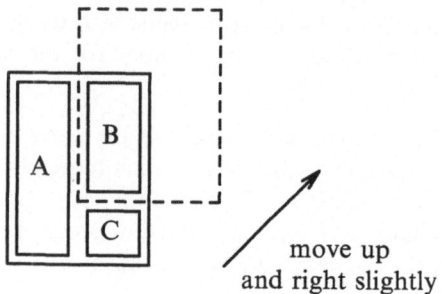

move up
and right slightly

Rectangles must be moved
in the order B C A

Figure 6.2

6.4.3 Graphical Output

The window management system needs to provide fast updating of graphical information in the windows. In Sapphire, we differentiate between graphical output to
covered and uncovered parts of windows. For uncovered parts, drawing is performed directly to the screen memory with a clipping imposed by the kernel. For
covered parts, updating is performed using the inter process communication mechanism of the Accent operating system.

The problems arise when you want to support even faster graphics by adding
microcode to draw circles and other special graphics. It is difficult to see how protection of the various windows can be achieved and still make good use of the
hardware.

6.4.4 Move and Grow

Some theoretical results give some order of relative cost of operations in a covered
window environment. If N is the number of windows, a RasterOp is inherently of
order N^2 which contradicts the claim of Rob Pike that it is of order $N\log N$.

'Move and grow', which Pike decided not to provide in BLIT because they are
too complicated, are provided in Sapphire and they are extremely complicated. The
reason for the complexity is that an attempt is made to retain all the information
that is possible. The picture is automatically redrawn in the new window. As both
the source and destination of the window may be covered or partially covered, the
picture update is complicated. A major question is whether it is sensible to attempt
to redraw the picture. As the window has changed in size, the application is likely to
want to redraw the window contents immediately to fit the new size window in
which case the updating is immediately overwritten by the application. However, if
the application has requested Sapphire to provide memory to remember the picture,
you cannot assume that the application has the ability to redraw the picture.

6.4.5 Separate Processes

Several problems arise when you consider how the window manager is implemented with respect to the operating system with which it is associated. The Accent operating system is based on a system of asynchronous message-passing primitives and Sapphire uses these as its inter process communication mechanism. It is natural in this environment to think of the window manager as a process to and from which other processes send and receive messages. However, messages take a finite time to arrive and this can cause problems.

For example, imagine a file is being typed into a window with the text scrolling up the screen. Suppose another window partially obscures this window so that text disappears and reappears as it scrolls underneath this window. If the window manager is requesting the application to redraw the uncovered parts, by the time the message is received by the application, the text has moved and it is likely that the application will refresh the wrong piece of text. There is no way round this *fixup* problem without providing more synchronization. This may not be possible with some operating systems.

Another problem that the application has in a window management environment is whether it can get sufficient of the processor time to ensure reasonable feedback when it is working in a real-time environment. This may affect the way the application is structured as well as the window manager.

Finally, there is the issue of how closely the graphics package should be integrated with the window manager. Cedar, for example, is built on top of a fairly sophisticated graphics package and the APPLE Macintosh has a similar structure. The alternative approach is to assume the graphics package (say GKS) sits on top of the window manager. The problem is that the window manager itself does graphics. The 'move' operation, titling of windows, drawing borders, constructing icons are all graphical operations and the window manager would like to use the flexibility of a full graphics package to do this. This is shown in the Macintosh where the windows are much more elaborate in terms of the pictures presented because it has a graphics package it can use. Integrating the graphics package and window manager produces a large system. If the window manager is to be portable it should sit on top of the graphics package and not vice versa.

6.5 SUMMARY

When you are designing a window manager, there are many tradeoffs and the design decisions are interrelated. Sapphire attempts to provide a rich user environment and this leads to complexity. We have found that users do make use of the options provided. In particular, progress indicators and cursor-picture changing have been much appreciated and used. As a result, applications running under Sapphire tend to have a richer user environment than if these facilities had not been provided by the window manager. Users tend not just to port an application without change but rework their application to make extensive use of the facilities provided.

6.6 DISCUSSION

Chairman - Austin Tate

Teitelman: In Sapphire, you allow the application to tailor the environment including changing the icons. Will this not leave the user with seeing many different environments together rather than a consistent one?

Myers: Sapphire is similar to the environment on the Macintosh in as far as you provide a bunch of facilities which you allow the application to change. The application is aware that if he does not use the standard facilities, it will look different to everybody else. There is a continuum between having no functionality and providing the entire interface. The claim is that the more you provide, the more the application is likely to use.

Teitelman: You mentioned the additional complexity of specifying the listener when you have multiple input devices. Did all the devices move to a different window when the listener changed? Is this not an argument for not having so many devices?

Myers: Not necessarily, the point is that the user is interacting with an application program far more often than he is interacting with the window management system. He creates a window, brings it to the top and then may interact with the application for half an hour. If you can provide a better interface to the application by providing six input devices, that is what you should be doing to make the user most effective. If another application also requires six input devices, that needs to be provided too. The window manager has to deal with this situation not because it is easy for the window manager and makes it better but because it makes the application programs better.

In Sapphire, we tried hard not to constrain what we gave to the application. It has access to all the buttons on the puck and all the keys on the keyboard while it is the listener so that it can have the best interface it can come up with. You should not say you can only have two buttons because the window manager needs the third. The window manager is not that important in the real scheme of things in terms of the user's requirements.

Rosenthal: The property of being the listener for each input device potentially has to be separate to allow flexibility although it should be possible to cluster devices which move with the listener.

Butler: How many Sapphire users are there?

Myers: There are about 20 companies or so using Sapphire but I don't have any information on usage.

7   A Modular Window System for Unix

Dominic Sweetman

7.1 INTRODUCTION

Whitechapel Computer Works is a UK company founded in April 1983 which manufactures a workstation running a Unix operating system. The company is situated in the East End of London, a step or two away from Silicon Valley! This paper describes the window manager for the workstation, gives some background to the design decisions and attempts to forecast problems likely to arise in the future.

7.1.1 Whitechapel MG-1

The Whitechapel MG-1's design goal was to produce a personal workstation of similar performance to existing workstations but set at a price equivalent to that of a personal computer.

Unlike most of its competitors which use the Motorola 68010, the Whitechapel MG-1 is based on the National Semiconductor 32016. The important characteristics of the design as far as the window manager is concerned are:

(1) *Video refresh from main memory*: the display of 800×1024 pixels is refreshed directly from main memory. There is no intermediate frame buffer. The refresh rate is 57 Hz.

(2) *RasterOp processor*: provides a full set of 16 functions operating anywhere in the memory space.

(3)   *Separate hardware cursor*: a 64 × 64 bitmap anywhere in memory can be video mixed with the main screen image. Its position is controlled by a separate processor which tracks the mouse position. Rapid switching by hardware between alternative cursors gives fast cursor picture change.

The MG-1 currently runs a variant of the Unix 4.1BSD system (Genix) but will be moving to Berkeley 4.2 in the near future.

The first system was delivered in August 1984 and the window manager was released recently to beta-test sites.

7.1.2 Goals of Window Manager

The window manager design started in the late summer of 1984. A major concern initially was whether to use the overlapped or tiled window model. The overlap model has the advantages of giving more efficient use of the screen, and the desktop metaphor on which it is based is generally more familiar than the tiled model where the pages are continually rearranging themselves. Creating a new window or changing the size of an existing one in the tiled model implies a reorganization of the screen and this potentially causes more interference to the application.

The overlap model does demand more of the machine. As Whitechapel anticipates other people putting different window managers on the MG-1, if the MG-1 is capable of supporting an overlapped window model efficiently, it will also be capable of supporting a tiled model. The main design decision was to go for an overlapped window paradigm.

7.2 ARCHITECTURE

7.2.1 Introduction

The simple model of a window manager is as shown in **Figure 7.1**. Applications generate graphics which are displayed. If the hardware was able to support multiple contexts, no window manager would be needed at all. However, with current systems, hardware and software, the situation is not like that. A single mouse has to be multiplexed between a number of applications. Also, the operating system imposes structure on both the application and the window manager. With the firm decision to use a Unix operating system, the architecture of the software system had to fit with the basic strengths and limitations of Unix systems.

7.2.2 What is in the Kernel?

One of the major problems in the design of a window management system for a Unix operating system is that of determining the degree of functionality to embed in the kernel. Ideally, very little of the window management system would be represented in the operating system kernel; but because of the inadequate inter process communication mechanisms and susceptibility to scheduling delays under heavy load such a system would not offer fast enough feedback for a good user interface.

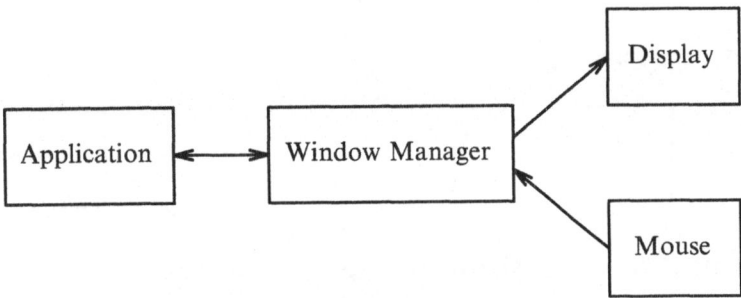

Figure 7.1

There is also the question of how applications will be structured. Although it appears attractive to build applications out of a large number of cooperating processes, it is likely that single processes will be used for the most part, not because this is a good way to structure programs but because it works. Unix programs are either in user space and find it hard to communicate with each other and hard to communicate with devices, or they are in the kernel in which case they are hard to program and hard to debug.

The decision was taken to split the window manager into two parts one of which was in the kernel and the other in user space. The window manager cannot be taken totally out of the kernel because time-critical tasks of window update and feedback, mouse control etc have to be carried out without a scheduling delay and, consequently, have to be in the kernel. On the other hand, one cannot have the application program having to do all graphics updates via an IPC mechanism.

That implies that the part of the window manager that actually deals with graphics should go into the kernel in some sense and you leave outside the parts of the window manager that do user interfacing. There is no question of embedding the user interface into the kernel as that would be disastrous. The problem that arises is what is the appropriate level of the division between graphics operations inside the kernel and window operations outside.

The application, of course, just sees a single collection of functions that can be called and is unaware of the split. The revised diagram of the window manager is shown in **Figure 7.2**.

The Whitechapel window manager has two main objects that are manipulated, *panels* and *windows*. The application deals with panels which have no user interface properties. The user deals with windows which are much more of interest to the user than the application. The kernel resident part of the window manager only knows about panels. All the window management functions are in a user process ('window manager').

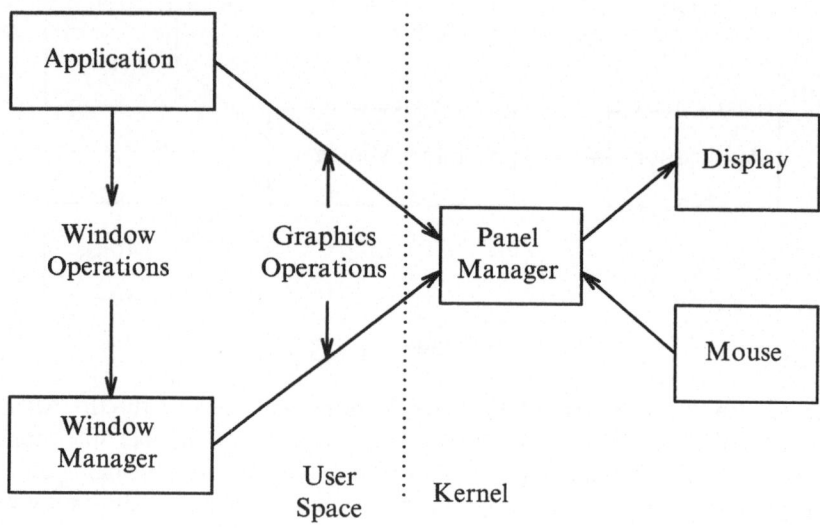

Figure 7.2

7.2.3 Panels

A *panel* is a rectangular area which is a viewport onto a client or application bitmap. Applications output graphical and textual information to panels. A major design decision is at what level does information pass from the application to the part of the window manager implemented in the kernel and responsible for updating the panels? Because the kernel is difficult to change and it is envisaged that applications run in a single system, the decision was taken that the interface should be at the bitmap level.

Applications call graphics primitives in libraries which maintain a bitmap copy of the image that they are displaying. The information passed from the application to the kernel is either the complete bitmap (when the panel is created) or a subrectangle when part of the panel needs updating. Incidentally, a paper study has shown that this system can be mapped on to hardware which uses display lists and where there is no access to bitmaps, provided clipping can be done efficiently.

Panels have a position and priority on the display so panels give you a division of the screen into a set of possibly overlapping rectangles. Panels are organized in a hierarchy with each panel having only one parent but it may have several child panels. The positions of children's panels are relative to the parent. Consequently, it is possible to build a family of panels all descended from a single parent which will move around the screen as the parent moves.

Support for pop-up menus is achieved by creating a new child panel containing the pop-up menu. The pop-up menu is deleted just by deleting the child panel from the hierarchy.

7.2.4 Windows

The part of the window manager in the kernel manages panels, while the part running as a user process manages windows. Messages to the window manager currently use an IPC mechanism which is actually a pseudo TTY in order to provide some portability between Berkeley 4.1 and 4.2.

The window manager creates and manipulates windows for the user. The window consists of a set of panels some of which are provided for the application to use while others (borders and title) are created by the window manager. A typical window is shown in **Figure 7.3**.

The window manager reserves the corners and title bar for its own use, only allowing the application to change the text in the title bar. The edges of the window are owned by the application with library routines being provided to allow functions such as scrolling, splitting, changing size etc.

The window manager organizes the desktop; window creation and destruction (by explicit Unix commands) and provides corner controls for reorganizing the desktop (move, resize etc). The window manager itself does not have any menus nor does it

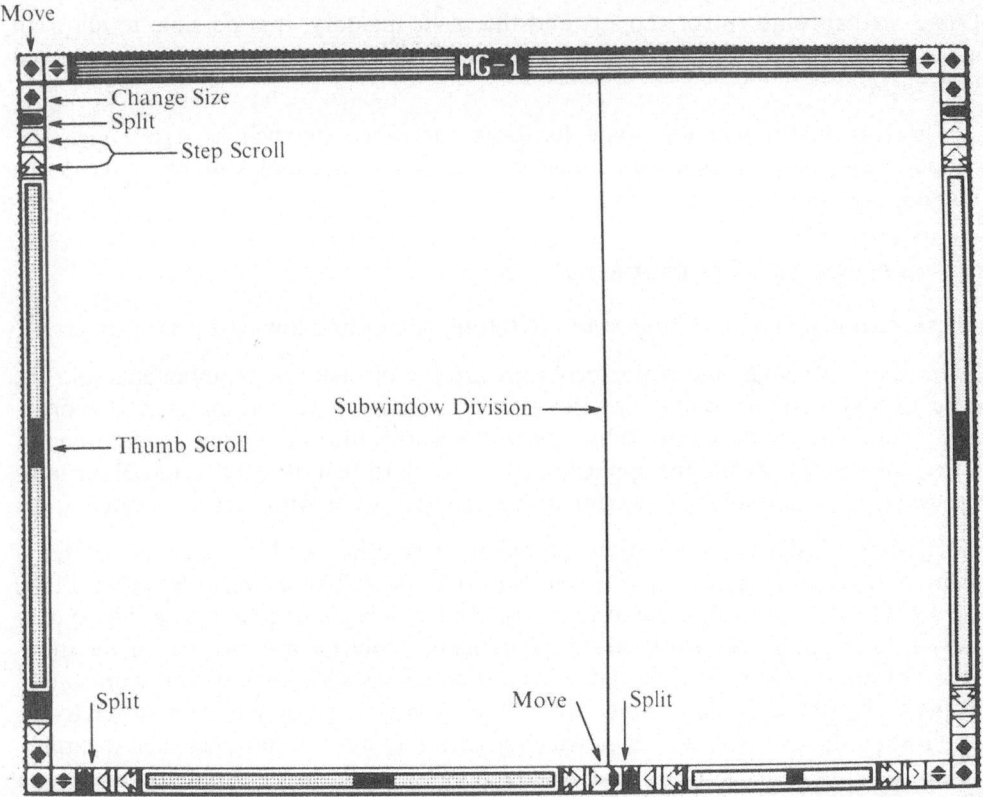

Figure 7.3

predefine any button use. The window manager regards all buttons on the mouse as equivalent. This it is believed will cause the minimum interference with any application.

7.2.5 Redrawing and Cursor Control

In the kernel, the panel manager is responsible for handling the hierarchy of panels which are displayed as a set of overlapping rectangular areas. The main strategy has been not to expect too much from the application. Consequently, all redrawing of windows that become uncovered is the responsibility of the panel manager. The view was that it was unreasonable to send a signal to the application that certain parts of the display need to be redrawn.

To accomplish the redrawing, the panel manager has off-screen in memory the complete bitmap of each panel. The experience so far is that performance implications are reasonable.

With the hardware support for cursor changing, it is sensible for all cursor changing to be done in the kernel. Effectively, the window manager and application tell the panel manager which cursor should be displayed in each region of the display. Using the hardware cursor support and the cache memory, it is possible to allow an arbitrary number of regions on the screen with different cursor pictures associated with them.

The kernel also provides some feedback for functions such as wireframes and rubber bands. Other functions could be added but the aim will be to keep the number of options as low as is reasonable.

7.3 FUTURE REQUIREMENTS

We see two main areas of interest in the future, colour and low-cost laser printers.

In terms of colour, the major problems are the diversity of requirements and the need to retain compatibility with the existing monochrome system. A major problem is how you handle colour tables when the workstations are likely to have one or a few colour tables while the applications are likely to require a different colour table per window. The problem is similar to the one that arises with cursor pictures.

The second area is the ability to output to laser printers. It is clear that within a short timeframe the cost of laser printers in the UK will be down to less than £1500 per workstation (possibly $500 in the USA) and it is beginning to be possible to consider a laser printer per workstation. The major problems are the cost of the interface and the resolution of the laser printer which exceeds that of the workstation display. This implies that output to the laser printer must derive from closer to the application than the bitmap image which is currently our interface between the application and the Unix kernel panel manager. This leads to the need for defining a higher level interface. Until the talk by James Gosling, my view had been that PostScript seemed impossibly complex actually to do real-time image updates. I would like to be proved wrong!

7.4 DISCUSSION

Chairman - Austin Tate

Gosling: I would like to prove you wrong! You are currently using 4.1 IPC which does not have reasonable communications mechanisms. Does your design decision concerning the slowness of IPC stand up for 4.2 where the IPC is reasonable?

Sweetman: It depends what you mean by reasonable. Compared with the multiprocess systems that I am used to, Unix IPC is unbelievably slow in 4.2. Process to process message passing takes several milliseconds. It does not permit you to structure applications into communicating subcomponents unless they communicate relatively infrequently.

Gosling: I agree but this is not really a problem. One of the things you have to do is to batch together requests. This makes the overheads of message passing acceptable. It will not work if you send out one packet for each line you draw.

Sweetman: We did not assume IPC was out of the question but we did believe batching was unnatural.

Williams: Batching is all very well, but you cannot do that in the inner feedback loop. That is where it really breaks down.

Gosling: IPC works when the ratio of the number of pixels to be drawn is large compared with the number of bits sent in the packet.

Sweetman: So you can use it for operations that naturally happen once or twice for each user input but you cannot use it for operations which might happen 50 times.

Rosenthal: You said that resize causes the kernel to update the display. Do applications get resize information?

Sweetman: Yes, they get sent an event in the event queue and they can optionally ask for a signal. Obviously some applications when you resize their window will want to resize their picture. For windows becoming uncovered or covered, they do not get told.

Bono: If applications cannot suppress the redraw, does this not lead to flashing when the kernel redraws the picture and the application does it immediately afterwards?

Sweetman: It is certainly possible but we have not noticed this effect.

8   Standards Activities

John Butler

8.1 INTRODUCTION

The ANSI X3H3 (Graphics) arena is concerned with standardization of data exchange, virtual terminals, and the user interface. Over the last six months a number of meetings have taken place between people interested in the Window Management area, beginning with a request for a standard expressed at SIGGRAPH 84. During December of the same year an *ad hoc* meeting of 12-15 people was held, where it was clear that there was enough interest to proceed. In January 1985, at a meeting of the X3H3 Committee which had some European involvement, interest initially centred on the Computer Graphics Interface (CGI) proposal [30]. The group felt that some modifications to this proposal were called for, such as the introduction of complex clipping areas and the ability to direct primitives to a specific window. A further *ad hoc* meeting was held in February, where it was decided to explore standards based on the shared resource model, and standards at the applications interface level. A useful line to explore is whether there are limited ways to construct systems; if so it may be possible to build configurable interfaces.

As part of the SIGCHI 85 conference in April a User Interface Workshop was held. The view from the Human Factors community expressed there was that it might be possible to standardize at the application program interface level, but not at the user interface level. A further workshop is to be held in May at the Boston meeting of X3H3.

Other ANSI committees with interests in Window Management are X3H5 (Virtual Terminal and User Interface), X3T5 (OSI), and X3V1 (Documents). The *ad hoc* group feels that there is a need for a new committee to consider virtual terminal and user interface standardization, and to coordinate with the existing standards committees.

As a caveat, the author would like to state that this presentation represents his personal opinions, and little has been presented to X3H3 yet. Other workers have advocated a more limited view; for example, that at present only the application interface can be standardized. Possible Committee actions range from none, to the formation of a new task group. The X3H3 members at the Workshop [Butler and Bono] were interested both in raising the level of awareness of issues already formulated, and in learning as much as possible about implementation issues from other Workshop attendents.

8.2 MODELS

8.2.1 Basic Program Models

Present models of interactive systems have evolved each with its own terminology. There needs to be agreement on terminology and the basic model before standards can be defined. At the most basic level the model in **Figure 8.1** can be drawn. A more detailed version of the model is shown in **Figure 8.2**.

Specific knowledge about the interactive hardware is needed by an application to interact with a user, and abstraction is required to enable portability. The adaptation layer is provided as a layer below the system level to provide abstraction from real devices. A language for portable systems is at this level; below this, items are system-specific.

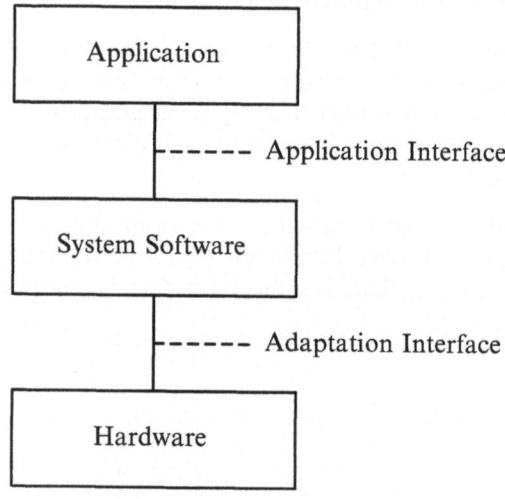

Figure 8.1

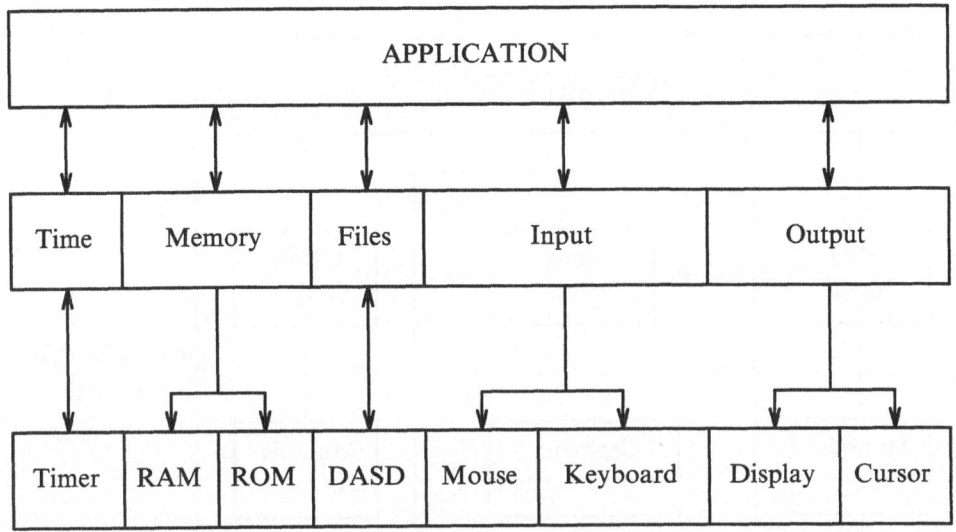

Figure 8.2

8.2.2 Reference Model

Figure 8.3 shows a reference model for interactive programs (DI = Device Independent, DD = Device Dependent).

The centre column of functions shows links or *sneak paths* which might be utilized to short-circuit the complete user ⟷ application sequence if necessary. At the lowest level this is tracking (for example, of the cursor) while at the DI level it is echo (using the GKS input model terminology). Multiple stream and UIMS levels generate links corresponding to segment transformations and menus, forms or dialogues respectively. Languages are needed (and exist) to allow the application to control these sneak paths. Not all architectures support such controls.

8.2.3 Model of User

Similar notions and levels exist in the model of a user given in **Figure 8.4**. Note the similar cross links to those in the graphics model; for example the knee jerk reflex at the lowest level, hand withdrawal at pain or pressure, head turning to sound of thunder/flash of lightning, and a greeting at the complex multisense level. The tactile feedback of a key click is different in type to the character feedback on screen or paper.

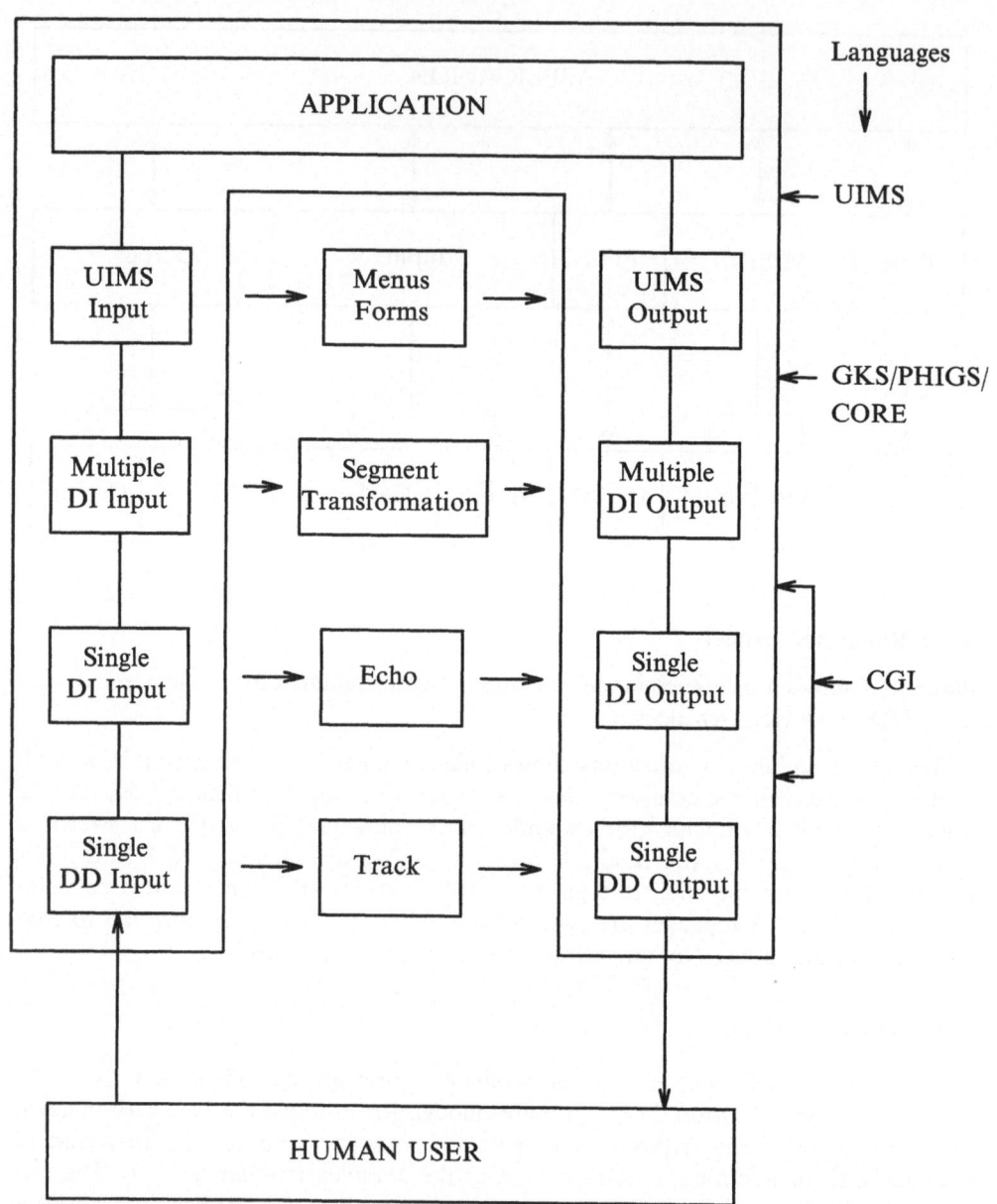

Figure 8.3

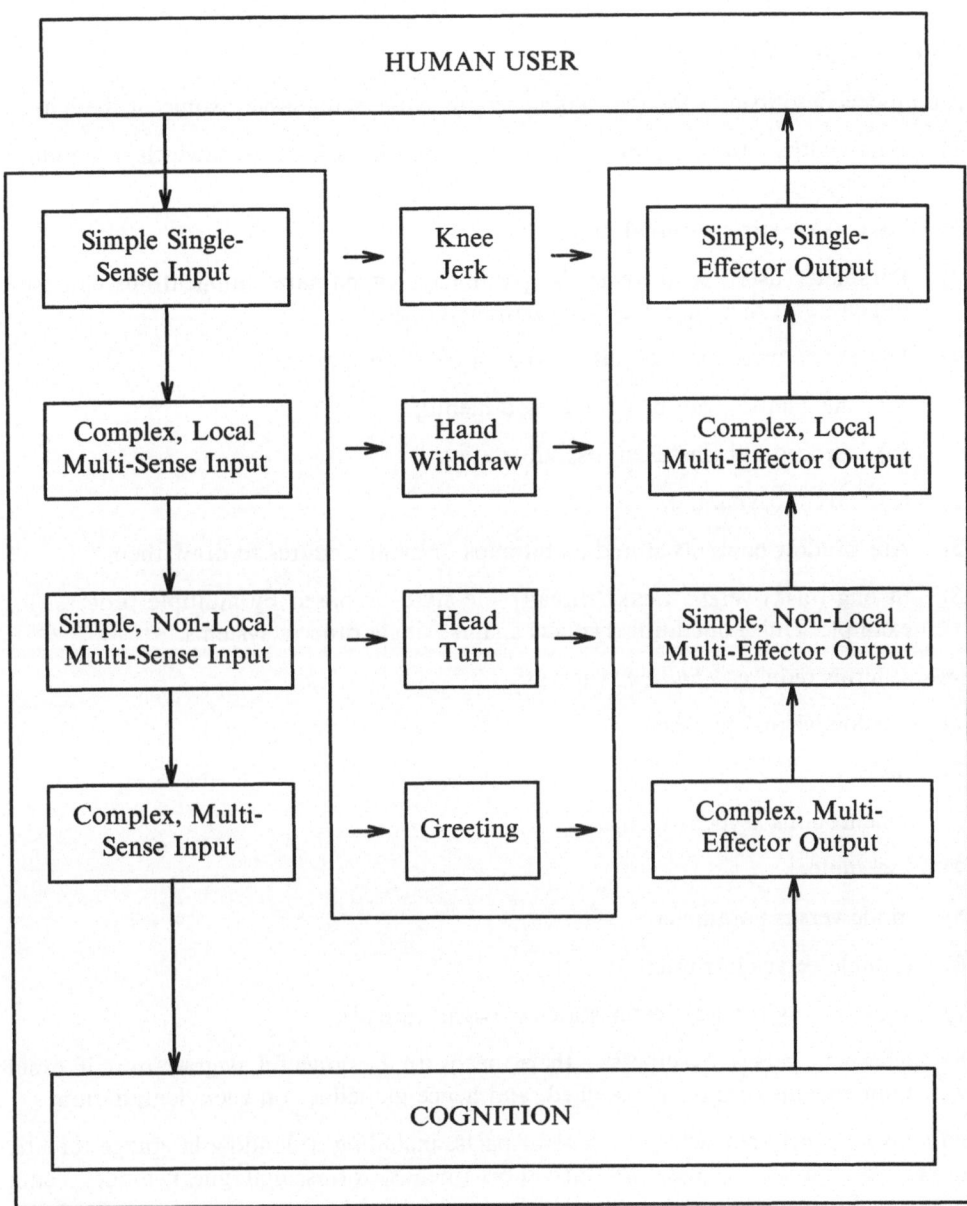

Figure 8.4

8.3 UNRESOLVED MATTERS

The models described in the preceeding section raise many issues; some of these are:

(1)   Bandwidths - the PC, for example, can use all its CPU bandwidth in handling the display.

(2)   Task ⟷ virtual terminal mapping.

(3)   Parameter lists - who owns the parameter, eg bitmaps; applications can have difficulties if there are very long parameter lists.

(4)   Parameter types and default actions; some examples are:

    (a)   file (static - can be edited, eg a menu);

    (b)   procedural (installed, pseudo-static);

    (c)   event (dynamic).

(5)   Are window contents stored as bitmaps or as procedures to draw them?

(6)   Strong (task) versus weak (thread) - ie styles imposed by multiple process (for example, Unix) operating systems against single process systems.

Several terms require *definition*, such as:

(1)   window/virtual terminal;

(2)   task;

(3)   synchronous/asynchronous;

(4)   lock/unlock;

(5)   mode versus parameter;

(6)   settable versus intrinsic;

(7)   state (strong thread) versus stateless (weak thread);

(8)   efficiency versus exactness - there needs to be graceful degradation if exact requirements cannot be matched, and hence guidelines on such degradation.

Standards in this area will have several parts, including a window language (create, move, size and so on), user interface tools (menus, forms, dialogues), models, data exchange formats (eg extracting cells from a spreadsheet to pass to another program), and bindings (both procedural and datastream).

9 A Graphics Standards View of Screen Management

Bob Hopgood

9.1 INTRODUCTION

Major users of a screen management system will be applications programs written using one of the existing or future graphics standards. The standards will be responsible for the graphical information sent to and received from the screen and its associated input devices. While this will not be the only system requiring access to the screen, it may be useful to identify the constraints placed on a screen manager by the graphics standards, and possible solutions to problems may be sensible in a wider context.

The examples used here will relate to GKS - the Graphical Kernel System [28] - but should be relevant to both PHIGS [6] and GKS-3D [29] also.

9.2 VOCABULARY

The use of the word *window* in the screen management context is certain to cause confusion in the graphics standards arena. The ISO Graphics Vocabulary and the graphics standards use the word *window* in the well established window to viewport coordinate transformation paradigm. If coordinates are to be mapped in the transformation pipeline from a higher level (closer to the user) coordinate system to a lower level (closer to the device) coordinate system, the window defines the area in the higher level coordinate system to be mapped on to the *viewport*, an area defined in terms of the lower level coordinate system.

It is likely that a screen management system will not control just the contents of a viewport but will also control information associated with the viewport including details of how its boundary is to be displayed, possible titles and control points just outside the viewport boundary etc.

To avoid confusion, this paper will use the term *frame* to describe a viewport on a virtual bitmap screen together with any associated graphical or non-graphical information related to it. The software responsible for organizing the contents of the bitmap screen will be called the Frame Management System (FMS).

The (FMS) is responsible for the control of information displayed on a single bit-map screen. The system allows a number of separate processes to share the screen resources and associated input devices under the control of a single user. The FMS simulates several virtual devices on the single screen where each virtual frame corresponds to a single virtual device. The basic goal of FMS is to allow a single user to interact with several processes at the same time.

9.3 INTERFACE TO GKS

GKS is a graphical kernel system which allows a single application to provide graph-ical interaction with a user in control of one or more real devices. GKS is divided into a virtual and real part. The application is allowed to define output using a variety of coordinate systems which are mapped on to a single virtual coordinate sys-tem, normalized device coordinates (NDC). Particular devices map NDC space on to their own device coordinate systems retaining the aspect ratio of the NDC space. This is illustrated in **Figure 9.1**.

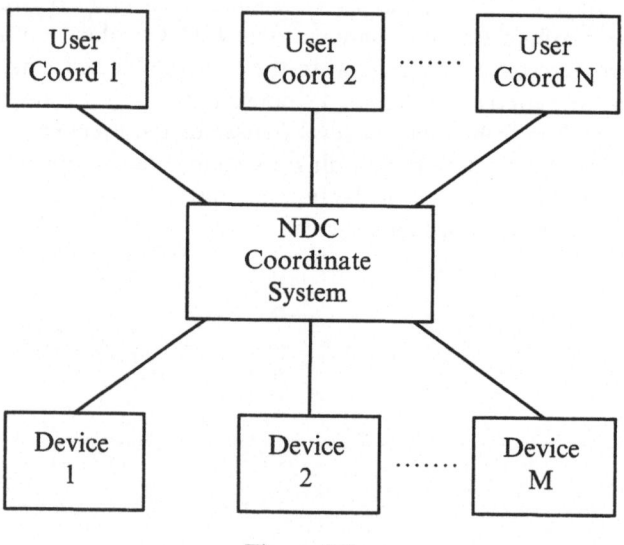

Figure 9.1

An initial decision has to be made as to where the interaction exists between GKS and FMS in **Figure 9.1**. The greater part of GKS is concerned with producing and manipulating images created in the NDC coordinate system. It would be difficult for existing GKS applications to work with an FMS above this level. GKS would still need to be responsible for the conversion of application coordinates to NDC.

Assuming the interaction between GKS and FMS occurs below the NDC level, the FMS's role will be to multiplex several GKS workstations onto a single screen from a single application and to multiplex output on a single screen from several applications controlled by a single user.

If we consider a single application and device in GKS, the transformation pipeline is as shown in **Figure 9.2**.

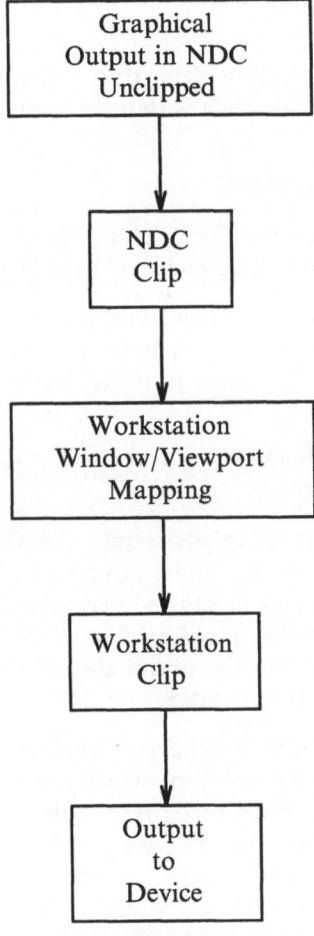

Figure 9.2

In GKS, it is possible to clip graphical data at the boundary of the window which is used to transform coordinates from world to NDC. The operation of this clip is delayed with the picture in NDC space being stored as unclipped NDC coordinates together with a clipping rectangle. The reason for this is that it allows this clip to be amalgamated with the mandatory clip against the boundary of the workstation viewport if the hardware can do that efficiently.

The obvious place where the FMS would take over from GKS is somewhere below the workstation window to viewport mapping. The two possibilities are before and after the workstation clip. Because the NDC clip should be efficiently performed by amalgamation with the workstation clip, the two possibilities are:

(1) FMS receives graphical output defined in bitmap coordinates but unclipped. The FMS performs the necessary clipping. Note that for efficient implementation of GKS, the clipping rectangle should be specified independently of the frame boundary.

(2) FMS receives graphical output defined in bitmap coordinates and clipped so that all output is known to reside within the boundary of the frame.

9.4 SUBDIVISION OF FRAMES

Some existing FMSs (for example, ToolKit/32 [70]) provide facilities for controlling subareas of the complete frame. Two concepts have been introduced:

(1) *Panels*: it is assumed that the application program has the ability to divide the complete frame into one or more panels with each panel giving a view of an object to be displayed. Control is provided for scrolling and adjusting the view of the object.

(2) *Panes*: a panel can be divided into a number of panes. Each pane can contain a different view of the object.

It is difficult to fit either panels or panes into the GKS model. Composition of graphical information into a single picture is performed at the NDC level in GKS. Only a single view of NDC space is allowed per workstation. In GKS-3D, multiple views are allowed and correspond in some sense to the panels of ToolKit/32. However, no constraints are placed on the positioning of views in GKS-3D. For example, it is possible for two panels to overlap.

In terms of graphics standards, it is unclear whether an FMS with either panes or panels would have any advantage over one which just treated the frame as the lowest level of subdivision. For the FMS to be responsible for controlling the display of information in panels or panes, the graphics standards would require it to control much more of the viewing pipeline than at present, being responsible for all the workstation functions. In GKS-3D this would require it to do the 3D perspective and viewing transformations.

9.5 ASPECT RATIO AND POSITIONING WITHIN A FRAME

The graphics standards assume that changes in aspect ratio occur above NDC in the transformation pipeline. A circle in NDC coordinates will appear as a circle on all devices. Consequently, any FMS must have the capability of ensuring no change to aspect ratio in the displayed picture.

Any change of frame size by the operator will require information to be returned to the application program if the picture is to be updated to accommodate the new frame size. It is not the responsibility of the FMS to do this for the application.

The graphics standards assume output is to a device of fixed size (apart from continuous page plotters). It assumes maximum device coordinates for a specific device and allows the application to specify that output should be directed to a subarea of the complete screen. For a virtual device controlled by an FMS, some of this flexibility is probably unnecessary. It may well be sensible for the graphics standard to specify effectively the whole of the viewport as the frame size. There appears to be little advantage in defining the workstation viewport as a subpart of the frame unless output to the frame is anticipated from the application which does not come from the graphics system.

9.6 OUTPUT CONTROL

The major reason for sending graphical information to a workstation being used in an interactive mode is to allow the operator to view the output. In an environment with an FMS where the operator is multiplexing several output devices on a single screen, it is quite possible that the operator will not see the graphical output, certainly while it is being generated and possibly ever. This clearly may or may not make sense in the case of an application using a graphics standard.

The standards recognize that it is possible that a number of situations occur concerning graphical output:

(1) *Output need not be visible on a specific workstation*: an example could be the case of output being sent frame by frame to a plotter with the operator having the ability to view selected frames on another device to check accuracy of production. This is achieved in the graphics standard by having the ability to activate or deactivate particular workstations.

(2) *Output must be generated but timing is unimportant*: in GKS, a workstation can be put into the mode ASTI (At Some TIme). This allows the workstation to batch updates until an appropriate time occurs to output it (useful in the context of a plotter).

(3) *Output must be up to date on workstation before next interaction*: in GKS, a workstation can be put in the mode BNIL (Before Next Interaction Locally). This recognizes that input should only be accepted at a workstation if the view on that workstation is up to date.

(4) *Output must be up to date on all active workstations before next interaction*: in GKS, a workstation can be put in the mode BNIG (Before Next Interaction Globally). This recognizes that input should only be accepted at a workstation if the views on all the active workstations are current.

(5) *Output must always be up to date as soon as possible*: in GKS, the mode ASAP (As Soon As Possible) requires output to be sent to all workstations as soon as is possible.

It is sensible to see how these modes of handling frames are mapped for an application running in the context of an FMS and what requirements it places on the FMS.

A sixth possibility exists in GKS but is not particularly catered for. That is where output is being generated and the operator may or may not be aware of it. An example might be where the output is giving status information. GKS does not differentiate between the two situations.

Commenting on the five modes above in an FMS environment:

(1) If generation of output is time consuming, it is still sensible to stop output to a frame when it is not required.

(2) A workstation working in ASTI mode assumes that either the operator sees the output or it is recorded in a permanent media. This mode has little use in the FMS environment.

(3) The modes BNIL and BNIG effectively require the selected frame or all frames to be visible and current before an interaction takes place.

    BNIL mode implies that input can only occur to the selected frame if it is visible.

    BNIG is a more stringent mode of operation. In the context of an FMS, it at least requires the virtual frames to be current even if all are not visible.

    In both modes, the FMS could save updates to a frame and not apply them as they arrive.

(4) The ASAP mode implies at least that the virtual frames are updated as graphical information is output.

It is clear that if the FMS supports ASAP mode, it satisfies the requirements of the other modes in terms of frames being current but does not really address the visibility issue. Effectively, the graphics standards assume output to be visible.

In summary, the graphics standards require an FMS to have the following capabilities:

(1) to output to a virtual frame;

(2) to force output to be current on a visible frame;

(3)   to force output to be current on all frames owned by an application before the next interaction;

(4)   to force output to be current on the current frame before the next interaction;

(5)   to support a mode whereby all graphical output is made visible. This could be by a switch which requires output on a frame to be made visible before the frame is cleared and another displayed.

9.7 INPUT

Most FMSs will work in an environment where a single keyboard and mouse with buttons will be multiplexed as a set of input devices for each frame.

The graphics standards divide input into six types of logical devices:

(1)   LOCATOR;

(2)   VALUATOR;

(3)   CHOICE;

(4)   STRING;

(5)   PICK;

(6)   STROKE.

Any real input device can be used to simulate these logical devices. A workstation provides the simulation and is required to provide certain types of echoing. In GKS, this echoing must appear on the workstation's screen but not necessarily in the workstation's viewport.

In an FMS environment, the LOCATOR, STROKE and PICK devices must be closely related to the frames controlled by the application. It does not seem unreasonable for the other logical devices to be simulated differently. For example:

(1)   VALUATOR: could use a separate temporary frame to input the value;

(2)   CHOICE: pop-up menus could be used;

(3)   STRING: echoing of input need not be in the current frame.

Although it would be possible for all the echoing to be done by a workstation sitting on top of the FMS, it is likely that the performance of certain operations can only be achieved effectively if the FMS takes responsibility for echoing. The FMS is likely to need to support:

(1)   *LOCATOR tracking*: it must be possible to echo the current position of the mouse.

(2)   *Rubber band lines*: it must support a rubber band line from a specified point to the current position of the mouse.

(3) *Highlighting*: of current CHOICE being pointed at followed by feedback of CHOICE selected.

Input in GKS is available in the modes REQUEST, SAMPLE and EVENT. An FMS must be capable of handling input in all three modes. This may require a particular input device to be switched between logical input devices and different modes as well. GKS also allows more than one logical input to be activated by the same TRIGGER. Thus an FMS should be capable of generating, say, a LOCATOR input and a CHOICE by a specific button hit on a mouse. It is also possible to time input requests and modify the action depending on whether input arrives or not.

9.8 ICONS

Some FMSs provide an icon facility. Its use varies from one to another. Some models are:

(1) *Process creation*: an icon is used to represent a dormant process. Picking the icon effectively causes a frame to be created and the relevant process started. It can be regarded as a macro facility for frame creation and process start-up.

(2) *Virtual frame identification*: obscured frames or ones completely off the screen can have an icon associated with them which can be used to make the frame visible.

(3) *Process status*: an icon is used to signify the status of a frame not currently visible. It might give information such as whether a process has completed, is waiting for input etc.

In the case of an application using a graphics standard as interface to the FMS, it should be possible for it to run unchanged in the environment of an FMS with icons. GKS has associated with each workstation a Workstation State Table which contains information concerning the workstation. This could be used to contain information such as icon form in case (2) above. In general, I would not anticipate much control of icons being necessary by the graphics application.

9.9 SUMMARY

The properties of a frame management system suitable for GKS and the other graphics standards should have the capabilities given below.

(1) The FMS should control information displayed on a single bitmap screen.

(2) The FMS is responsible for the management of a set of frames several of which can be associated with a single application.

(3) The FMS must know which frames are associated with the same application.

(4) Frame creation must be possible from the application program.

(5) Graphical primitives should be passed to the FMS in frame coordinates.

(6) Either the frame is in the memory of the workstation and it is responsible for bitmap updating, or the FMS must be capable of handling GKS primitives at the workstation level.

(7) If clipping is provided by the FMS, it should be to a specified boundary rather than the boundary of the frame.

(8) No subdivision of frames is necessary. Any requirements of this type should be handled by the graphics system or the workstation.

(9) The aspect ratio of output is defined by the application and not the FMS. Changes in frame size must be reported back to the application if any effect on the output is expected.

(10) An FMS should work in ASTI mode. Conceptually, virtual frames are updated as the output appears.

(11) The FMS should be able to indicate to the operator that input is required and in what mode from which logical device.

(12) The FMS should be capable of providing logical input in all three modes and from all six logical input classes. The separation of tasks between the workstation and FMS could vary.

(13) The FMS should support input from a keyboard with the ability to send an event report when 'end of string' is indicated.

10 Windows, Viewports and Structured Display Files

Colin Prosser

10.1 INTRODUCTION

Here is a selection of issues for consideration by anyone interested in discussing the merits of making more explicit use of the traditional graphics concepts of windows and viewports, and structured display files in windowing systems.

10.2 WINDOWS AND VIEWPORTS

Adopting the traditional graphics distinction between a *window* and a *viewport*, the former denotes an area in some source display space and the latter denotes an area in some destination display space. The displayed destination image appears to be clipped to lie within the viewport boundary. Some systems, like the currently issued PERQ PNX windowing system, present a window and viewport as one and the same entity. This can be regarded as a special case of one-to-one window to viewport mapping. Initial hiding of the implicit window to viewport mapping does not necessarily prevent later exposure. This approach has the advantage of simplicity and allows deferral of solving any complexities of the more general case. It has the disadvantage that the user is denied, at least in the short term, several potentially desirable facilities made feasible by fuller manipulation of window to viewport mappings.

Examining some of the possibilities for manipulating window to viewport mappings poses some interesting issues:

Issues

1. Should the window to viewport mapping be explicit?

2. Should more than one source space be permitted per windowing system?

3. Should more than one destination space be permitted per windowing system?

4. Should many window to viewport mappings be permitted per source?

5. Should clipping of output to a window boundary be mandatory or under application or user control?

6. Should it be possible to constrain a particular window to viewport mapping such that it depends on another window to viewport mapping?

7. Should it be possible to specify the destination of a window to viewport mapping to be part of a source (ie: allow hierarchies of window to viewport mappings)?

8. Should viewports be permitted to overlap?

9. Should overlapping viewports mutually interfere?

10. Should output appearing in any viewport be permitted to modify the appearance of the image in another viewport, without the mutual consent of the application(s) associated with those viewports?

11. Should the inverse window to viewport mapping(s) apply to input?

12. Should window to viewport (and inverse) mappings be restricted to unique pairs of window and viewport?

13. Should input events outside those window to viewport mappings directly accessible to an application be detectable by that application?

14. Should a manipulation to one window to viewport mapping, which has the effect of changing the visibility of parts of the viewport of another unaltered mapping, be a notifiable event to any applications associated with the affected mappings?

As is well known from traditional graphics, manipulation of a window to viewport mapping permits operations such as:

(i)   repositioning of the viewport on the display surface;

(ii)   scrolling or panning effects by moving the window in the logical display space;

(iii) scaling or resizing of the displayed image;

(iv)   controlling the visibility of a window.

When deciding how or whether to allow these operations in a window management system, several more issues might be considered.

15. Should applications be permitted to manipulate window to viewport mappings independently of any user facility for doing so?

16. Should it be possible to position viewports partially off the display surface?

17. Should control over the visibility of windows be permitted?

18. Should there be some mechanism for notifying applications of the status (or changes to the status) of window to viewport mappings?

19. Where should responsibility lie for update of images in the destination space?

20. Should it be possible to specify viewports in alternative destination spaces (eg: printer, remote screen across a LAN)?

21. For bitmap images, should the window to viewport mapping only map pixels one-for-one?

22. Should there only be one style of presentation for manipulating window to viewport mappings?

23. What makes for a good style of presentation?

10.3 BITMAPS AND STRUCTURED DISPLAY FILES

Given a one-for-one window-pixel to viewport-pixel relationship, it is attractive to consider the source space in bitmap form. One can readily imagine rapid panning and scrolling of a window over a larger display area, without having to recompute the image. Additional measures need not be taken to save information for refreshing the contents of partially obscured viewports when they are later revealed. In practice, optimizations might be made, for instance, to economize on memory utilization by avoiding duplicate copies of unobscured portions of viewports. Given multiple mutually constrained window to viewport mappings, independent images may be combined easily so as to appear in the destination space as if a single image, but with differing areas being potentially under the control of independent applications.

A bitmap image representation has some disadvantages, however. Limitations on physical resources may severely constrain the possible size of a bitmap. Transfer of information among display spaces (cut and paste) is limited to bitmap form which may have undesirable consequences if the resolutions differ. Any structure that may have been used by the application to construct the image is lost so it might be difficult to identify logical components of the image.

Another possibility is to introduce a structured display file. The disadvantage of having only a structured display file is the time taken to regenerate complex images. Perhaps some combination of structured display file and bitmap might be more appropriate than either alone.

Issues

24. How should display space images be represented? Bitmap, structured display file, combination of both?

25. Where should the source space reside? Application or windowing system?

26. Should optimizations on bitmap memory utilization be the sole responsibility of the windowing system? Or may it depend on applications honouring requests for display updates?

27. Should the windowing system support any structured display file?

28. In what form should a structured display file be maintained?

29. Should a structured display file be maintained on a per window or per source space basis?

30. Should it be possible to transfer information among windows independently of the applications which generated the images?

31. Should it be possible to store and retrieve images independently of the applications which generated the images?

11   Partitioning of Function in Window Systems

James Gosling

11.1 INTRODUCTION

What is a window system? It is a manager for graphical display devices that divides the display surface into several *windows* along with a graphics library that understands them. In a multiprocess environment each window may be supported by a separate process. This paper examines the architectural issues involved in constructing a window system in such an environment. Emphasis is placed on the communication and synchronization problems that arise.

Client processes, running in parallel, invoke the window system to manipulate windows and to perform graphic operations in them. A window system is faced with several client programs which all need access to windows. One of its hardest tasks is to coordinate client access to windows, while at the same time providing maximum performance and avoiding synchronization problems.

As an example of the synchronization problems that can occur, consider moving a window. The user sitting at the workstation issues a command that causes a window to move. This is happening *in parallel* with the client programs which are all madly drawing in their windows. A process whose window becomes partially obscured can find itself halfway through drawing a line with a window that is no longer the shape it thought it was. The drawing of the line and the moving of the window must be synchronized to avoid collisions of this type.

Because of its existence in a multiprocess environment the window system must be partitioned. The various bodies of code that make it up must be placed somewhere. Partitioning has a strong effect on synchronization and performance.

There are three basic ways in which the function of a window system can be partitioned:

(1)   it can be in the same address space as the client process, replicated for each client;

(2)   it can be outside the address space of the client process, in the kernel of the operating system;

(3)   it can be outside the address space of the client process, in a server process that is not a part of the kernel.

The distinctions are rather fuzzy since the partitioning usually ends up being a mixture of these three: some part is in the kernel, some part is in each client process, and some part is often in some other server process. The question is really one of emphasis. The choice amongst these is based on the usual considerations of functionality, performance, flexibility and ease of programming.

11.2 WHO PAINTS THE BITS?

One way of looking at the partitioning of a window system is by asking the question "Who paints the bits?"

11.2.1 The Kernel

Many operating systems force at least the graphics primitives to be in the kernel since client processes are not able to access devices directly. In operating systems where client processes can access devices directly, like 4.2 BSD Unix systems, the kernel can be completely separated from graphics operations.

Nonetheless, the kernel is often a convenient place to put device support. It also provides a centralized synchronization point. But it is susceptible to all the usual problems of placing anything into the kernel: the debugging tools are usually wretched at best, any bug that does escape detection threatens the integrity of the entire system, development cannot proceed in parallel with other uses of the system, and it usually commits a large body of code to wired-down memory.

What often happens in such systems is that only those functions which must be done by the kernel are done by the kernel. Graphical operations and synchronization are usually in the kernel, while window management is not. There are special kernel calls that only the window system uses that manipulate the kernel's data structures. These data structures contain such things as the window boundaries that the kernel must know in order to perform the graphic operations. This organization is illustrated in **Figure 11.1**.

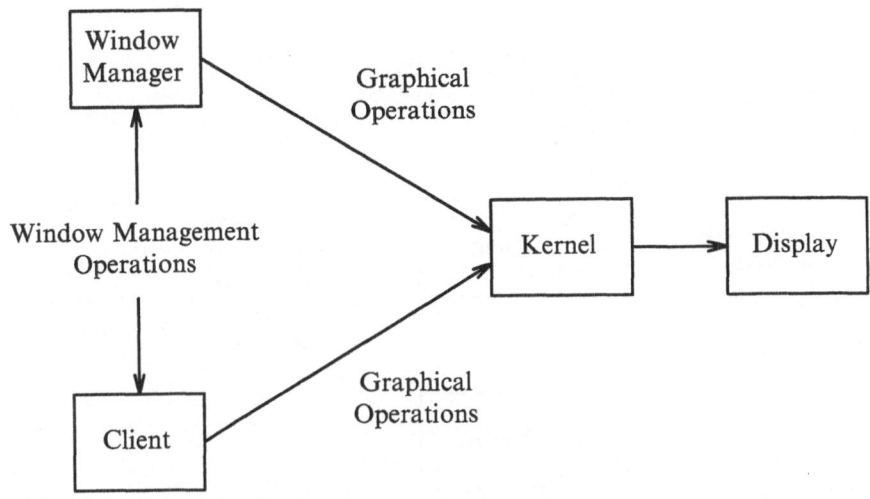

Figure 11.1

11.2.2 The Client

On systems where client processes can directly access the display hardware, one very seductive organization is to place all of the graphics code in each client process. Implementing this involves duplicating much of the code of the window system in each process. This gives clients the most direct possible access to the display. Not even a kernel call is required. The usual motivation for doing this is to provide the maximum possible performance. This scheme is illustrated in **Figure 11.2**.

Often the expected performance does not appear. There are several possible reasons:

- *Synchronization*: the clients must synchronize amongst themselves for access to the display hardware. It is usually impossible for two processes to be accessing the device registers in parallel. For example, before drawing a line a client must make sure that no other client is drawing lines and only when the hardware is idle may it finally draw the line. This checking and locking can be very expensive, sometimes as expensive as a kernel call, and can overshadow the expense of drawing the line. This expense can be reduced by increasing the granularity of locking: instead of locking on every line, lock before drawing a group of lines, then unlock afterwards. This has the disadvantages of being error-prone and of exposing locking concerns to higher levels of the system.

  Some displays, however, do have special features that allow multiple processes to access them in parallel. One way of doing this is by having the hardware support multiple request queues and assigning one queue to each client.

  Synchronization in the form of agreement about window layout also needs to be dealt with. When a client is drawing a line, other clients must be prevented from moving their windows and affecting other clients' clipping. This also implies that clients cannot precompute clipping information outside of the

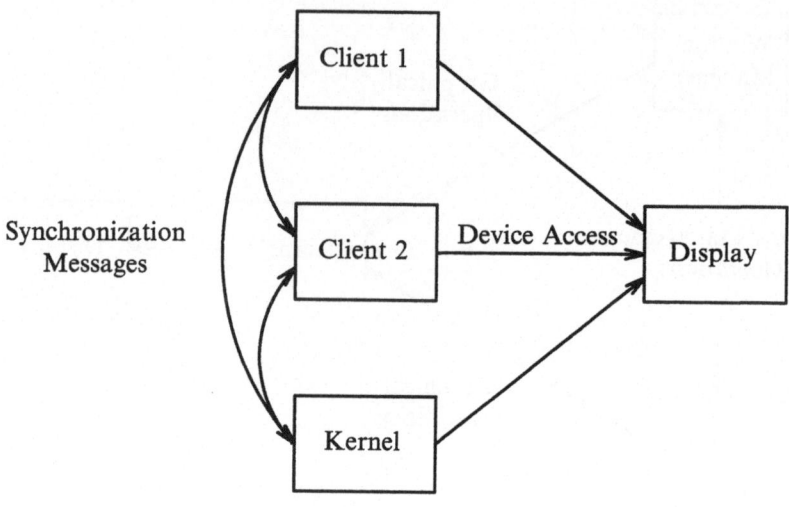

Figure 11.2

locked regions of code.

- *Paging*: if the hardware provides little support for graphics operations, as many simple frame buffers do, then the graphics library that is replicated in each client can become large. If there are many different display devices and operations to be supported then the amount of replicated code can become enormous. In systems with virtual memory, this can cause substantial paging delays.

- *Attempts to keep code small*: if a large amount of code is being replicated and its sheer bulk is causing problems, attempting to keep it small appears attractive. But this often involves exploiting fewer special cases and avoiding other optimizations that make operations faster but larger.

Putting such a large body of code into each client process also introduces logistical problems. It becomes much harder to make changes since every client must be relinked to access the new routines. This has a strong impact on bug-fixing since it takes quite a bit of effort to propagate the fixes. It also hurts device independence since each new display device forces a complete relink. New display devices also increase code size which has interactions with paging behaviour and hence performance.

Such an approach also requires either that client programs are *well-behaved* or that the hardware is sophisticated enough to cope with those that are not. For example, if the hardware doesn't provide clipping or if clients are able to change their clipping boundaries, then a client which runs amok can destroy the image on the entire display, not just within its window.

11.2.3 A Separate Process

Parts of the window system may also be placed in a user level server process that is not a part of either the kernel or the client. Operations are performed by sending messages to the server. Often, at least the window management functions are done this way, but the graphics library may be done the same way. This technique is dependent on the existence of an inter process communication (IPC) mechanism. When IPC is integrated with networking, as it is in 4.2 BSD Unix systems, it allows the window manager and its clients to be distributed across many machines. This scheme is illustrated in **Figure 11.3**.

Under this scheme, all of the graphics and window management code is placed into one process. The window layout database, clipping regions and all other relevant information is centralized. It solves most of the problems of the other organizations:

- The synchronization issue is solved by sidestepping: the window system has only one thread of control and complete access to all information. Synchronization occurs by the act of serializing the messages coming into the process.

- As a user level process it is much easier to develop and maintain. It doesn't threaten the integrity of the whole system.

- It provides a good basis for device independence. To achieve independence one must be very careful in specifying the semantics of the messages that get exchanged.

Passing messages can substantially increase the overhead of performing operations. There are a number of techniques for reducing the cost:

- Make sure that the basic IPC mechanism is fast. Shared memory in non-networking environments works well.

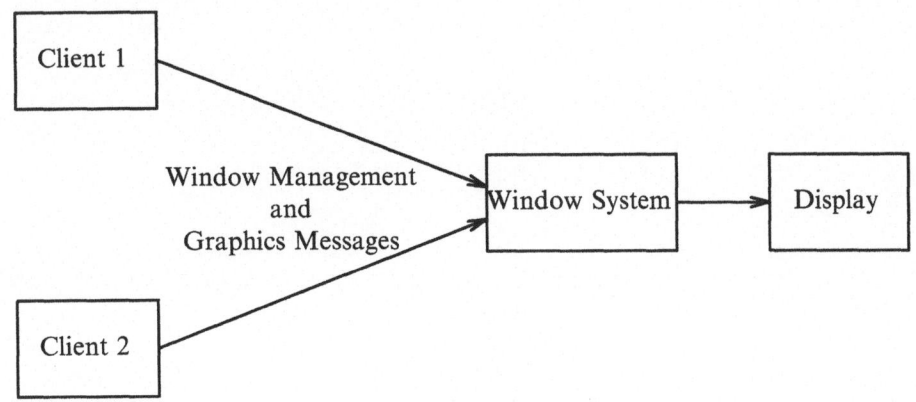

Figure 11.3

- Batch requests. If a request to the window system doesn't require a reply (like "draw a line") then it can be batched with following requests into a single message. With a large enough message size and a protocol specification that requires few replies, the per-message setup cost can almost be made to vanish.

- It is important to keep low the ratio of bits passed in messages to bits altered on the screen. This reduces the cost per pixel of message passing. A very good way of doing this is to design a protocol which deals at a fairly high level of abstraction. For instance, it is perfectly possible to design a protocol that allows only bitmaps to be sent to the window system from the client. Thus, when a client wants to draw a text string, all the bits for all the characters must be sent. In this case, the window manager has a complete, simple model, but it will have poor performance. On the other hand, if the protocol includes notions like *font* and *string*, then text can be shipped down in a very compact form. The same goes for circles, arcs, filled polygons and many other operations: the more that the window system understands at an abstract level, the better the performance of message passing will be.

11.3 CONCLUSIONS

Window systems can be partitioned by placing the bulk of their code in either the kernel, each client process, or some separate server process. It is important to observe that for all three partitioning schemes some information must be passed. There are processes that are trying to cooperate, not blindly ignore each other. This cooperation has a price, and that price is the passing around of information. Window systems that are built with each client independently performing graphics operations are often seduced by performance promises but often don't achieve them due to unexpected synchronization problems. The centralized server technique solves most of these problems with an added message passing cost, but this cost can be substantially reduced.

12 System Aspects of Low-Cost Bitmapped Displays

David Rosenthal and James Gosling

ABSTRACT

The design of low-cost bitmapped displays is reviewed from the perspective of the implementors of a window manager for a Unix system. The interactions between RasterOp hardware, the multiprocess structure of Unix software, and the functions of the window manager are discussed in the form of a checklist of features for hardware designers.

12.1 INTRODUCTION

Chip manufacturers are announcing products designed to improve the performance and reduce the cost of bitmapped displays. Workstation manufacturers are marketing systems featuring a Unix operating system and a window manager on such displays. The window manager has an overwhelming effect on the perceived performance of the workstation it is running on.

We have recently designed and implemented a window manager (see Chapter 13) for a 4.2BSD Unix system. It is intended to be easy to port between displays. It runs on the SUN workstation, and throughout its development we have been reviewing designs for other displays that are to be used in the future. In attempting to obtain the best performance from the SUN displays and remain portable to these others, we have encountered many interactions between display hardware features and window manager software; what follows is a compilation of our experiences.

12.2 MODELS

To provide a context for the discussion of these interactions, we set out the range of hardware and software we are concerned with.

12.2.1 Hardware

Workstation hardware typically consists of a processor, memory management hardware, memory, and I/O devices including a mouse, keyboard, and monochrome display. The display may have either:

● pixels visible in the CPU's address space, with RasterOps performed by the CPU (possibly with special hardware assistance);

● pixels not addressable by the CPU, but manipulated by an autonomous RasterOp processor, communication with which is via registers or command queues in the CPU's address space.

12.2.2 Software

This hardware typically runs a form of the Unix operating system, whose importance for this discussion is that it supports multiprocess interaction. When multiple interactive processes compete for a finite real screen resource, arbitration is undertaken by some form of window manager, either:

(1) a part of the Unix kernel, accessed via special system calls, or

(2) a special user level process, accessed via inter process communication channels.

The RasterOps affecting the parts of the screen resource allocated to each client may be performed by:

(1) the kernel, when the client requests them using system calls;

(2) the user level window manager process, when the client requests them using remote procedure calls;

(3) the client directly, if it has the pixels or RasterOp processor control registers mapped into its address space.

The goal in all cases is to provide clients with a *protected* RasterOp, one that can affect only those pixels allocated to the client.

12.3 CHECKLIST

After providing memory to store the pixels, and a mechanism to generate the video output, the designer of a low-cost bitmap display is faced with the question of how much RasterOp support is required. With careful design, at least for the MC68000 (which can exploit autoincrement addressing), many cases of monochrome RasterOp are close to the limit set by display memory bandwidth even if they are done entirely in software. Next-generation microprocessors typically have barrel shifters, making the alignment shifts of software RasterOps much faster. If special RasterOp hardware is to be cost effective compared to a software solution, the following points should be considered.

(1)   Can user processes operate on the bitmap without system call overhead?

(2)   If special RasterOp hardware is provided, can a client access the bitmap without using it?

(3)   Can a client given access to the bitmap be prevented from accessing other I/O devices?

(4)   If special RasterOp hardware is provided, can multiple user processes access it?

(5)   If the RasterOp hardware is an autonomous processor, does it support one or many command queues?

(6)   Can the RasterOp hardware be used off-screen?

(7)   Does the RasterOp processor implement clipping?

(8)   If the display has a colour map, can it be shared between multiple windows?

(9)   Does the display support a cursor?

(10) Can the display track the mouse autonomously?

(11) Does the hardware allow non-rectangular RasterOps?

(12) Can the display draw characters fast?

12.4 DISCUSSION

Can user processes operate on the bitmap without system call overhead?

● Either the bitmap itself, or the registers and command queues controlling the RasterOp processor, or both must be capable of appearing in the address space of one or more user processes. In this way the process can do RasterOps directly; the cost of a system call (perhaps 0.3ms) per RasterOp is prohibitive.

If special RasterOp hardware is provided, can a client access the bitmap without using it?

● The presence of RasterOp hardware does not eliminate the need for the CPU to access the pixels directly. Unless the function set of the RasterOp processor matches the application requirements exactly, some display operations will need to be implemented in software. Inappropriate support that cannot be programmed around is worse than none.

Can a client given access to the bitmap be prevented from accessing other I/O devices?

● A corollary of the need for user processes to address the bitmap is that the system's memory management and protection unit must be capable of controlling access to the I/O space at a relatively fine grain. It should not be necessary to trust a graphics process with access to the disc controller hardware.

If special RasterOp hardware is provided, can multiple user processes access it?

- If user processes can access the RasterOp hardware directly, its internal state such as source and destination coordinates, function codes, mask bits, and so on must be regarded as part of the state of a process. They must in general be saved and restored across context switches; the performance impact of doing so can be severe (even if hardware permits it).

- The overall impact of saving and restoring the RasterOp processor's state can be reduced if processes using it can be identified. The analogous problem for floating point processors has traditionally been solved by initializing them to a state in which an attempt by the processor to use them will cause an interrupt. At that point the process is known to use the processor, and can be marked as needing the extra context. Thus, if the processor has any context to save, either the memory management unit or the processor itself should be capable of generating an interrupt on all access attempts.

If the RasterOp hardware is an autonomous processor, does it support one or many command queues?

- Designs with autonomous RasterOp processors can reduce the need to save and restore RasterOp context by implementing several independent command queues and multiplexing these queues together. The window manager can then assign a queue to each window and treat them as if they had independent processors. A means to drain the queues before changing the shape or position of a window will be needed.

Can the RasterOp hardware be used off-screen?

- Many window managers require RasterOps that operate uniformly on rasters both on and off the screen. Off-screen rasters are typically in process virtual address space. If the RasterOp support cannot be applied to these rasters, the window manager will have to implement a software RasterOp even if it is not used on-screen.

Does the RasterOp processor implement clipping?

- A major role of a window manager is providing client processes with a protected RasterOp, that is in ensuring that a client can draw only within its assigned area of the screen. Thus, much of the window manager's processing is devoted to clipping. The window manager must apply a clipping rectangle to all the client output, though within these limits the client may wish to impose a smaller clipping rectangle. Hardware support for clipping is useful, but it would be much more useful if it provided both a *system* clip rectangle that could not be changed from user mode, and also a *user* clip rectangle. Output would be clipped to the intersection of the two. The window manager would set the system rectangle to the window, and the client would set the user rectangle as desired. Even better would be clipping to the union of a *set* of rectangles for each mode, to permit clipping to partially overlapped windows.

If the display has a colour map, can it be shared between multiple windows?

● Just as the pixels are a real resource to be shared among competing clients, so also are the entries in the colour map. Clients should also be able to use a number of different pixel values and corresponding colour map entries without being aware that other windows are also using the colour map. For example, all windows should be able to use pixel values from 0 to some limit.

Hardware assistance for this sharing would be useful. The window manager should be able to specify a number of rectangles, in each of which the relationship between the pixel value and the colour map entry it selected would be different. These rectangles might select from a number of independent full-size colour maps, or provide a base register to be added to the pixel value before the colour lookup (and perhaps a limit register to truncate the range).

Does the display support a cursor?

● An essential feature of a window system is a cursor, tracking a pointing device around the screen. The cursor can be displayed either:

(1) by temporarily changing some pixels in the bitmap from which the screen is refreshed, or:

(2) by mixing the video from two separate bitmaps, one for the screen image and one for the cursor.

The first is often preferred for low-cost systems; it requires little or no extra hardware but can impose significant performance loss. The problem is that if the cursor affects pixels in the screen bitmap, it must be absent during any RasterOp that affects those pixels. There are two approaches to ensuring that the cursor gets removed:

(a) The process performing the RasterOp can handshake with the process maintaining the cursor before every RasterOp. (Ideally, it would do so only when the source or destination rectangles overlapped the cursor, but this is normally impracticable.) The cost of the necessary system call on every RasterOp, or at least on every RasterOp when the cursor is displayed, is very significant, and the cursor will flicker badly.

This problem recurs in a milder form even if the process performing the RasterOps is also the process maintaining the cursor. The synchronization cost is less, but the cursor flicker is still present. It is particularly offensive because the cursor is typically the focus of the user's attention.

(b) If the video refresh controller is capable of interrupting when a specified scanline is reached, the interrupt routine can arrange for this to happen shortly before the first scanline containing the cursor. It can then put the cursor into the bitmap, wait at interrupt level until the refresh has passed the cursor, and then remove it. No user RasterOps can occur while the cursor is in the bitmap, and the cursor will not flicker, but the cost is the fraction of the CPU corresponding to the ratio of the cursor height to the screen height.

Video-mixed cursors are normally regarded as too expensive for low-cost displays, because they require either a complete second bitmap, or a smaller bitmap plus extra logic to position the cursor. But their effect on overall performance is so great that this may be a mistake. They should be considered in the design of advanced video generator and controller chips.

Can the display track the mouse autonomously?

●   Another major load on the system is tracking the mouse. Autonomous display hardware sufficiently intelligent to monitor locations in main memory for the mouse coordinates, and to position the cursor to correspond, would off-load significant processing. The off-load would be greater if it supported a *clip* rectangle for the cursor, and could interrupt if the cursor tracked across the boundary. Many window systems wish to change the cursor shape as it tracks across windows, or even regions within windows.

Does the hardware allow non-rectangular RasterOps?

●   Non-rectangular RasterOps such as 'fill trapezoid' can significantly improve the performance of applications using polygonal graphics, but need careful implementation. In particular, if they are to abut correctly it must be possible to save and restore the error parameters of the Bresenham or other algorithms tracing their edges. This is an example of the need for subpixel addressing, which also occurs in greyscale and other antialiased applications.

Can the display draw characters fast?

●   The overwhelming majority of RasterOps will paint a character. The cost of these will be dominated by setup time unless the font contains very large characters, or the client sends long strings of contiguous characters. Note that single character RasterOps are important as echos of user typeins. "What you see is what you get" (WYSIWYG) editors are major applications for this class of display, and their performance is dominated by repainting characters as the user types.

Thus, the design of RasterOp engines should consider making character-drawing a special case, so that the hardware understands the font tables, knows the amount of shim space to add between printing and space characters, and so on. This spreads the setup time across as many characters as possible.

●   Typical windows may contain characters from a large number of fonts; twelve per window is not uncommon. The stored fonts from which characters are drawn are frequently stored in the 224×1024 pixel off-screen area of an 800×1024 pixel display. Thus, specialized RasterOp hardware can be used to paint characters even if it can access only the bits in the hardware bitmap.

Unfortunately, Parkinson's Law shows that this space is insufficient to store all the required fonts, so that the off-screen space can at best be a cache for active fonts, and cache misses will occur. The code to manage free space in the font cache, to gather usage information, and to perform cache reloads on misses is difficult to write, and imposes disturbing performance irregularities. Font definitions, and the individual glyphs, are variable-size, adding to the normal problems of writing a pager.

If the RasterOp hardware is not restricted to accessing the pixels in the hardware bitmap, but can access the whole of physical memory (even at reduced bandwidth), the problem is easier. The font cache can now be larger, stored in wired-down pages of system physical memory. But it is still only a cache.

If, however, the hardware support for RasterOp is applicable even in process virtual address space the fonts can be stored in virtual memory, and the system's pager can deal with the problem of ensuring that the fonts in use are readily accessible. Virtual memory RasterOps are normally available only if the RasterOp is implemented by the CPU, either in software, microcode, or as a processor extension chip.

12.5 CONCLUSION

We have set out a number of points worthy of consideration in the design of low-cost bitmap displays intended to support multiprocess interaction. Although RasterOp hardware may appear attractive, it needs careful design if its potential is to be realized fully, particularly for drawing characters. Assistance with cursor drawing and sharing of the colour map may be more cost effective uses for limited hardware resources.

12.6 ACKNOWLEDGEMENTS

This work originates from insightful critiques of some proposed hardware designs given by Bob Sproull. Bob Sidebotham, Andy Palay, Fred Hansen and Bruce Lucas helped implement the ITC's window manager.

Anyone attempting to design bitmap displays should read the paper by Pike, Locanthi and Reiser [52].

13   A Window Manager for Bitmapped Displays and Unix

James Gosling and David Rosenthal

ABSTRACT

A window manager for workstations with bitmapped displays has been developed. It exploits the inter process communication mechanism of the 4.2 Berkeley Unix system, and the DARPA TCP/IP protocols to support remote access to windows. One user level window manager process runs on each workstation; it tiles the screen(s) with windows, and manages a mouse, keyboard and pop-up menus. Client processes make remote procedure calls requesting the window manager to create or destroy windows, and to draw text and graphics in them. The window manager asynchronously requests clients to redraw their images when windows change size.

"You will get a better Gorilla effect if
you use as big a piece of paper as possible."
Kunihiko Kasahara, *Creative Origami.*

13.1 INTRODUCTION

The style of interactive user interface exploiting multiple windows, multiple processes, bitmap graphics, pop-up menus, and a mouse originated with the Xerox Alto, and has traditionally been confined to environments that, like the Alto, provide the application with memory bandwidth access to the bitmap.

Two examples demonstrate that a careful choice of interface substantially reduces the bandwidth requirement. Pike's window manager [51] for the Bell Labs BLIT terminal [50] provides multiple processes with a low level interface to a set of overlapping windows. All obscured pixels are remembered in the terminal, so that the window system can recover from changes in window arrangement without intervention by the application. The system provides adequate performance despite being driven over an RS232 link.

In a recent paper [36] Lantz and Nowicki describe a window system for a network including powerful personal workstations providing multiprocess interaction. Their system (VGTS) supports remote and distributed access to windows, and provides adequate performance despite the limited network bandwidth by maintaining a *structured display file*. The application specifies modifications to this file; the window system is responsible for recreating the image from the display file when required.

We present a window system that supports remote and distributed access to windows using the same underlying network technology as VGTS, but provides applications with a much lower level interface, similar to that of the BLIT. It differs from both systems, however, in that the window system maintains no memory of the image in a window other than the actual pixels. The application is notified whenever the window must be redrawn, and it must recreate the entire image. Despite this, the system provides adequate performance for many advanced user interface techniques, such as WYSIWYG editors. It also differs from both systems in that it is implemented entirely at user level in an unmodified widely used Unix system, Berkeley's 4.2 BSD [31].

After eighteen months of production use on a network of about 80 workstations, it supports a wide range of applications. Examples include a document preparation system providing dynamically reformatted text editing, diagram editing, and page preview facilities, an iconic interface to Unix commands, help facilities, mail, bulletin board and conference call programs, terminal emulator, clock, performance monitor, database query programs, and a range of educational applications. Client processes using the window manager to perform bitmap operations are *portable*, in the sense that they will run without source modification on any 4.2BSD system on the network, and *device independent*, in that they can have no *a priori* knowledge of the hardware being managed on their behalf.

13.1.1 User's View

The user of a workstation running this window manager sees one or more screens *tiled* with windows. The windows completely cover the screen, without overlapping one another. A user's initial window layout is specified in a profile file, though it may be changed at any time. Each window has a headline, containing an identification of the client program attached to it, and the machine the client is running on. As the mouse is moved, a cursor tracks it on the screen, changing as it moves from window to window, or as clients use it as a feedback mechanism. Characters typed on the keyboard appear in the window containing the cursor, assuming the window is one to which it is sensible to type. Characters typed at the clock, for example, simply disappear.

When the mouse buttons are pressed, various window-specific things happen; menus pop up, items are selected, objects move, and so on. Menus normally pop up on the down stroke of the middle mouse button. They appear near the cursor, overlapping the windows under them. A selection is made on the up stroke of the button whereupon the menu vanishes. While the mouse button is down the menu item under the cursor is highlighted. Menus form a hierarchy: any menu item may have a submenu, which will pop up nearby when the cursor is in the parent. If the cursor is moved into the submenu, the process repeats.

Using a window menu that appears when the middle button is pressed in a window headline, the user can change the size of a window and reposition it. A window may be hidden; it then appears as an item in a submenu and will reappear when selected. New windows may appear on the screen at any time, as client processes request them. They cause existing windows to be resized or hidden at the whim of the window manager; creating a window does not involve interaction with the user. In fact, users cannot create windows directly; they can only create processes that will create windows.

13.2 CLIENT'S VIEW

13.2.1 Design Principles

The client program interacts with the window manager by means of function calls, file descriptors, and signals. The design of this interface has two objectives.

(1) It should be as simple as possible. The role of the window manager is to arbitrate among competing requests for real resources, such as the screen, the colour map, and the mouse. Within the limits needed to protect others, clients should be free to use the resources they are allocated as they see fit.

(2) Clients should regard their requests for resources as *hints*. The window manager will use its best efforts, but cannot guarantee to satisfy requests exactly.

The simplicity of the window manager client interface achieves three objectives:

(1) Application programmers are encouraged to use it since they need make only a small investment of time in learning how.

(2) Applications using it will become popular, since a small fast window manager provides a responsive interface. Inefficiency in the primary user interface tool is unlikely to be tolerated.

(3) A simple window manager forms a base on which layers implementing more advanced graphical techniques can be implemented. For example, programs needing homogeneous coordinates and transformations can use a subroutine library that calls the window manager. Including these facilities in the window manager would burden all applications with them.

Viewing resource requests as hints has three effects:

(1)   The user, who after all has to look at the result, can override the window manager's policies at any time.

(2)   Clients are more robust. At times when resources are short, requests typically succeed at least partially, instead of failing. The client can use the resources allocated to ask the user for more, for example by displaying a plea to "make me bigger".

(3)   Clients must take device independence seriously; they cannot predict the properties of their *virtual device* because the properties will change at runtime.

13.2.2 Resource Model

Clients see windows as rectangular spaces of integer coordinates in which they can draw. The window manager ensures that the origin of the space is at the top left of the allocated screen space, and that output outside the rectangle from the origin to (*Xsize*, *Ysize*) is clipped away. The client may inquire the values of *Xsize* and *Ysize* if it wishes to adjust its image to fit the allocated space.

Each pixel in this array may be regarded as containing one of a contiguous range of indices into the colour map. The client may hint as to the number of indices it requires, and inquire as to how many it has actually been given. It can manipulate the colour map entries corresponding to its current set of indices. On a monochrome display or a colour display without a hardware colour map manipulating these entries will have no visible effect.

Characters may be drawn into this pixel space in any of several fonts. A client may define a font using a string name (eg *TimesRoman12*), and the result will be a handle that may be used to select it. The window manager will use its best efforts to supply a suitable approximation. The client may inquire about the bounding box of any character in the font.

Whenever the window manager changes the allocation of resources so as to affect a particular client, that client is notified. It is expected to inquire what the new allocation is and redraw the image in its window to suit. The values that may have changed when a notification is received are:

●   the size of the window;

●   the range of accessible colour map indices;

●   the actual font represented by a handle (and thus the size of each character in it).

13.2.3 Control Functions

Some of the functions used to pass control information between the client and the window manager are:

w = DefineWindow(h)

>   Creates a window *w* on the host named *h*.

SelectWindow(w)

>   Makes *w* the current window.

GetDimensions(&Xsize, &Ysize)

>   Sets *Xsize* and *Ysize* to the dimensions in pixels of the current window.

SetDimensions(minX, maxX, minY, maxY)

>   Hints to the window manager about the desired size of the current window.

DefineWindow takes only one parameter, the host on which the window is to be created. It creates an inter process communication (IPC) channel between this process (the application) and the window manager process on the named host. It returns a handle giving access to the window's resources, actually a pointer to a structure containing information including the Unix file descriptor for the IPC channel.

Many parameters affect the initial allocation of resources to a newly created window. Conceptually, they are all defaulted, and the client must use the normal window manager calls to request changes. In practice, the window manager uses lazy evaluation of window creation, so that change requests made early in a window's history are likely to affect its initial allocation. Clients need not know the complete parameter set, an important consideration in an evolving system.

Clients are expected to deal with windows of any size. The size specification given in *SetDimensions* is only a hint. Either the user or the window manager may decide to change the size of the window, disregarding the hint. Clients allocated windows they cannot readily use are free to ask the user to change their size.

Notification that resource allocations have changed (for example, that a window has changed size) could be either *synchronous*, via synthetic input events, or *asynchronous*, via a Unix signal. Only asynchronous notification is currently implemented. The window manager makes no attempt to preserve the contents of the window being resized (or having other resources changed). There are two reasons for this apparent lack of courtesy:

(1)   Different clients need to respond to resizing in different ways. For example, an editor may reformat a document to suit the new space, a clock may centre its face in the window and scale it to be as large as possible, or a chart may rescale its borders and show more detail.

(2)   Window managers that save window images often develop clients that do not cope adequately with resizing. Insisting on redrawing forces clients to deal with resizing too.

A client may have many windows, but the window manager calls affect only the *selected* window. Newly created windows are selected automatically, but other windows may be selected at any time. This technique is common in graphics packages [5, 24]; it allows complex lookups without severe performance costs and shortens parameter lists (and thus messages).

13.2.4 Primitive Attributes

Among the functions setting the attributes applied to graphic output are:

$f = DefineFont(n)$

> Returns a handle for a font whose name is the string n.

SelectFont(f)

> Selects the defined font f for subsequent text drawing.

$c = DefineColor(n)$

> Returns a handle for a colour whose name is the string n.

SelectColor(c)

> Selects the defined colour c for subsequent drawing.

DefineFont takes as its only parameter the name of the font to be defined. For example *"TimesRoman12b"* defines 12 point Times Roman bold. If the font library does not contain exactly the required font, something "close" will be substituted. For example, *"TimesRoman12"* may be substituted for *"TimesRoman12b"* if no bold-face Times Roman exists. It returns a handle that can be used to *select* the font.

The value returned by *DefineFont* is actually a pointer to a structure that describes in great detail the properties of the font. It is important to note that fonts are window-specific. '*DefineFont("TimesRoman12b")*' in two different windows might return two different values if, for example, the windows were on two displays with different properties. Since the user may reposition a window from one display to another, the values in the font structure may change dynamically. They are obtained from the window manager, and are updated when the client is notified of a font change.

13.2.5 Output Primitives

The client draws using a functional interface. The primitives available are:

DrawTo(x,y)
MoveTo(x,y)

Moves the current position to (x,y), with and without drawing a line on the way.

RasterOp(sx,sy,dx,dy,w,h)
RasterSmash(dx,dy,w,h)

Applies the current RasterOp functions to the destination rectangle, with or without a source rectangle.

FillTrapezoid(xl,yl,wl,x2,y2,w2,f,c)

Fills the specified trapezoid with the character c from the font f.

Text is output using the normal Unix 'write' system calls on the file descriptor for the window's IPC channel. It appears at the current (x,y) position using the selected font. There are routines for drawing strings relative to a positioning parameter. These apply only to the selected window. For example:

> *DrawString(WindowWidth/2, WindowHeight/2,*
> *BetweenLeftAndRight\BetweenTopAndBaseline,*
> *"Center");*

draws the string *Center* centred vertically and horizontally in the current window. Use of *DrawString* obviates the need to remember parameters from the font structures that may change at any time.

13.2.6 Input Functions

Characters typed on the keyboard are routed by the window manager to the process owning the window containing the cursor. The client process can read them from the file descriptor for the window's IPC channel in the normal way.

AddMenu(s,r)

Adds the string s as an item in the pop-up menu of the selected window. The response string is r.

When a menu item is selected, the effect is as if the response string had been typed. In this way, menus can easily be added to existing programs.

SetMouseInterest(mask)

Informs the window manager of the type of mouse events the client is interested in.

SawMouse(&action,&x, &y)

Sets *action* to the event code, and x and y to the position in the window.

Whenever an *interesting* mouse event occurs, the untypeable character *MouseInputToken* appears in the input stream. The client should then call *SawMouse* to decode the following few characters. Interest masks and actions are composed by or-ing together values including *LeftButton*, *DownMovement* and *UpTransition*.

13.3 IMPLEMENTATION

The window manager process maintains the state of all windows, performs all the primitive graphic operations, receives all mouse inputs, and routes keystrokes, menu selections, and redraw requests to the clients. It communicates with the clients via a remote procedure call (RPC) mechanism implemented using 4.2BSD sockets.

The client interface was designed with the idea of implementing it by mapping the bitmap and the display device registers into each client process. Unfortunately, the SUN 1.5 hardware we had could not save and restore the display registers on context switches, so the display could be mapped into at most one process. Thus, the window manager is currently implemented as a single user-process that communicates with the screen, mouse, keyboard and all the clients. We use the SUN-supplied device driver to map the bitmap and the display device registers into the window manager's address space. All other I/O uses standard 4.2BSD system calls. No kernel changes are needed.

13.3.1 RPC Implementation

A *socket*, as defined by 4.2BSD, is one end of a communication path. It has an associated type, naming domain, and protocol. The type defines the semantics of I/O operations on the socket; we use *stream* sockets, providing byte streams much like pipes. Every socket has a name and a protocol in some domain; we use the Internet naming domain and the TCP/IP protocol for compatibility with other machines. A socket may be connected to another socket having the same domain/protocol pair. A connection between sockets within one machine is much like a named pipe in other Unix systems. In fact, 4.2BSD implements pipes as connected pairs of sockets. The socket mechanism is especially elegant in that it makes inter-machine boundaries transparent. Neither the client nor the window manager really knows whether there is a machine boundary between them.

All window manager calls in the client turn into messages sent via these pipeline connections. (The RPC protocol is asymmetric, in that the window manager may not call the client.) The RPC protocol supports C-style parameter passing, with at most one variable-length argument (typically a string). Functions may return results directly, or through pointer arguments. The common operations are output primitives and attribute selections, which do not return values. These are accumulated in *stdio* buffers until explicitly flushed, or until a result is required. Typical interactions between the window manager and the client consist of a single message from the client containing many operations.

13.3.2 Window Creation

When the client requests the creation of a window, a communication path is set up to the window manager which creates a structure in its address space describing the properties of the window, but does not actually create a visible window until a request is received that requires its existence. Thus, the window creation heuristics can use any information sent to the window manager in the meantime.

The window creation heuristics use four parameters: the minimum height and width, and the *preferred* height and width. We have tried several sets of heuristics. The most complex, and one of the shortest lived, involved considering each window to be a rectangular frame with springs holding the sides apart. A system of equations was relaxed to minimize the energy in the compression of the springs. This was very uncomfortable to use - it almost always completely rearranged all windows every time a new window was created. The present heuristics pick one window and split it to give some of its area to the new window. The window to split, and the position and orientation of the split, are determined by minimizing an error function that attempts to balance areas and preserve aspect ratios.

13.3.3 Font Support

Since the most frequent request to the window manager is to draw characters, the performance of this operation is crucial. Just as the remote procedure call mechanism batches together window manager requests, character drawing requests are batched together. The lowest level routines that draw characters then receive long strings. This allows the precomputation costs to be spread over many characters: clipping is done based on strings, not characters; and some RasterOp setup is removed from the inner loop.

A *font* as used by *DefineFont* and the character drawing routines is broken into two parts: some general information about the font as a whole and an array of *icons*. The general information includes the name of the font and a maximal bounding box for all of the icons in the font. An *icon* is a drawing, in some representation, that may be placed on the screen. Usually these icons correspond to the shapes of characters from the ASCII character set, but they need not. There are many representations possible for an icon. For example, they may be described by a bitmap specially aligned for the SUN hardware or they may be described by a set of vectors. Icons are split into two parts: the *type specific* part, and the *generic* part.

The type specific part of an icon contains all the information that depends on the type of representation used for the icon, while the generic part contains the information that is independent of the representation. When a client program defines a font, the information returned to it contains only the generic information for each icon in the font: all of the type specific information is eliminated. This allows the window manager to implement a font in a way that is tuned to each type of display device while insulating clients from the differences and still allowing them sophisticated access to the properties of the font.

13.4 APPLICATIONS

One of our applications is an editor [23], similar in spirit to Bravo [35] or LisaWrite [8]. It deals with kerned, proportionally spaced fonts, left and right justification and filling, using redefinable style sheets similar to those of the Scribe [54] document formatter. Unlike Scribe, where formatting is a batch process, it reformats the document at every keystroke. One might expect that this would be feasible only if the editor had full knowledge of, and an intimate association with the hardware. However, only a small performance degradation is imposed by using IPC channels and our window manager.

The editor is fast enough to be used as a general user interface tool, in effect a replacement for the Unix *teletype driver*. Users generally use the Unix shell via a typescript manager implemented from the same code. It keeps a complete transcript of their session, permits scrolling, string search, and text to be cut and pasted. (The window manager provides a ring of cut buffers, permitting text cut from one window to be pasted into another, even across machine boundaries.)

Another application is a diagram editor, implementing primitives such as lines, arcs, ovals, boxes, arrows, and text. The primitives may be collected into symbols; both primitives and symbols may be placed in the diagram and linked by connectivity constraints at *magic dots*. Objects stay connected even though the dots are moved. The window manager supports this adequately except that dragging objects around the screen is too slow. (The mouse event has to pass through the window manager on its way to the diagram editor, and the response has to pass through the window manager on the way back. Three processes must be scheduled.) As a result, almost all users turn dragging off.

13.5 ASSESSMENT

13.5.1 User's View

It is usual for window managers to permit windows to overlap [9, 38]. Tiling window managers are rare. Our decision to experiment with tiling was based on two observations of overlapping window managers in use:

(1)   Experienced users typically lay out their screens so that the windows do not in fact overlap.

(2)   Creating a new window is traumatic. The user has to point out opposing corners of the screen space to be allocated to the new window, and often adjusts several other windows.

It seems that only transient windows overlap others; the reason they do so is the disproportionate number of interactions needed to adjust the layout.

In contrast, the constraint that windows must tile the screen allows the window manager to use heuristics when allocating space for new windows, and to adjust the screen layout autonomously. The heuristics need not be complex, the user can override the window manager's decisions if the investment in interaction would pay off.

A common complaint from users is that the layout process is unpredictable. We are experimenting with Cedar-style fixed-width columns of windows as an alternative. Clients are, of course, unaware of the layout policies being followed by the window manager.

13.5.2 Client's View

Because the interface is at a very low level, the window manager provides clients with very few services. Fortunately, this has not deterred people from writing client programs. For many clients, the use of clipped and shifted pixel coordinates is natural and efficient. We expect also to provide a higher level interface, supporting floating point coordinate spaces, by means of a library.

It can be claimed that the requirement to redraw the window makes client programs more difficult to write, but experience with this and other systems [57] does not support the claim. Programs need to be restructured, moving the code that initially calculates scales and draws borders to a procedure that can be reexecuted. It is more a matter of discipline than of extra work. New programs have no difficulty meeting this requirement.

13.5.3 Device Independence

Device independence is essential; the campus network will be an open system, and applications must operate on incompatible workstations. All access to the display hardware is mediated by the window manager, effectively insulating applications from its peculiarities [14]. The window manager currently has device drivers for three SUN displays, the earlier 1024×800 monochrome display with RasterOp hardware [10], the more recent 1152×900 monochrome display without RasterOp hardware, and the 640×480 colour, and for the MicroVAX display. Experience shows that it can normally be ported to a new display in less than a week.

13.5.4 Performance

When we discovered that we would have to implement the window manager using inter process communication (IPC) rather than direct access to the hardware, we expected the performance to be unacceptable. Traditionally, the use of IPC in Unix systems has had severe performance penalties. But, to our surprise, the performance of the window manager is respectable. Common operations, such as drawing text, scrolling and clearing windows are almost indistinguishable from the same operation performed directly on the hardware. Line drawing, and small RasterOps between the screen and client address space also work well. Drawing grids of individual points, and large RasterOps between the screen and a client run much too slowly, because of the large volume of data that must flow through the IPC connection.

Window manager calls which return values, requiring a full handshake between the two processes, typically take about 19ms each if both the client and the window manager are on the same machine. This slows to 22ms if they are on different machines. Most operations, however, do not return results and therefore do not require a full handshake. Notable among these are the frequently used drawing and attribute selection functions.

The Emacs text editor [22] provides an example of performance, It takes 360ms to redraw the screen completely when it is run on a SUN with direct access to the display. The same test under the window manager takes 530ms. This is 47% slower, which is hardly perceptible. Performing this test again with Emacs and the window manager on different machines yields an interesting result: the full redraw takes 390ms. Only 8% slower - the two machines are effectively dividing the computational load.

One item in the window manager's menu sends a redraw signal to all visible windows. With a typical screen layout of 6 windows, this takes about 2 seconds, scheduling among the window manager and the clients to repaint every pixel.

The reasons for the acceptable performance are simple:

- For the common operations, including character drawing, the number of pixels affected per byte transferred via the IPC connection is large.

- The underlying IPC mechanism - 4.2BSD sockets and TCP/IP - performs very well.

- Remote procedure calls that do not return values get buffered-up with subsequent calls. The RPC mechanism builds large buffers of requests and avoids sending unnecessary messages.

- Few procedures in the window manager interface return values, and those that do are called infrequently.

13.6 FUTURE WORK

Eventually we would like to move to a hybrid implementation: one in which a client may choose to use direct device access if the window is local. Even if direct device access is possible, most clients are unlikely to use it. Few need the extra performance, and loading the extra graphics library will make them much bigger. Above all, most will prefer to remain device independent.

There is a limit to the number of simultaneous clients that the window manager may service. It is imposed by the limit on the number of open file descriptors available to a Unix process. Each socket accessible to a Unix process uses one file descriptor. Typically Unix processes are limited to 20 file descriptors. The implementation of 4.2BSD allows this limit to be increased by recompiling the kernel, but only to 30. Normally the limit is not a problem; more than a half-dozen windows visible on the screen looks cluttered and confusing.

Unfortunately, we would like to support a large number of hidden windows, and each of these also takes up a file descriptor. We do not know of a satisfactory solution to the problem. One possibility that we considered was to use connectionless datagram sockets. The window manager would need only one socket on which to receive from all of its clients. The problem here is that at present only unreliable datagrams are implemented; datagrams get through with some probability between 0 and 1, exclusive.

An alternative is to pass the descriptors for closed windows in messages to another process. The window manager can then close the descriptor, sharing the limit on file descriptors among the visible windows only. We plan to experiment with a receiving process that maintains a window full of icons representing hidden windows and returns the appropriate descriptor to the window manager when one is selected for exposure.

13.7 ACKNOWLEDGEMENTS

Bob Sproull has been an invaluable source of advice. The other members of the ITC's User Interface group, Fred Hansen, Tom Peters, and James Peterson, rushed in where others feared to tread, and suffered the consequences. Bob Sidebotham, Andrew Palay, and Bruce Lucas have all implemented significant parts of the system as it now stands.

APPENDIX - LIST OF FUNCTIONS

Function	Description
wm_AcquireInputFocus( )	force input focus to the current window
wm_AddMenu(s)	add *s* to menus in the current window
wm_BrushRegion(id)	brush save buffer *id* using mouse
wm_ClearWindow( )	make the current window all white
c = wm_DefineColor(r,g,b)	get handle for colour (r,g,b)
wm_DefineColorElement(i,r,g,b)	colour element *i* becomes (r,g,b)
f =wm_DefineFont(f)	get handle for font *f*
wm_DefineRegion(id,x,y,w,h)	rectangle becomes region *id*
wm_DeleteWindow( )	destroy the current window
wm_DisableInput( )	typeins in the current window discarded
wm_DisableNewlines( )	text off bottom lost (not scrolled)
wm_DragRegion(id)	drag save buffer *id* using mouse
wm_DrawString(x,y,op,s)	draw string *s* at (x,y) with alignment *op*
wm_DrawTo(x,y)	line from the current position to (x,y)
wm_DumpRegion(id,fn)	write save buffer *id* to file *fn*
wm_EnableInput( )	typeins in the current window obtainable
wm_ExposeMe( )	make the current window visible
wm_FillTrapezoid(x1,y1,w1,	
x2,y2,w2,f,c)	fill trapezoid with char *c* in font *f*
fp = wm_FontStruct(f)	get pointer to info about font *f*
wm_ForgetRegion(id)	destroy save buffer *id*
wm_GetColorIndices(n)	**n* gets size of colour map for the current window
wm_GetColorMap(n,cp)	fill *cp*[ ] with *n* colour map entries
wm_GetDimensions(w,h)	set (w,h) to size of the current window
wm_GiveupInputFocus( )	previous window regains input focus
wm_HideMe( )	make the current window invisible

wm_HandleAcquisition( )	
fp = wm_infile(w)	get input file pointer for window *w*
wm_InvertRaster(dx,dy,w,h)	invert colours in destination
wm_LinkRegion(n,o)	region *n* becomes part of region *o*
wm_LoadRegion(id,fn)	read save buffer *id* from file *fn*
wm_MoveTo(x,y)	set the current position to (x,y)
wm_NameRegion(id,s)	region *id* gets name *s*
w = wm_NewWindow(h)	create window on host *h*
fp = wm_outfile(w)	output file pointer for window *w*
wm_print(x,y,op,f,a,...)	like *print(f,a...)*
wm_RasterOp(sx,sy,dx,dy,w,h)	perform current op on source and destination
wm_RasterSmash(dx,dy,w,h)	perform current op on destination
wm_ReadFromCutBuffer(n)	get size and contents of cut buffer *n* steps away
wm_RestoreRegion(id,x,y)	copy from save buffer *id* to screen
wm_RotateCutRing(n)	rotate the ring of cut buffers *n* steps
wm_SaveRegion(id,x,y,w,h)	save rectangle in buffer *id*
wm_SaveMouse(action,w,y)	decode mouse event from *winin*
wm_SelectColorIndex(e)	new output in colour index *e*
wm_SelectFont(f)	new output in font *f*
wm_SelectRegion(id)	current region of the current window becomes *id*
wm_SelectWindow(w)	make *w* the current window
wm_SetCharShim(s)	*s* pixels of shim between printing chars
wm_SetClipRectangle(x,y,w,h)	clip to rectangle within the current window
wm_SetCursor(f,c)	set cursor to char *c* in font *f*
wm_SetDimensions(minx,maxx, miny,maxy)	set preferred size of the current window
wm_SetFunction(f)	set current op to *f*
wm_SetMenuPrefix(s)	
wm_SetMouseGrid(n)	set mouse motion granularity to *n*
wm_SetMouseInterest(mask)	set mask for interesting mouse events
wm_SetMousePrefix(p)	
wm_SetPixelDepth(n)	set preferred depth of the current window
wm_SetProgramName(s)	set name in headline to *s*
wm_SetRawInput( )	do not buffer chars typed to the current window
wm_SetSpaceShim(s)	*s* pixels of shim between space chars
wm_SetStandardCursor(c)	set cursor to char *c* in font *icon12*
wm_SetTitle(s)	set title in headline to *s*
wm_StdioWindow( )	stdin/stdout is a window - select it
wm_StringWidth(s,x,y)	set (x,y) to far end of string *s*
wm_WriteToCutBuffer( )	following null-terminated bytes to cut buffer
wm_ZoomFrom(x,y,w,h)	

14   Issues

14.1 INTRODUCTION

The individual participants were asked to provide at least a one page summary of their activities of relevance to the Workshop and also to indicate their views on the major issues. From this, it was possible to establish the initial list of issues and to define the structure for three Working Groups which would most likely achieve the desired focus on the main issues.

The participants were split equally between industry and academia/government with the majority coming from the UK. Six of the participants were from the USA and Canada and provided a much needed injection of experience in building and evaluating window managers.

John Butler of Microsoft provided input from the emerging standards activities in the USA under ANSI. A particular concern of the participants in their introductory statements was the question of standardization. Was it too early?

Some of the views of the participants expressed in their introductory statements are grouped together under the headings of the three Working Groups;

(1)   Application Program Interface (API);

(2)   User (ie Operator) Interface;

(3)   Architecture.

Finally, the lists of issues which were drawn up as a result of considering position papers are presented. These issues are listed under the headings of the Working Groups and provided a starting point to motivate Working Group discussions.

14.1.1 What is a Successful Window Manager?

A window manager is not a useful program in itself; it is valuable only in so far as useful and interesting applications use it. A successful window manager is one that persuades many people to write applications for it.

The most important factors in persuading people to write for a window manager are:

- *Simplicity*: application developers must invest in learning the system before writing for it. They won't do so if the investment outweighs the reward. Rich features will be a *disadvantage*.

- *Portability*: applications are very dependent on the window managers that they use. It is a lot of work to port from one to another. A window manager wired into a manufacturer's proprietary kernel, or dependent on spiffy hardware features will put people off. One that is visibly portable will experience the same boost that the Unix system itself did.

- *Code availability*: a body of existing applications, forming a mine of techniques and code, will encourage further application development. A library on top of the window manager, implementing high-quality text and graphics interactions, is even better.

One way to get a successful window manager is to write a simple but adequate one with lots of applications and libraries, and then give it all away. This is the strategy that the Information Technology Centre (ITC) at Carnegie-Mellon University is trying to follow. However, one that provides many built-in features, such as the Macintosh, will make applications with easy-to-use user interfaces easier to write.

14.2 APPLICATION PROGRAM INTERFACE

There was a general view that if progress was to be made towards establishing a methodology, it was more likely to happen at the API than elsewhere. A central issue that came from several people was the question of whether applications already in existence could run without change when put to work in the environment of a window manager. The obvious advantages are the saving in cost. However, a number of people indicated that the constraints this may put on the architecture of the system and its efficiency might be such as to make the application difficult if not impossible to use under the control of a window manager.

Assuming that the application is not asked to redraw output unless the window manager requires it, and that the covered window paradigm is assumed for the window manager, then it is almost essential that the architectural model is one where the window manager has available the current contents of all windows irrespective of whether they are visible or not.

The model as far as the application is concerned consists of a virtual terminal with a virtual screen and virtual input devices. Several virtual screens can be multiplexed on the same physical screen by the window manager. The application should be able to run unaware that a set of physical terminals is not in use.

While the above requirement was necessary, the advantages of having several separate contexts being presented in one overall context were real and it was felt that new applications could make use of the ability to transfer information between windows. This raised a number of issues as to how such interchange should take place, and at what level. Moving bitmaps may be relatively easy but, for the application, moving higher level data structures is much more important.

Existing graphics systems such as GKS [28] and PHIGS [6] provide segmentation or structuring facilities which allow graphical information to be superimposed on a single display with control of visibility of the individual segments similar in concept to window management. Are windows just segments in disguise? Should not the segmentation facility be extended to include the window concept of a rectangular region surrounding the graphical/textual information?

14.3 USER INTERFACE

Nearly everybody was against rigid standardization in this area. From the industrial side, cosmetic changes in the area of the user interface are selling points widely used in industry now and are likely to continue in the future. However, it should be possible for a user to move from one system to another without major changes in the model of the interface. Using as an analogy the motor industry, users frequently wish to tailor certain parts of a car (seat position, mirrors, luggage/passenger space, etc) while most would be seriously annoyed and in danger if the car wheels turned left when the steering wheel was moved clockwise.

Assuming a multiprocess environment with several processes outputting to the screen and requiring input from the operator, there is a major problem in identifying which process should receive input and how input should be echoed. There is also the problem of how the window manager can help users monitor and control multiple processes running in parallel. Some systems have introduced the icon with some kind of progress indicator (e.g. sand falling in an hourglass) to help the user. Icons have been used for many distinct tasks. The view of what an icon is and how it interacts with windows is clearly a major issue. Is an icon or pop-up menu a window or not? If not, does the window manager control more than just windows?

In considering what the user and application require, it soon becomes evident that conflicts could occur between the two if the same function is available to both. For example, both the application and user may require different windows to be visible. If both windows are large and cannot both fit on the screen, which has priority?

Finally, there are a number of issues concerned with the richness and appropriateness of the tools available to the user. What is the best locator device and how many buttons should be associated with it? Does it make sense defining a user environment which works equally well with and without a locator device? Using the motor car analogy would a voice-operated car have similar constraints to one that uses a steering wheel?

The window paradigm itself also needs to be questioned. Many existing systems have followed the cluttered desk scenario while only a few seem to provide the orderly interface we are insisting on at the application interface in terms of good software engineering practice.

14.4 ARCHITECTURE

A major problem in any window management system is resource sharing. In particular, the display upon which windows are viewed is a resource shared between the processes with scheduling being required by the window manager itself, the individual processes and the user/operator.

While the display is the major resource to be shared, many of the functions required of a window management system will make use of RasterOp/BitBlt hardware for moving information. Such functions include picture creation, window movement and changing window attributes (inverse video etc). In each of these cases, the process which makes use of the RasterOp is a different one. Hence, RasterOp is a resource that needs to be shared between the competing processes. While RasterOp is one example, many display systems have other fast general-purpose picture-generating hardware such as colour lookup tables, geometry pipelines etc. Again, the window manager should be capable of cooperating with such hardware.

With Unix operating systems being the most widely used on most high-powered single-user systems, a major issue to resolve is how to retain the existing software investment while introducing windowing techniques as a central feature of the system environment. This involves allowing for established conventions and operations for naming, accessing and representing objects so that existing applications require no changes. At the same time, system facilities must be extended to provide support for more sophisticated styles of interaction. Windows allow several separate contexts to be presented in one overall context. From the latter viewpoint it seems natural to specify relationships and operations which apply across the separate contexts as well as within those contexts.

At some stage, the structure of the window system needs to be established. Do we just have a set of independent windows or are windows specified hierarchically with a single root window, within which all other windows lie? Child windows would then be defined relative to the origin of their parent, and might or might not extend beyond the boundary of their parent. Siblings might have relative priorities, to define which has precedence when they overlap. If such a system is defined, who is responsible for regenerating information within a window? Do we need a procedure associated with each window whose function is to regenerate it? How is this reconciled with the need to run existing applications unchanged?

14.4.1 Two Types of Window Manager

Two possible models on which a simple portable window manager can be built are:

(1) *Direct access*: client processes can be allowed to map the actual pixels into their address space, and trusted to perform the correct clipping and synchronize with other clients.

(2) *Remote Procedure Call (RPC)*: client processes can access the display via RPCs on a server process that has access to the display. Clients therefore see some abstraction of the real display; with some difficulty this abstraction can be kept simple enough to span a wide range of devices.

The first approach only works well if RasterOp is part of the CPU's instruction set, or if there is no hardware support for RasterOp. Unfortunately, it is very difficult to prevent hardware designers wasting resources on inappropriate RasterOp support; when they do they normally make the direct access model impossible. Further, it is impossible to provide direct access except to processes running on the workstation itself, a problem in a networked environment. Even when this model has been implemented, as with the SUN system, it has proved less popular than expected. On the other hand, a full implementation of RasterOp in hardware such as on the PERQ, can provide a great deal of added speed for graphics.

The second approach, surprisingly, works well in practice. The Bell Labs BLIT, the MIT, and the ITC systems are all examples using low-level abstractions (lines, characters, and RasterOps with pixel coordinates). The Stanford system VGTS [36], and its predecessor at Lawrence Berkeley Labs, use a higher-level abstraction, namely a *structured display file*.

An RPC based window manager has several major advantages:

● It provides distributed access to graphics for free (if the underlying IPC mechanism copes with the network).

● Since applications contain no device-specific code, they are portable by definition. Once the window manager is up on a new display, all the applications can use it *without relinking*. Relinking in a large network may be impossible.

● Direct access window managers need to synchronize access between multiple clients using some interlocking scheme. Typically, this costs almost as much as the IPC mechanism, so their potential performance edge may not be realized.

The bandwidth limit imposed by RPC window managers is unpleasant in some cases, but they can provide competitive performance if they satisfy the following requirements:

● They handle fonts and character drawing well. The overwhelming majority of client requests draw characters.

- They provide (unlimited) off-screen buffers for applications to save screen parts in, and operate on invisibly.

- They provide some form of programmability, for applications to download specific behaviour. The BLIT, PostScript, and use of dynamic linking by ITC are examples.

Another, orthogonal, distinction is whether windows can change size. Forbidding size changes, as on the BLIT, is simple but probably unacceptable. Allowing windows to change size means that applications must respond to a signal, and regenerate their display. Applications like this turn out to be much easier to port.

14.4.2 Relationship to User Interface Management Systems

A problem is how the window manager interacts with User Interface Management Systems. Since a window manager may have a fairly complex user interface, it is desirable that it be created by a UIMS. If applications' user interfaces are created by the same UIMS, then the various user interfaces will be consistent. A UIMS, however, may require a window manager for its operations, so there is an unfortunate circularity. Also, no current window manager has been created by a UIMS, and this may be very difficult to accomplish.

UIMSs require drawing operations which are often supplied by a graphics package such as GKS. Similarly, window managers also need a certain level of graphics operations to draw title lines and handle the covered portions of windows. How a graphics package fits in with window managers and UIMSs is another problem.

14.5 THE ISSUES LISTS

Consideration of the position papers submitted by participants resulted in three lists of issues being drawn up. The issues divided into the three categories of Application Program Interface Issues, User Interface Issues and Architecture/ Hardware/ Operating System Issues and they are listed below under these three headings. Participants at the Workshop split into three Working Groups covering these areas. The groups spent part of the Workshop working in parallel considering the issues relevant to their area of concern in order to try to resolve at least some of them.

14.5.1 Application Program Interface Issues

P1. Is the window manager or the application responsible for redrawing the contents of a window when it becomes visible?

P2. Should the user (operator) be able to change the size of a window? What effect will it have on the information in the window?

P3. What input primitives and modes should the window management system support, as presented to the application?

P4. Should an application be allowed to write directly to the screen, or should all output be via the window system? How can high performance be achieved without compromising integrity?

P5. How should positioning of windows be described, and what functions should be provided to manipulate the depth-order of windows?

P6. What graphic primitives, if any, should be supported by the window manager (ie other than direct bitmap manipulation)?

P7. How should conflicts between user and application requests be resolved, in cases such as window priority or current input destination?

P8. Should clipping to the window boundary be the responsibility of the window manager or the application? Should applications be trusted (if they so request) to remain within the window?

P9. Is grouping of windows a necessary function?

P10. Is substructuring of windows a necessary function? Should the window manager support it?

P11. Can the virtual window be larger than its portion of the screen? Is scrolling done by the window manager, or by communicating with the application?

P12. Should any title/borders associated with a window be defined by the window manager or by the application? How might the contents/appearance be specified or altered by the application?

P13. Should the window manager support colour displays and/or colour images, and if so how?

P14. Should applications be at all aware of window position, rank etc, or the existence of other applications or windows?

P15. Should input be associated with windows, subwindows, window groups, processes, or process groups?

P16. How should cut and paste between windows and applications be supported? How should the user invoke these functions, and how should the applications be informed (if at all)?

P17. Should applications be able to change window size, priority, position autonomously?

14.5.2 User Interface Issues

U1. Is the overlapping windows paradigm the correct one?

U2. Should the user (operator) be able to change the size of a window? What effect will it have on the information in the window?

U3. How should positioning of windows be described, and what functions should be provided to manipulate the depth-order of windows?

U4. How should conflicts between user and application requests be resolved, in cases such as window priority or current input destination?

U5. What set of functions operate on windows? (For example, clear, close, change depth position, move, change size, set background colour, iconize window, windowize icon.)

U6. Should the window manager provide an undo command?

U7. What styles of control structure should the window manager support or impose?

> Reactive - user in control;
> Active   - application in control;
> and/or mixed initiative.

U8. How should window manipulation functions be invoked? Pop-up or fixed menus; sensitive spots on borders; dedicated mouse button?

U9. How should cut and paste between windows and applications be supported? How should the user invoke these functions, and how should the applications be informed (if at all)?

U10. How should the user indicate to which window the input should be directed? How are multiple input devices dealt with?

U11. Should applications be able to change window size, priority, position autonomously?

U12. What is an icon? What attributes has it? What can the user do with it? How do icons differ from windows?

U13. What performance or functionality limitations may be imposed by the use of any special hardware, eg on- versus off-screen images, single versus multiple process access, colour table sharing, dynamic feedback (eg in remote processor)?

14.5.3 Architecture/Hardware/Operating System Issues

A1. Should the window management system be responsible for other objects on the screen such as icons, or must all objects on the screen be windows?

A2. Is the window manager or the application responsible for redrawing the contents of a window when it becomes visible?

A3. Should the window management functions provided to the operator be a subset of those provided to the application?

A4. Is grouping of windows a necessary function?

A5. Is substructuring of windows a necessary function? Should the window manager support it?

A6. Should an application be allowed to write directly to the screen, or should all output be via the window system? How can high performance be achieved without compromising integrity?

A7. Should text windows be a special class (visibly so, to the application or user)?

A8. What graphics primitives, if any, should be supported by the window manager (ie other than direct bitmap manipulation)?

A9. Should off-screen and partially obscured windows be held in full as off-screen images?

A10. How should conflicts between user and application requests be resolved, in cases such as window priority or current input destination?

A11. Should clipping to the window boundary be the responsibility of the window manager or the application? Should applications be trusted (if they so request) to remain within the window?

A12. What set of functions operate on windows? (For example, clear, close, change depth position, move, change size, set background colour, iconize window, windowize icon.)

A13. Can the virtual window be larger than its portion of the screen? Is scrolling done by the window manager, or by communicating with the application?

A14. Should any title/borders associated with a window be defined by the window manager or by the application? How might the contents/appearance be specified or altered by the application?

A15. Where is the boundary between the graphics package and the application? For output: low level primitives versus modelling (eg PHIGS); for input: abstract input events (eg GKS CHOICE versus physical device actions). What abstraction level is provided to applications, and how is it mapped to the physical devices?

A16. Should the window manager support multiple graphics packages, multiple imaging models?

A17. What is the input model and minimum input devices required?

A18. Should fine-grained feedback be performed by the window manager? If so, (how) can interface designers specify the behaviour? How can feedback dependent on application data be achieved?

A19. Should input be associated with windows, subwindows, window groups, processes, or process groups?

A20. Should *good practice* (eg in display layout) be imposed at a basic level, or achieved through a higher layer implementing such policies? (The implication is that the latter might potentially be subverted.)

A21. How should simple teletype-driven applications be supported and integrated?

A22. Should sharing of windows among processes (in the sense of Unix processes) be allowed? If so, how, and to what degree?

A23. What styles of control structure should the window manager support or impose?

> Reactive - user in control;
> active   - application in control;
> and/or mixed initiative.

A24. How should cut and paste between windows and applications be supported? How should the user invoke these functions, and how should the applications be informed (if at all)?

A25. Should applications be able to change window size, priority, position autonomously?

Part III

Part III

15 Application Program Interface Working Group Discussions

15.1 INTRODUCTION

The Working Group membership was:

> Peter Bono (Chairman)
> John Butler
> Gordon Dougan
> Paul ten Hagen
> Bob Hopgood
> Colin Prosser
> David Rosenthal

The Working Group decided not to tackle the issues it had been given directly but first attempted to produce one or more models that captured the main points of concern at the application interface. The Architecture Working Group was responsible for the overall model but the Application Program Interface Working Group felt that it needed a model relevant to its activities as a mechanism for allowing constructive discussion.

The confusion between choice of names with the phrase *user interface* being used for both the programmer and operator interface led the Working Group to use the term API to stand for the Application Program Interface.

15.2 PROPERTIES OF A WINDOW MANAGEMENT SYSTEM

The Working Group attempted to narrow the discussion by establishing a set of basic principles that were agreed upon for window management systems. A summary of the discussion relevant to the properties given in the final report (see Chapter 16) is included below.

15.2.1 How Many Surfaces Does a Window Manager Control?

Nobody believed that an application would be restricted to outputting to a single window. Consequently, the application needed to specify at the API to which window output was directed. Consequently, it would not be difficult for a single window manager to control a number of display surfaces. It already had to control output going to different windows and whether they were on the same screen or not did not complicate the situation much. The SUN workstation, for example, with an attached colour display treated the two surfaces as a single entity. For simplicity, the majority view was that a window management system should control a single display space where two display surfaces with a well-defined positioning relative to each other could be regarded as a single display space.

If an application wished to set up a window on a second display space, this could be done but it would effectively be done by network communication between the window managers controlling the two display spaces.

15.2.2 Relationship between Applications and Windows

There was general agreement that a single application should be able to output to more than one window. The view was that the application was able to output to one or more drawing spaces and the window management system was responsible for displaying parts of these drawing spaces in the display space in windows.

There was a long discussion concerning whether more than one application could draw to a single window. It clearly complicates the model if this happens. In particular, are input events in this window passed to both applications and what happens if both respond? There was a general view that drawing to a window was a capability that should only be owned by a single process at a time. However, an application consisting of a number of processes might pass the capability between them.

15.2.3 Existence of Windows

Windows can either be regarded as entities in their own right or have a closer attachment to an application. If an application dies, does the window continue in existence? If it continues to exist, the window manager is forced to be responsible for updating it and this leads to the need for a full bitmap to be kept by the window manager for this particular window. If windows are regarded as files, they should continue in existence after the application dies. The consensus was that windows should be regarded as having close attachment to an application. Their purpose was to provide a communications medium between the operator and the application.

15.2.4 Role of the Window Manager

At some level of abstraction, the application does not have a great deal of interest in what constitutes the window manager and what constitutes the library support for graphics etc which sits between the application and the window manager. However, the system builder has to have a clearer definition of the interfaces.

The window manager's prime functions are resource management, protection and providing an interface to the user. A major function is ensuring that application output does not stray outside the window boundary. It would be feasible for the window manager to assume that applications were correct and did not draw outside their allocated display spaces. It would also be possible for the window manager to ask the application to clip to a desired boundary. However, the view was that a primary function of the window manager is to provide protection against applications going outside the allocated resource. It was something it could not give away or neglect to do.

It was less clear what should flow across the API interface. Cases can be made for high-level graphics primitives, low-level ones or bitmaps. Each has advantages and disadvantages. For a simple 'draw line' operation, the number of possibilities is large.

Consider 'draw line from (x1,y1) to (x2,y2)' as an output request from the application. It is assumed that the coordinates are already in the bitmap coordinates of the display. Almost certainly the application will require such a graphical command to be clipped against an application-defined clipping boundary. The window manager also requires a clip to be performed against the window boundary. Finally, the visible part of the line needs to be turned into a set of screen positions to be changed on the raster. These three functions can be done in any order and the two clips can be amalgamated. The interface between the application and window manager can be above, below or in the middle of these functions. This provides a whole range of possible alternatives some of which require added functionality in the window manager (for example, ability to clip at rectangles other than the window boundary).

The only agreement was that the window clip should be performed by the window manager.

15.3 ISSUES

The Working Group was presented with a set of issues to discuss. Half a day was spent in discussing these with a mode of working as follows:

(1)   Understand the issue. If it can be interpreted in more than one way, subdivide into separate issues or, at least, refine the issue until its meaning is clearer.

(2)   Discuss the issue, identify possible solutions and the advantages and disadvantages of each.

(3)   Attempt to come to a conclusion or at least indicate which alternatives are preferred even if a clear cut decision cannot be made.

The advantage of this approach is that the write-up of the issues, description, alternatives and arguments gives a good view of the depth of the discussion leaving the reader to assess the merits of the conclusion. The approach has been widely used in the graphics standards circles originating with the original discussion of the GSPC CORE proposal.

The write-up of the set of issues in the final report encapsulates the activities of the second and third periods that the Working Group met.

Presentations of the conclusions reached on issues at plenary sessions suggested that there was considerable common ground between this group and the Architecture Working Group. Instead of having two separate meetings for the fourth period, the two groups came together to attempt to come to a joint consensus on the issues or at least extend the arguments.

The combined groups identified two major areas of concern that had absorbed considerable discussion time in both groups. These were:

(1)   the level of the API interface;

(2)   what substructuring facility should be provided below the window level.

While the final reports of the two Working Groups were being written, Task Groups were formed to look at these two specific issues and report back. Their conclusions are given in Chapters 21 and 22.

While leaving many issues unresolved, the Application Program Interface Working Group felt it had been usefully employed discussing the issues in some level of detail and hopes its conclusions and arguments may be of use to others.

16 Application Program Interface Working Group Final Report

16.1 DEFINITIONS

A *window* is a region on a display surface whose size, position, and display priority relative to other windows may be changed at will by the operator. Different windows may vary in their appearance: presence of title bars, border style, kind of scroll bars, etc.

Several windows may appear on a *display surface*. Conceptually speaking, a display surface may extend across several physical *screens*.

A *Window Management System (WMS)* is a system service that provides for the creation, deletion, and modification of windows. The WMS allocates scarce resources (represented by on-screen real estate, entries in a colour map, use of mouse and keyboard input devices) among contending applications.

16.2 PROPERTIES OF A WINDOW MANAGEMENT SYSTEM

A WMS has the following characteristics:

(1) A WMS controls the resources associated with only one display space.

(2) A WMS manages a set of cartesian coordinate systems (*drawing spaces*) from one or more applications concurrently. A subset (possibly all) of each drawing space is presented in a single window.

(3)   Only one application at a time can write into a drawing space (and, conse-
      quently, to each window). The application is said to *own* the drawing space
      and the associated window.

(4)   A single application can own several windows concurrently.

(5)   A display space and its associated window does not exist without being
      attached to an application. Consequently, windows go out of existence when
      the application that owns them goes out of existence.

(6)   An application may transfer ownership of a window to another application.

(7)   The WMS is responsible for ensuring that the owner application does not draw
      outside the window boundary.

16.3 CONTROLLING THE WINDOW MANAGEMENT SYSTEM

There are two methods by which an operator can control the WMS: indirectly via an
application (the application program interface, API in **Figure 16.1**) and directly via a
special layout task (the operator interface, OI in **Figure 16.1**).

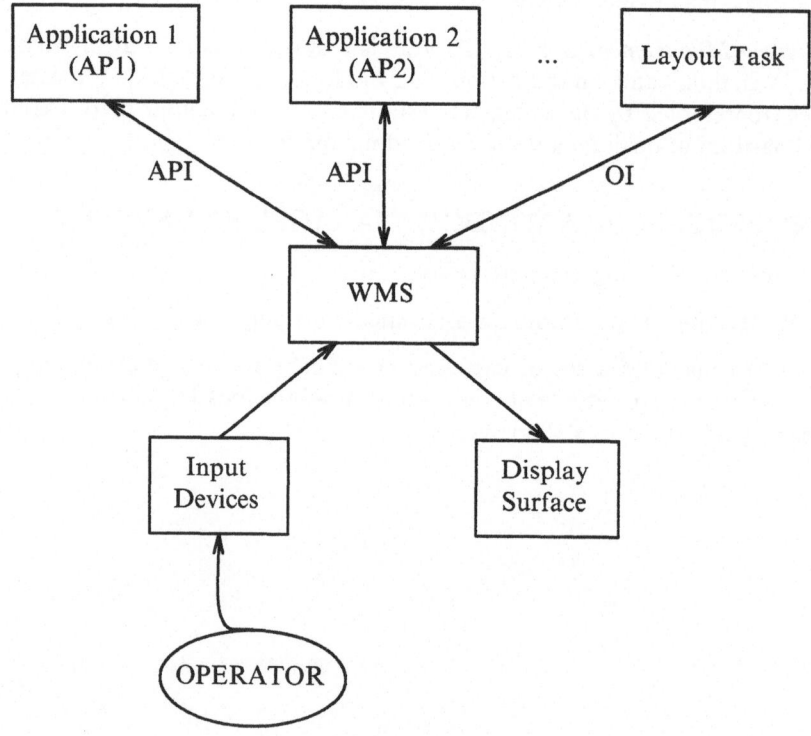

Figure 16.1

Some of the functions expected to be included in the API are:

(1)   creating and destroying windows;

(2)   redrawing images in windows;

(3)   providing titles for windows;

(4)   requesting the allocation of colour table entries;

(5)   requesting a sampling input from the mouse, keyboard, or function button.

Some of the functions expected to be included in the OI are:

(1)   resizing and repositioning a window;

(2)   changing a window display priority;

(3)   reassigning an input device from one application to another.

The exact relationship between the API and the OI (in terms of the functions supported) is not yet agreed. Possibilities include:

(1)   the functionalities are identical;

(2)   the functionality of OI is a subset of API;

(3)   the functionality of API is a subset of OI;

(4)   the API and OI functionalities are totally disjoint;

(5)   there is some overlap of functionality, but each has some functionality of its own.

16.4 MODELS OF THE APPLICATION - WINDOW MANAGER INTERFACE

A major problem in the resolving of issues in the Application Program Interface was getting a clear idea of the model and level of the interface. To aid discussion, the following three models were introduced.

In Model A (see **Figure 16.2**), the assumption is that existing packages for graphical (GR) and text (TTY) output are used by the applications, and interface to the window manager (WM) at a relatively low level. This could be in terms of a bitmap but might also include some standard primitives. Existing applications would effectively be making changes at the device driver level in order to run in a window management environment. An example of a window manager along these lines is the one on the Whitechapel MG-1. The major attraction is that little change is required to the application. On the other hand, because the interface to the window manager is at a low level, it is likely to be less device independent than other models. As the window manager is responsible for resource protection, the window manager will need to check and possibly clip output presented to it by the GR/TTY modules.

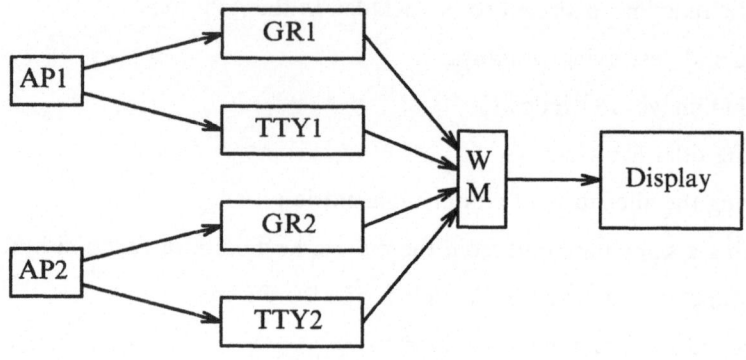

Figure 16.2 Model A

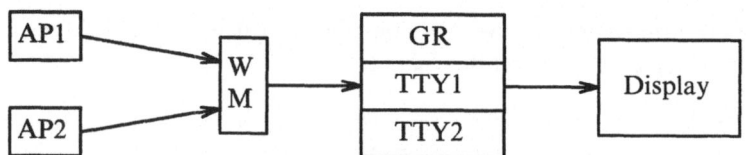

Figure 16.3 Model B

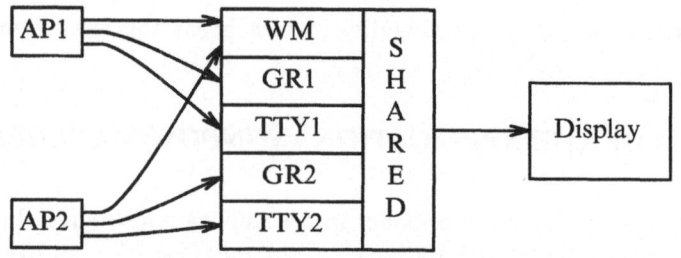

Figure 16.4 Model C

In Model B (see **Figure 16.3**), the window manager interfaces to the application at a high level and has a full range of Graphics/Text Primitives as part of it. An example of the protocol level between the application and window manager would be something of the same order of richness as PostScript, extended for input.

Each application would need to replace its existing interface to the graphics system associated with it by one to the facilities provided by the window manager. The advantage of this approach is a higher level of device independence and also gives the window manager the ability to use special hardware functionality if and when it becomes available.

In Model C (see **Figure 16.4**), the existing GR and TTY subsystems are integrated with the window manager so that the reconstructed graphics system etc is forced to provide the necessary protection to ensure that it does not write outside a window.

The advantage of this approach is that the functionality of the graphics system for clipping etc can be used by the window manager under its control to ensure the necessary resource protection.

To a large extent Model C is a compromise between the first two models.

16.5 ISSUES

These are listed on the following pages. A summary of the issue titles, their origins and the Working Group's recommendation on each is contained in the table following.

No.	Issue	Derivation	Recommendation
1	Can an application running under the window manager turn off the window manager's protection mechanism?	P4 reworded	No
2	Should the window manager notify an application when resources allocated to it change?	P14 part 1	Application can ask to be notified about changes in specific resources.
3	Should an application be aware of resources allocated to it?	P14 part 2	Yes
4	Should an application be aware of resources allocated to other applications?	P14 part 3	No
5	How should cut and paste be supported between applications under the control of the window manager?	P16	NONE
6	Should the operator be able to change the size of a window, change colour table etc continuously?	P2	NONE
7	If both application and operator can change size, colour tables etc and thus use of resources over time, how are conflicting requests for changes handled?	P7	NONE
8	Can the application change the listener?	P7 addition	Majority for Yes

No.	Issue	Derivation	Recommendation
9	Should there be the capability for a separate listener for each input device?	P7 part	Yes
10	Should applications (other than the layout manager) be able to change window size, position, priority etc continuously?	P17	NONE
11	Who is responsible for drawing (part or all of) the contents of a window when it becomes uncovered?	P1	Application can volunteer to redraw - default is window manager.
12	Who is responsible for clipping to the window boundary (in later terminology, the panel boundary)?	P8	Window manager
13	How is scrolling done?	P11 part	NONE
14	Should the virtual window (the off-screen window image, or picture) be the same size as its portion of the screen?	P11 part	No conditionally
15	Should the application program interface for the window manager provide support for substructuring of windows?	P10	Yes
16	How is input handled in the window manager?	P3	NONE
17	At what level should the interface between the application and window manager exist?	P1	NONE Task Group formed

Issue 1: *Can an application running under the window manager turn off the window manager's protection scheme?*

Description:

The issue was originally written as to whether an application should be allowed to write directly to the screen. The issue was rewritten to avoid assumptions about the method by which the screen is accessed to make clear that mutual protection of windows by enforcement of clipping is a major role of the window manager.

Alternatives:

(1)   Yes.

(2)   No.

(3)   Only under certain circumstances.

Arguments:

(a) CON 1,3: MS-DOS illustrates that in an environment where there is a standard way of doing something and a faster non-standard one, the non-standard way will be used all the time irrespective of the need for speed.

(b) CON 1,3: Would allow applications a closer knowledge of the hardware and could lead to certain displays not being suitable for window management graphics, for example, no memory map.

(c) CON 1: Forbids use of server-style window managers.

(d) CON 2: The graphics system already provides a clip at the workstation boundary. If this is the same as the window boundary, an unnecessary clip takes place. If this is smaller than the window boundary either the window manager must be capable of clipping to an area smaller than the window boundary or clipping will take place twice when only once is required.

(e) CON 2: Assumes a way of working that may be applicable today but possibly not in the future. A default method of being non-standard could be useful.

(f) CON 2: Overhead will almost certainly mean that some applications will not be able to run smoothly and effectively in a window management environment. An application that is well-behaved should be able to reduce window management overhead to a minimum.

(g) CON 2, PRO 3: Necessary protection of window manager could be achieved by saving and restoring the world so that allowing application access to screen does not necessarily lose all protection.

Recommendation:

Alt 2 (unanimous).

Issue 2: *Should the window manager notify an application when resources allocated to it change?*

Description:

The operator can perform a number of operations on a window which could potentially be of value to the application - for example, the position of the window on the screen. Other changes, such as resizing the window, can give poor visual results unless the application redraws the window.

Alternatives:

(1)   Always.

(2)   Never.

(3)   Application can ask to be notified about changes in specific resources.

(4)   Window manager could decide which changes need to be notified.

(5)   Resources are never changed.

Arguments:

(a) PRO 3: Application may not be exploiting all the allocated resources and may not be interested in certain changes. For example, may be happy to run however much of CPU is allocated. May be able to run whatever the window size.

(b) CON 2: Impossible to write programs that use resources effectively. For example, an editor needs to reformat text when window has changed in size.

(c) PRO 5: Operator should not be allowed to change resources required by application. It could leave the application with insufficient space or resource to work at all.

(d) CON 2: The role of the window manager is to allocate resources to competing demands. This allocation can be static through the lifetime of an application, or it may change. Forbidding change is too restrictive.

(e) PRO 3: While some applications may be able to use information passed to them, others may not. It may not even be possible for the window manager to send information to the application. Thus both (1) and (2) are too restrictive.

(f) PRO 4: Given enough intelligence, window manager could perhaps separate critical changes from others.

(g) CON 3: A filter of this type complicates the interface.

Recommendation:

Alt 3 (unanimous).

Issue 3: *Should an application be aware of resources allocated to it?*

Description:

This is a general statement concerning all resources. These could include current size of window, amount visible, how much CPU time allocated to this process, whether there is off-screen memory associated with the window etc. It is assumed that the operator and/or window manager can change the original allocation of resource in some way.

Alternatives:

(1) Yes.

(2) No.

Arguments:

(a) PRO 1: An application's request for resources cannot be guaranteed to be fulfilled as the window manager is a resource allocator. Consequently, there is a need for the application to be able to enquire whether the resources given are sufficient for it to run and the allocation could affect its method of running.

(b) PRO 2: Application should be unaware that it is running under a window manager.

(c) PRO 2: Application may not be able to deal with resource changes.

(d) PRO 1: Window manager methodology allows operator to change window size. Application must have the ability to find out whether change has taken place.

(e) PRO 1: Colour table may be the resource and application may not be able to run if it is not set to its requirements.

(f) PRO 1: Windows could be marked as changeable by operator so application could be helped.

Recommendation:

Alt 1 (unanimous).

Issue 4: *Should an application be aware of resources allocated to other applications?*

Description:

An application may need to know what resources are allocated to other applications running at the same time in order to decide how to run. For example, CPU time may need to be scheduled between several processes.

Alternatives:

(1) Yes.

(2) No.

(3) Privileged applications only.

Arguments:

(a) PRO 2: Too complex an interface otherwise.

(b) PRO 1: Could be necessary in some models of cut and paste.

(c) PRO 2: Cut and paste should be done as a negotiation between applications, with each enquiring of its own resources; otherwise security could be lost.

(d) PRO 1,3: Unless at least one application has the ability to enquire of all resources, it is impossible to define an application-level program which tidies up the screen.

(e) CON 2: Cannot write layout process or clear screen.

(f) PRO 3: If we distinguish between the layout application and normal applications, the latter should be protected and mutually unaware - the former should be all powerful.

Recommendation:

Alt 2 (unanimous).

Issue 5: *How should cut and paste be supported between applications under the control of the window manager?*

Description:

In window managers such as the Macintosh it is possible for an application to take part of the information in another window and use it. The information passed in this way could either be the bitmap on the screen or the data structure that produced it. Both need to be allowed for.

Alternatives:

(1)   Not supported at all.

(2)   Window manager maintains an uninterpreted cut buffer. Applications can read and write bytes to the buffer. Cut and paste are thus *asynchronous*.

(3)   Window manager arranges for a connection between the cut application and the paste application (cf: a pipe). Cut and paste are thus *synchronous*.

(4)   One level of window manager supports cut and paste via alternatives (2) and (3), a lower level does not.

(5)   Window manager interprets the contents of the cut buffer for applications.

Arguments:

(a) PRO 2,5: Applications using a server-style window manager on a network may not be able to use a common file name space to provide cut and paste outside the window manager.

(b) PRO 1: Common practice - few existing window managers support cut and paste.

(c) PRO 4: While seeing the attraction of cut and paste, it is clearly not always necessary as existing systems do not use it. Consequently, a level option would allow a choice of implementation.

(d) PRO 2, CON 3: Simpler and requires less of the operating system.

Recommendation:

None - more support for Alt 2 than others.

Issue 6: *Should the operator be able to change the size of a window, change colour table etc continuously?*

Description:

Changing the size of a window may change the amount of resources needed by an application. Allowing the operator to change size, colour table etc at will, implies that applications are not guaranteed access to resources which are stable over time. This is substantially different from file or memory resources which, once allocated, are secure.

Alternatives:

(1)   Yes.

(2)   No.

(3)   Some windows allow such change, specified at creation.

(4)   Application can specify whether it allows changes.

Arguments:

(a) PRO 3: Windows such as pop-up menus should not have their size changed by operators while others should allow it.

(b) PRO 1: The application can never get a guarantee of the resources it requests. So allowing the operator to change it does not change the situation. For example, two applications cannot have the colour tables set to their requirements if they are incompatible. The memory required for a new window may not be available etc.

Recommendation:

No support for Alt 2. No agreement for any of the others.

Issue 7: *If both application and operator can change size, colour table use, etc, and thus use of resources over time, how are conflicting requests for changes handled?*

Description:

The dynamic reallocation of resources under application or operator control may be desirable for at least some windows. The API may be written so that it semantically excludes possibilities of conflict (ie, either operator *or* application may cause reallocation, but not both), or else it may permit conflicts.

Alternatives:

(1)   Application requests override operator's.

(2)   Operator requests override application's.

(3)   Either (1) or (2), specified for each window.

(4)   Either (1) or (2), specified for each window/attribute pair.

(5)   Semantically excluded, rendering the issue moot.

Arguments:

(a) PRO 5, CON 3, 4: Only sensible solution to avoid conflicts; (3) and (4) too complicated.

(b) CON 2: Probably outlaws pop-up menus in some systems.

Recommendation:

Only alternatives getting support were Alt 2 and Alt 5.

Issue 8: *Can the application change the listener?*

Description:

There is one window that currently receives input from the keyboard, called the *listener*. Some window systems allow only the user to change the listener. Applications may also have varying degrees of control over the attachment of input devices. Note that application here excludes that part of the window system providing operator control.

Alternatives:

(1)   Application can request listener change.

(2)   Application cannot change listener.

(3)   Application can change listener but only to another window also owned by it. Effectively if application already has listener, it is allowed to change it to another of its windows.

Arguments:

(a) PRO 2: Changing of the listener by the application may conflict with the desires of the operator. It could also affect the quality of the user interface if misused. (However, badly behaved programs would be avoided by the user!)

(b) PRO 1: Cases exist where it could be useful - a lock-up application to make keyboard/mouse unusable until released. Command and Control systems may have override requirements.

(c) PRO 2: A block by the operator is necessary: ie the applications can only request listener changes.

(d) PRO 2: Application could run wild.

(e) CON 1,2,3: It might be reasonable for the application to have the capability of giving away a listener rather than taking it. In that situation, the listener would become available for other applications to ask for.

(f) PRO 3: If we can transfer other capabilities, we can transfer listeners.

(g) PRO 2, CON 1: You could have an application on a network which kills windows on all machines. You need some protection.

(h) PRO 1: If a user is editing and running a debugger at the same time, it would be useful for the listener to move automatically to the debugger on a break point.

(i) CON 1: You might not want it to happen even if the debugger felt you should!

(j) PRO 3: In this editor/debugger scenario, the two programs need to be linked in some way so that the listener returns to the editor at the correct position.

Recommendation:

Majority for Alt 1 but not unanimous.

Issue 9: *Should there be the capability for a separate listener for each input device?*

Description:
Some window managers attach all the input devices to the same listener window, with variations for communication with the window system itself. It is possible for each input device to be attached to a listener independently of all other devices.

Alternatives:

(1)   Yes.

(2)   Only one listener window.

(3)   Keyboard and the rest - two listeners.

Arguments:

(a) PRO 1: Even more generality needed, you might want to input to several windows at the same time by one device.

(b) PRO 1: How else can you handle voice input sensibly.

(c) PRO 1: It is important that we can specify that different applications have control of different devices and keep them. For example, only one application might be using a digitizer and it would be crazy for it to be transferred to another window each time the operator stopped to do something else.

(d) PRO 1: Applications can be envisaged which would require typing in one window while using the mouse in another.

Recommendation:
Alt 1 (unanimous).

Issue 10: *Should applications (other than the layout manager) be able to change window size, position, priority etc continuously?*

Description:

It is usual to allow control of resources to be given to the operator. The query is whether such control should also be given to the application.

Alternatives:

(1)   Yes.

(2)   No.

(3)   Some windows - specified at creation time.

Arguments:

(a) PRO 1: Applications are able to change the amount of file and memory space required, so why not these other resources.

(b) CON 1: These resources are different from those given in (a) as the operator using the application is aware of the changes.

(c) PRO 2: The "principle of least surprise" and the principle of "the user is king" suggest that applications not be given the same authority over windows.

Recommendation:

Some feeling towards Alt 2.

Issue 11: *Who is responsible for drawing (part or all of) the contents of a window when it becomes uncovered?*

Description:

When the operator moves a window or moves one to the bottom, the parts of windows that become visible need to be redrawn. Either the window manager or the application can be responsible for the redrawing. It is even possible that the window that was doing the hiding should do the redrawing. Much depends on the interface between the application and window manager.

Alternatives:

(1)   Only window manager via virtual bitmap.

(2)   Only application.

(3)   Application can volunteer to redraw - default is window manager.

Arguments:

(a) PRO 1,3: It is in poor taste to *require* application to redraw.

(b) PRO 3: In some cases application may have faster or more compact representation of the image and it is in the application's interest for it to be responsible for the redraw.

(c) PRO 3: Fits in with other issues where it is sensible for application to be aware of the resources allocated to it.

(d) PRO 3,1, CON 2: Window manager should ask the application to redraw as infrequently as possible.

(e) PRO 2,3: Application may be easier placed to redraw only a small rectangle of the window.

(f) CON 2,3: In some window managers, it is easy for window manager to redraw and very difficult for application.

(g) CON 2: Do not like the model where application keeps receiving requests from window manager to repair windows.

(h) CON 2: Application may not be able to redraw. Perhaps it is a storage tube output graphics system or viewing previously-generated output. It may require a system between the application and window manager to save the current contents of the window in which case it might as well be the window manager.

(i) CON 2: Even if the application redraws the window, there is a need for the window manager to do the necessary clipping and this is not to the original window boundary. Window manager might not have this capability. Easier if application always redraws whole picture but there are then performance issues.

(j) PRO 2: If a window can be created that is not on top, the application rather than the window manager should do the clipping.

(k) PRO 3: The split of responsibility should be 99% window manager and 1% application.

(l) CON 3: Application may say it will take care of screen and then do nothing. Result is screen becomes a mess (rebuttal: is this a bad or bug-ridden program?).

(m) PRO 1,3: Memory is getting so cheap that worrying about window manager having a virtual bitmap is not sensible.

(n) CON 1: For a $2048 \times 2048 \times 24$ colour system with many windows, it will always be a large overhead.

Recommendation:
Alt 3 (unanimous).

Issue 12: *Who is responsible for clipping to the window boundary (in later terminology, the panel boundary)?*

Description:

The role of the window manager is to control the layout of information on the display. Given the right hardware it might be sensible for it to leave the clipping to the application. Also, if it cannot do clipping efficiently and the application can by use of specialized hardware at the application level, it may be necessary to trust applications to behave as the window manager instructs but it should probably be avoided if possible. The main issue is whether the role of the window manager is to ensure mutual protection for applications.

Alternatives:

(1) Window manager.

(2) Application.

(3) Shared.

Arguments:

(a) CON 2,3: If we are going to have integrity, application must not be allowed under any circumstances to draw outside the bounds of its window.

(b) CON 1: Not possible always in practice to implement this way.

Recommendation:

Alt 1 (unanimous).

Issue 13: *How is scrolling done?*

Description:

One of the principal uses of a window is to examine textual or graphical material which extends beyond the boundaries of the current window. Support is often provided in a window management system to allow the operator or application to scroll text within the window or to pan around a larger graphical picture. If there was a much larger bitmap kept by the window manager, it would be possible for many of these operations to be performed by the window manager without needing the application to be involved.

Alternatives:

(1)   Scrolling is not supported by the window manager.

(2)   Scrolling is completely handled by the window manager.

(3)   The window manager provides a *scroll indicator* specifying where display should begin, application does the actual repainting.

(4)   The window manager only supports scrolling across a display space which is larger than its image on the screen but finite.

Arguments:

(a) PRO 3: There are two problems, what bits need repainting and who paints them. It is clear that the window manager specifies the first. The second may be better done by the application.

(b) PRO 2,3: Eventually the application has to do scrolling as the window manager cannot keep an infinite buffer. Having it kept partly by the window manager complicates the model. Even if the window manager keeps a buffer it should be regarded as an efficiency issue with the model having the application doing it.

(c) PRO 1: The window manager functions should be kept to a minimum and this is not a necessity. Why stop at panning and scrolling. If you are going to do scrolling, it probably opens the door for a whole set of other functions.

(d) PRO 2: This can be achieved by the application passing to the window manager a procedure which does the necessary redrawing.

(e) PRO 3: The window manager has to provide the facility for interaction for scrolling, scroll bars etc. The application needs to get involved as the unit of scroll may be application dependent. The application may insist that text gets scrolled a line at a time.

(f) CON 4: Too complex a model.

(g) CON 1: Many existing window managers provide this facility via explicit operator tools and they are well used.

(h) CON 2: Not possible unless the application can pass procedures to the window manager to achieve the scroll.

(i) CON 3: Depending on the input model, it may not be possible to synchronize the request to repaint and the actual repaint. May always land up out of step.

Recommendation:
    None.

Issue 14: *Should the virtual window (the off-screen window image, or picture) be the same size as its portion of the screen?*

Description:

Some window systems make these the same size. Others allow the virtual window to be larger, and the window area may be panned over the picture without further application intervention. It was decided that this was a separate issue from allowing window manager to be responsible for scrolling as scrolling could be achieved by an exported procedure from the application to the window manager.

Alternatives:

(1)   Yes, should be the same size.

(2)   No, may be different size.

(3)   No, but the window manager should be able to say it does not have the resources to keep a complete virtual window of the screen area.

Arguments:

(a) PRO 1: The window system is simpler if they are the same size.

(b) PRO 2: Some applications (VLSI design) may require panning over the image faster than or decoupled from the generation of the image by the application.

(c) PRO 3: There is a resource allocation problem. The window system may not, or some may never, have the additional storage for the virtual window.

(d) CON 2: Requires additional operator functionality and, if provided by window manager, may not be compatible with other application interactions.

(e) CON 1,2: Both imply a virtual bitmap. The off-screen image could be a display file.

(f) PRO 2,3: Existing window managers already support larger virtual windows.

(g) PRO 2,3: System with large memory should be able to use it for this purpose.

(h) PRO 1: Dumb applications not capable of performing pan and scroll, could use an intermediate system to deal with it. There is no good reason for insisting that it is part of the window manager with an overhead for all systems.

Recommendation:

Alt 3 - not unanimous.

Issue 15: *Should the application program interface for the window manager provide support for substructuring of windows?*

Description:

Windows are often constructed with boundaries which are separate areas having different properties. The application could be made aware of these and treat the set of subareas as a window with perhaps different control of each. Alternatively, the application could be only aware of the drawing area with the window manager having responsibility for the boundary.

Sometimes the application would like to subdivide the drawing area in a way similar to the functions provided by the window manager. A substructuring facility would allow this.

Alternatives:

(1)   Yes - substructuring is provided.

(2)   No - substructuring is not provided.

(3)   Yes - but only special, predefined substructures are provided.

Arguments:

(a) PRO 1: It may be necessary for performance reasons that substructuring is provided and accessible to application.

(b) CON 1: Substructuring provided may not suit the application in which case it still has to be built on top.

(c) PRO 1: Windows are often constructed with special dedicated areas which have specific semantics. Such areas can be created by software above the window manager, but providing support at the window manager level may prevent needless duplication if such services are often used by the application.

(d) PRO 1: If window manager provides substructuring, windows will reflect this. Common implementation techniques and access to them will provide a more standard user and application interface.

(e) CON 1,2,3: The alternatives need to be more clearly expressed before the arguments for and against can be established.

(f) PRO 1,3: Some systems make heavy use of pop-up menus where the menu is fixed in place relative to the window it is associated with. It is effectively a substructure of the window even though it may have a separate boundary. As it moves when the window moves, it has to be supported by a substructure facility.

(g) PRO 1,3: A number of entities associated with windows have similar properties to windows in terms of screen management (pop-up menus) but are not true windows in the application sense (do not have titles, borders, etc). These are best handled as substructures.

(h) PRO 1,3: Everybody is agreed that the application is free to draw in the main part of a window. An issue is whether the window manager provides support to manipulate borders and subregions or does the window manager send signals to the application program. If the latter, it is likely that the application will need to be aware of the substructuring.

(i) PRO 1,3: If different mouse events are required in different subregions of a window, it is necessary for the application to have access to a substructuring facility.

(j) PRO 1,3: Some systems use a hierarchy of windows where the screen is the main window, the application windows are substructures of it and so on. In this model, substructuring is an intrinsic part and going to another level of substructuring is no problem.

(k) CON 1,3: If substructures get too complex, have different boundaries and have all the functions of windows, they become multiple windows. The only property different from an application having multiple windows may be whether they can be moved independently. A user can push a window away but not a substructure.

Recommendation:

Application Program Interface Working Group had no consensus but the combined Application/Architecture Working Group meeting came out strongly in favour of some kind of substructuring.

Issue 16: *How is input handled in the window manager?*

Description:

The existing window managers do not have the richness of control provided by GKS input where all devices can operate in REQUEST, SAMPLE and EVENT modes. Some window managers only support one mode or leave the application to do some of the work. The GKS input model does not address the problems specific to multiwindow environments where different windows may want to operate the same device in different modes. Also the window manager itself makes use of the input devices.

The Computer Graphics Interface (CGI) standard is at a lower level than GKS and should be the protocol used between a device and a GKS workstation. It may well be sensible to model the window management input on the CGI model.

Alternatives:

(1)   The GKS input model is provided.

(2)   The CGI input model is provided.

(3)   Something else applicable specifically to the window manager environment.

Arguments:

(a) PRO 3: It is feasible that you may wish to input to several windows at the same time and neither of the models currently existing support this.

(b) PRO 1: Applications are using this and so the window manager needs to support it.

(c) CON 3: We have one too many input models already.

Recommendation:

None.

Issue 17: *At what level should the interface between the application and window manager exist?*

Description:
The interface between the application and the window manager can be at various levels. Many existing window managers have the interface at the bitmap level with the application producing changes to bits in a virtual window. Others have a higher level interface where graphics functions are provided by the window manager for the application to use. There is also the possibility of the application sending procedures to the window manager to produce the output.

Alternatives:

(1)   At the bitmap.

(2)   Window manager has low level graphics functionality only - 'draw line' say.

(3)   All of GKS NDC functionality in window manager.

(4)   Interface is via procedure passing.

Arguments:

(a) CON 1,2,3,4: As long as the functionality provided to the application by the graphics system is the same, it is irrelevant which parts are in the window manager.

(b) PRO 3,4: The higher the interface level, the more device independent it will be.

(c) PRO 1: As all displays to first order have virtual bitmaps, this is the best way of achieving device independence.

(d) PRO 4: Appears to be the only way good flexible control of input by the application can be achieved.

(e) PRO 3: The higher the level of the interface, the more likelihood that the window manager functions can be taken over by hardware.

Recommendation:
A special Task Group should look at the problem (see Chapter 21).

16.6 PORTABILITY

16.6.1 A Portable Window Manager?

In general, the model of a bitmap monochrome display as an array of bits in memory with no other attributes and no special hardware to manipulate it results in software that is portable across a wide range of existing workstations. In some cases, this bit array may have to be maintained as a shadow of the screen, with modified regions or the whole screen moved to the real display memory at intervals.

Exploiting RasterOp hardware leads to another possible interface at which portability might be achieved: that of a 2D array of pixels with the 16 binary RasterOp functions. The need to apply them to process virtual address space reduces the usefulness of much existing hardware.

16.6.2 A Portable Window Manager for Unix Systems?

(1)   Should be a user process: kernel source code may not be available to port a window manager requiring kernel support. (Caveat: beware hardware which forbids user access to the display.)

(2)   Should assume that the display is an array of bits in memory with no hardware support, that there is no cursor support, and that the kernel does not interpret mouse input.

(3)   Should be prepared to exploit RasterOp hardware, cursor support and autonomous mouse tracking.

The CMU and MIT (X) window managers are of this type.

16.6.3 Portable Window Applications for Unix Systems?

Porting the window manager may not be necessary. If applications are written using a simple subset of window manager calls they can probably be moved with little effort. Example subset includes:

> Create/Destroy Window;
> Draw Line;
> Define Font - map string name to font descriptor;
> Draw String in selected font;
> Get Character;
> Get Mouse Event;
> Invert/Clear Rectangle;
> Set Cursor to Icon;
> Add/Delete Menu Items (menus should be regarded as shorthand for typing).

This was the objective of the design of the CMU window manager described in Chapter 13.

16.7 FUTURE WORK

The Working Group identified a number of areas where future work was required before any conclusions could be reached. Other areas were insufficiently explored to achieve any conclusion. This list contains items of both types and also indicates some areas of future work which would be worthwhile in order to resolve some issues or gain experience of conclusions reached.

(1) *Input model*: insufficient time meant that we were unclear whether a satisfactory input model could be obtained at this point in time. Issues arose over event queues (one or many?), type ahead/mouse ahead (are they allowed and if so how do you achieve correct ordering where necessary?). How is the listener defined and are there many? What are the logical input devices and their modes of operation?

(2) *High level application interface*: we have experience of window managers based on low level interfaces. Experience with one based on a high level interface with good control of feedback to the operator is an area where future work would be fruitful. Can a portable window management scheme be devised?

(3) *Structured windows*: there was general agreement that some subset structuring facility was desirable and this might be the route to incorporate pop-up menus and icons into the general model. More work needs to be done in defining such a model and testing it.

(4) *Window hierarchy*: should hierarchies greater than level 2 be supported? For what reasons is such a model desirable?

(5) *Cut and paste*: there was general agreement that a window management system should provide cut and paste facilities between applications. There was no consensus as to how this would be achieved or how cut and paste above the bit level would be achieved.

(6) *Sneak paths*: it was unclear to this Working Group whether sneak paths were harmful or should be fully integrated into the model. How do you provide them if conceptually they are not there?

(7) *Window classification*: many issues can be resolved by defining classes of windows which have restricted behaviour (for example, menus and icons etc). Is there a need to introduce window attributes as a method of simplifying the model? Is this a mechanism for tailoring systems to individual users or classes of users (novice versus expert)?

(8) *Operator/application conflicts*: if both application and operator are allowed a certain function, how do you avoid conflicts?

(9) *Icons*: icons are used for many purposes. There is still no model of how these fit into the overall window management system.

(10) *Level of portable window manager*: a number of principles have had broad agreement at the Workshop. Is it possible to produce a low level portable window manager?

(11) *Operator/application functionality*: should they be identical, a subset of each other or two overlapping sets? If the last possibility, what is in the overlap set?

17 User Interface Working Group Discussions

17.1 INTRODUCTION AND BACKGROUND

The Working Group membership was as follows:

> Austin Tate (Chairman)
> David Barnes
> Steve Cook
> Martin Cooper
> Arthur Foster
> Brad Myers
> William Newman
> Ken Robinson
> Warren Teitelman
> Harold Thimbleby

(Warren Teitelman joined the Architecture Working Group after the first two sessions.) The main goal of all the Working Groups was a better understanding of the issues involved in their respective areas. Given the wide range of user types, applications, and window managers seen by the Working Group, the difficulty of providing concrete, all-embracing *decisions* can readily be envisaged. The Final Report in the next chapter attempts to classify the influences on the User Interface (UI), and presents conclusions on some of the issues discussed. This chapter is essentially (if not essential) background reading to that report, providing some of the more detailed reasoning that underpinned some of the decisions, and presenting some matters which, although they did not appear in the report, nevertheless are of interest. The following sections are, for convenience of cross reference, numbered as in the final report.

As background, the seven functional uses that have been identified for windows [15] are worth quoting:

(1)   more information than a single frame;

(2)   access to multiple information sources;

(3)   combining multiple information sources;

(4)   independent control of multiple programs;

(5)   reminding (eg clock);

(6)   command context/active forms;

(7)   multiple representations of the same task.

These functions are needed to make a model of a window manager for a user, and are part of the problem-solving strategy.

The components of the user interface are the *command language*, *information display techniques*, and *feedback techniques*. The command language has commands (operations on selected objects), objects to be operated on, and states (or modes). Information display methods include displaying the state of the system (choosing an abstract representation (icons) when needed) and enabling the next command or task, with access to the relevant information. Feedback mechanisms - which might be considered as part of information display - are needed for immediate device feedback (eg cursors), echoing, and selection feedback. Consideration of the influences on the user interface leads to the diagram in **Figure 18.1**.

17.2 INTERFACE TECHNIQUES

Some of the issues supplied to the Working Group were felt not to be issues at all; as an example, tiled and overlapped windows were seen to be merely *options* that the user interface designer could use if appropriate. Indeed, a user connected to more than one host, one providing a tiling environment and the other not, might well have both mechanisms to interact with at the same time.

Window grouping and subwindows received some attention. A subwindow is not necessarily identical to a window: for example a subwindow receiving input it does not understand refers it to the parent for treatment, and if a parent window is deleted then so are its subwindows. Subwindows in some systems can overlap, while others permit only tiling. Title lines, which can be considered as a form of subwindow, may need to be accessible to the application.

Icons were considered to have a number of possible functions; for example in Cedar an icon is a representation of a window, while in Sapphire it is another, *concurrent* form of the window, displaying information such as completeness of the task being performed, and status. After some discussion, it was decided that icons, which should be associated with the application, could be representations of, or alternatives to, a window; a representation of a task; or a representation of data, plus some (implied) potential for functions which could be done. These last might not be conceptually consistent - for example, opening a document icon in one system gives a window with an editor operating on that document, but moving the document icon to the trash can icon deletes the document, not the editor ...

There was little discussion on colour. Non-application-oriented uses envisaged included highlighting to show the listener window, display of error messages, and so on.

The taxonomy presented in the final report provides a fairly complete structure and list of the various features and techniques available in the three main sections - window presentation, operations, and high level functions.

17.3 USER INTERFACE GUIDELINES

The final report contains a list of relevant guidelines to user interface design. During the discussion of these in the Working Group some other useful points came out which are recorded here.

Graphics such as icons can be very powerful if used intuitively - international road traffic signs give examples of good and bad usage of icons; the bad ones are non-intuitive. A cursor should be used to tell the user the current state, or next action available. All these exploit the bandwidth of the display. The spread of user experience can (at least partly) be accommodated by, for example, allowing holding a mouse button down to display help information. As user experience increases, the feedback used decreases. Another consideration is ease of use against power - a novice, when editing a document, could select a word by pointing at the first character and then extending the selection, while an expert would use a double click.

Cedar attempted to be *consistent* in its use of keys and buttons on the mouse. If < key > meant do < function >, then *shift* < key > meant do < reverse function >, so that a function key for (forward) search could be used with *shift* to provide a backward search, and *shift* with the *again* ('repeat previous operation') key meant 'undo'. Similarly, the left mouse button could be used for simple tasks and the right for more heavyweight ones; in a debugger, the left button could clear a breakpoint, while the right could clear all breakpoints.

Modes in general should be avoided where possible; *shift* is acceptable but *caps lock* is not. An *experienced* user could be allowed to specify modes, but these should persist visibly. One option used in Cedar was the concept of the *guarded button* - the first hit removes the guard for a few seconds, after which it returns. As a general rule, anything the user does is precious - for example, if a confirmation is required, any existing type ahead should be saved, and restored following the confirmation.

17.4 THE USER'S CONCEPTUAL MODEL OF A WINDOW MANAGER

This section also records some points arising during the discussion of this topic which are not recorded in the final report (section 18.4).

It is common to regard the screen as a fixed area that windows get placed in; an alternative, useful concept is to see the screen as a window on the user workspace, and the screen itself is moved over that workspace. In Cedar, the screen is just the current working set of a large (overlapped or tiled) system workspace; the system has the notion of multiple desktops. Alternatively, the total user view can be considered as a plane or a hyperspace. The system can save a screen set of windows, and restore a saved set of others.

A list of functions does not represent a conceptual model of a window manager; this model is high level, independent of the information displayed and the command language. It acts as a basis to start with when addressing a new user. The model describes *what* a window is and *what* can be done with it; the question of *how* the operation is done is separate. It is worth remembering the Foley and Van Dam description of the four parts of the user interface [conceptual, semantic ('move window'), syntactic ('how to move window') and lexical ('press left button')]. In general users have tasks to be done; they don't begin by moving windows, but by considering more macro-level tasks such as moving information between windows.

Representing the user model is difficult; many psychologists would say too difficult even to discuss. User interface designers tend to be more confident in talking about it as they don't understand well enough the complexity of the problem. It is worth bearing in mind that although the user has models of the window manager, the application and so on, these models are *not* additive. An outstanding issue is the need to separate the user's view of the window manager from that of the application - an example is that scroll and zoom are not part of the window manager.

17.5 APPLICATIONS DOMAIN AND WINDOW MANAGER DESIGN

The Working Group decided that there was a need to look at a set of applications and extract generic functions, common to a range of applications. Ideally, the whole universe of window manager uses should be considered; it might be that some areas could not be tackled; if so, reasons should be given. Subordinate applications should be noted - for example, in a spreadsheet system there might be a requirement for word processing software. There were some obvious implications, such as that a real-time application would require its windows to be unobscured, probably militating against the overlapping style of window management.

It was noted that, in terms of the functionality required, the window manager seemed slightly insignificant; research on commands and functions might be more worthwhile.

17.6 USER TYPES AND WINDOW MANAGER DESIGN

The common split between novice and expert was too simple. Users could be expert in one area and novices in another, or a computer-naive user could require a very sophisticated applications interface - consider an air traffic controller. The effects of stress might also need to be taken into account - users under pressure can revert to habits developed on a previous system. These ideas are taken further in section 18.6.

17.7 USER INTERFACE EVALUATION

Xerox PARC have done a lot of work in this area. At PARC, there was a feedback loop between the psychologists and the implementors of user interfaces; however it takes much longer to do a psychological study than to build the interface. The existence of a large community of critical users helped, but the psychologists tended to verify what was already known. The PARC measurements on keystroke efficiency and cursor movement overall had disappointing results. In a comparative study of editors (Roberts [56]), the only statistically significant result was that Teco was harder to use than the others. (As an aside, Teco was implemented by a very slow typist - slow typists are more willing to accept the cognitive load of short command names.) It is necessary to distinguish between metaphor and model - the metaphor is not a total function, and maps to a separate domain. With the desktop metaphor, one is mapping onto the paper office, but differences soon become important.

User interface characteristics are dependent both on the characteristics of the user and on the task being executed. It is important to consider the context in design; even using Teitelman's guidelines (see section 18.3) an enormous search space exists, and other methods must be used. Formal evaluation of a paper design for the interface can be undertaken; using formal methods means that tools can be used to estimate how appropriate the design is for a particular user and task. The process is time consuming, and there are often surprises when the interface is actually implemented. Various methods are available, including prototyping, when the general style of working is provided, not full functionality. Performance problems in prototypes can also affect the assessment of the interface.

Testing can be done by simulation (eg by using overhead projector slides for screen artwork, icon design and so on), trial implementations (with the need for feedback from users), and formal testing (classical human factors, laboratory condition experiments, statistics to make decisions about, for example, multiple button clicks).

Current work is patchy, based on comparative studies of single issues or small parts of a system. Methods that need to be used in the future can be classified into two types:

(1)   Collect the concepts of the user interface into a framework, and then use these to predict the outcome in particular circumstances. The model so prescribed can be used to generate parametric results. This is ambitious.

(2)   Look at higher order functions when interacting with an interface to develop a general theory of what people do when they interact with a computer. There are two categorizations, firstly, low level work on very fine-grained parts of the interaction (eye, mouse movements, posture, brightness and so on); and secondly, higher level conceptual model analysis of dialogues and contexts. The final report (section 18.7) highlights the need for more work in this area.

17.8 ISSUES

The list of issues assigned to the Working Group is to be found in section 14.5.2.

In addition to the issues covered in section 18.8, the Working Group also discussed the need to support some form of dialogue between disjoint applications. In cut and paste type operations support of dialogue between disjoint applications is required. In cut and paste type operations, the *cut* can be considered as bitmap, text or graphics, or the relationships between the items in the *cut* (consider a spreadsheet, for example). The requirements are application-dependent; all the window manager can do is to provide invocation mechanisms and a *conduit* for information flow between the applications, which can define what the data means.

17.9 FUTURE WORK

The Working Group saw the need for much more research in the user interface area especially in areas such as user's model issues, measurement and testing methods for assessing user interfaces, and User Interface Management Systems. An analysis of applications and their requirements would also be helpful.

18 User Interface Working Group Final Report

18.1 INTRODUCTION

The Working Group categorized the influences on user interface design and styles of interaction; these categories are shown in **Figure 18.1**.

The following sections consider these influences in turn, and list the options under these headings, attempting categorizations where possible. These should only be seen as a first pass and further work is needed in all areas to improve the classification of influences on user interface design and to enumerate the options in each area.

For each combination of system/application/task/user, the interface option selected changes. Almost all "How should...?" issues were changed into "What are the options for...?".

Group Motto: "IT DEPENDS".

A need for a design methodology for user interfaces was agreed. Central to such a methodology must be a means of representing the user interface design so that it can be specified, discussed, tested and implemented. For example, the user interface can be represented in terms of its command language and its conventions for information display. It is essential to apply such descriptive representations to window manager user interfaces so as to provide a basis for discussing their properties.

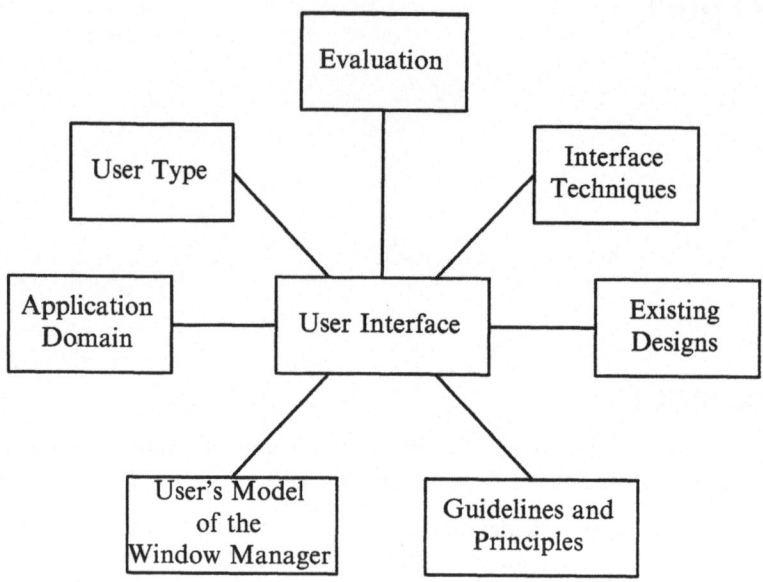

Figure 18.1

18.2 INTERFACE TECHNIQUES AND EXEMPLARS

Figure 18.2 is a proposed taxonomy of window manager user interface issues, based on a proposal by Brad Myers. This taxonomy attempts to list most of the properties that differentiate different window managers' user interfaces. It seems that a window manager can be characterized by choosing among the various issues listed here. Subissues listed depend on the decisions on the higher level issues. This list can serve as a guide to what choices need to be made when designing future window managers.

In addition, as a measure of the level of constraint placed on the user interface by different systems, window managers can also be described schematically, as shown in **Figure 18.3**.

Presentation of Windows

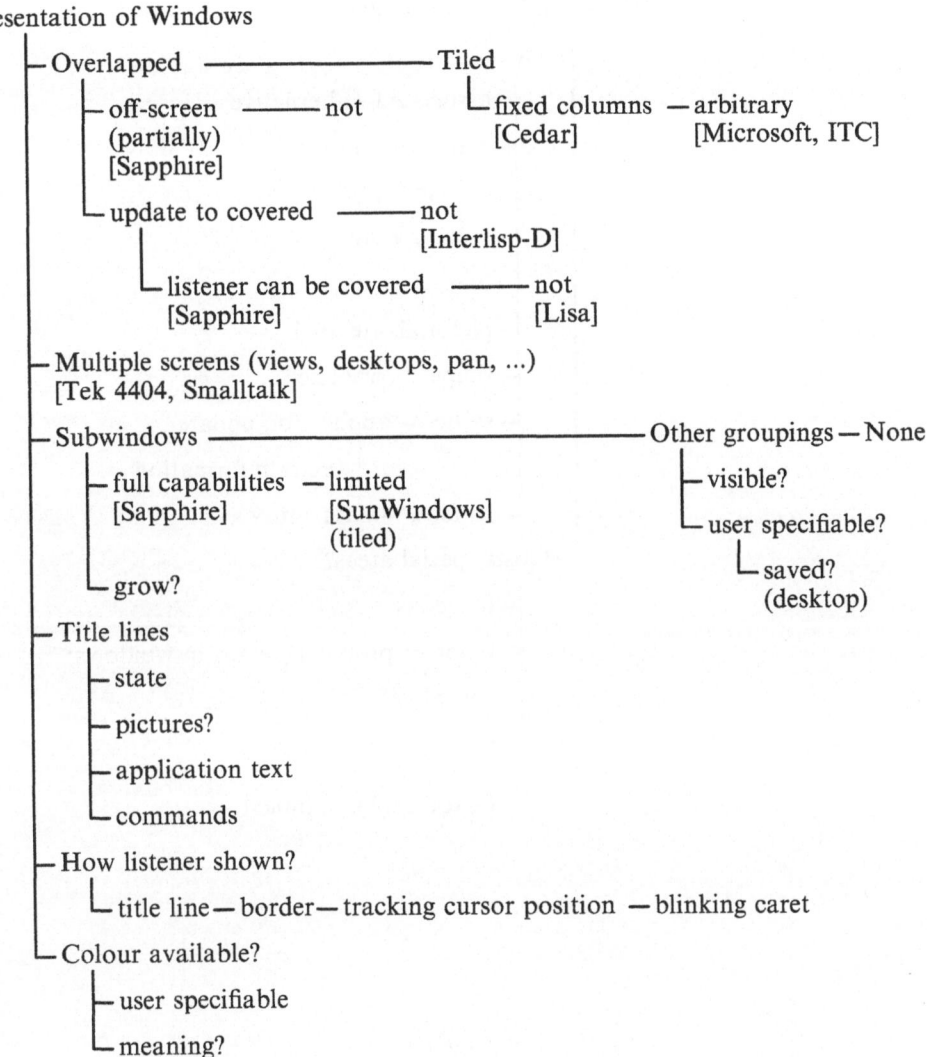

Figure 18.2

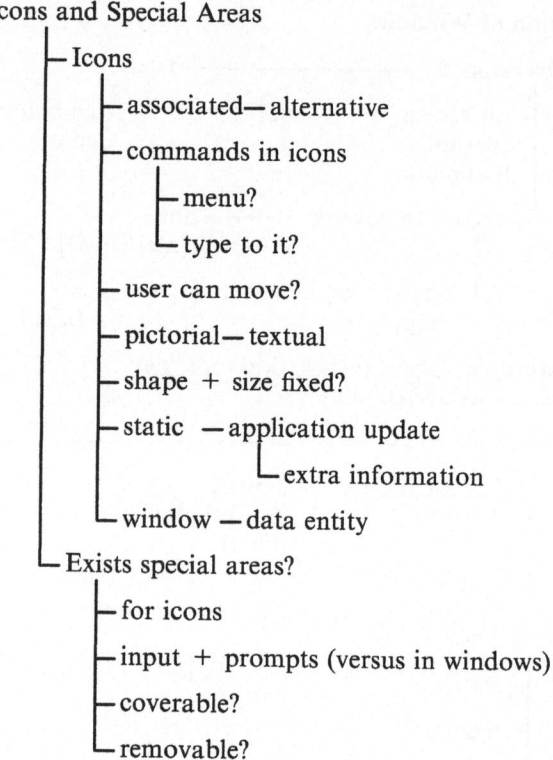

Icons and Special Areas
- Icons
  - associated— alternative
  - commands in icons
    - menu?
    - type to it?
  - user can move?
  - pictorial— textual
  - shape + size fixed?
  - static — application update
    - extra information
  - window — data entity
- Exists special areas?
  - for icons
  - input + prompts (versus in windows)
  - coverable?
  - removable?

Figure 18.2 Continued

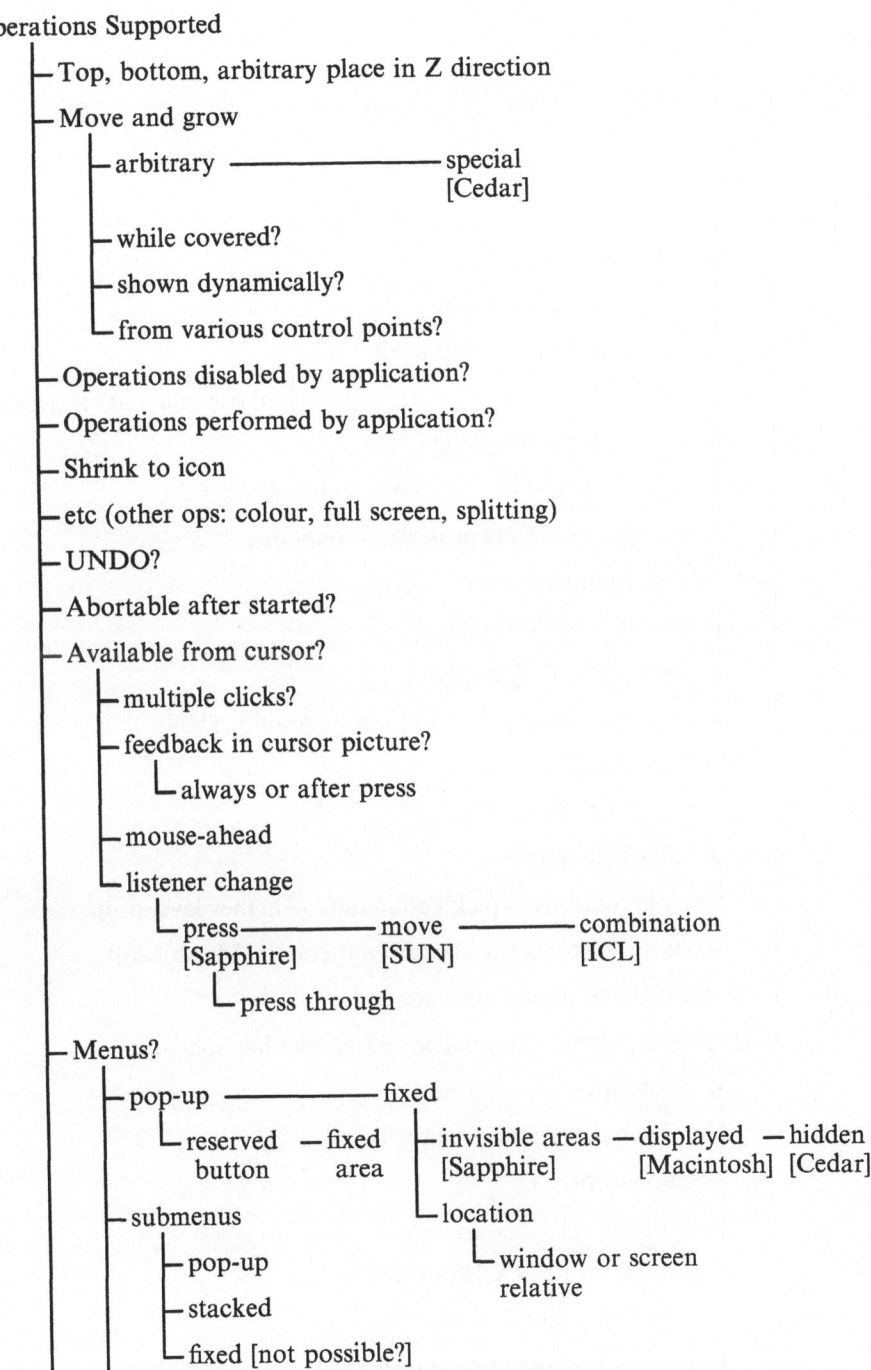

Figure 18.2 Continued

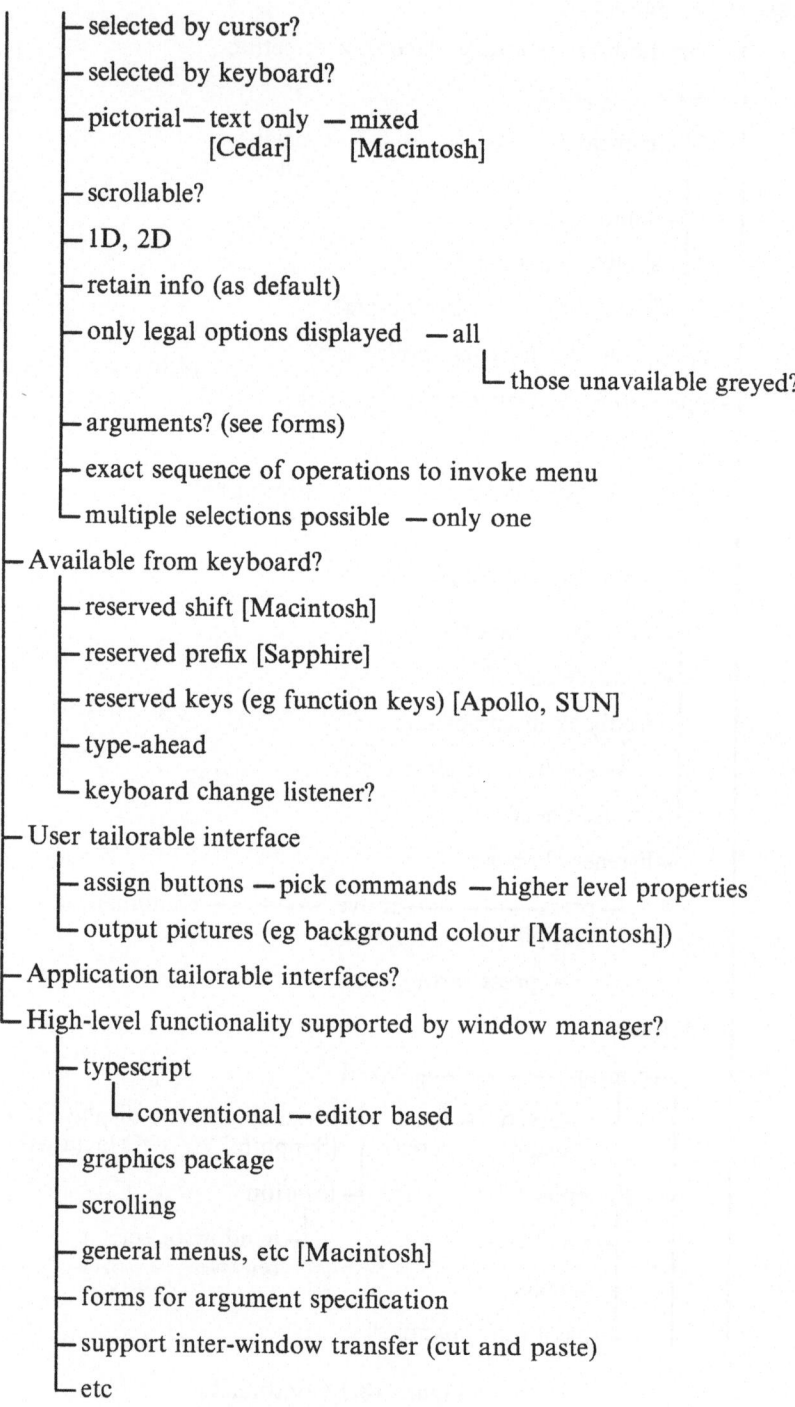

- selected by cursor?
- selected by keyboard?
- pictorial— text only — mixed
  [Cedar]   [Macintosh]
- scrollable?
- 1D, 2D
- retain info (as default)
- only legal options displayed — all
  - those unavailable greyed?
- arguments? (see forms)
- exact sequence of operations to invoke menu
- multiple selections possible — only one

- Available from keyboard?
  - reserved shift [Macintosh]
  - reserved prefix [Sapphire]
  - reserved keys (eg function keys) [Apollo, SUN]
  - type-ahead
  - keyboard change listener?

- User tailorable interface
  - assign buttons — pick commands — higher level properties
  - output pictures (eg background colour [Macintosh])

- Application tailorable interfaces?

- High-level functionality supported by window manager?
  - typescript
    - conventional — editor based
  - graphics package
  - scrolling
  - general menus, etc [Macintosh]
  - forms for argument specification
  - support inter-window transfer (cut and paste)
  - etc

Figure 18.2 Continued

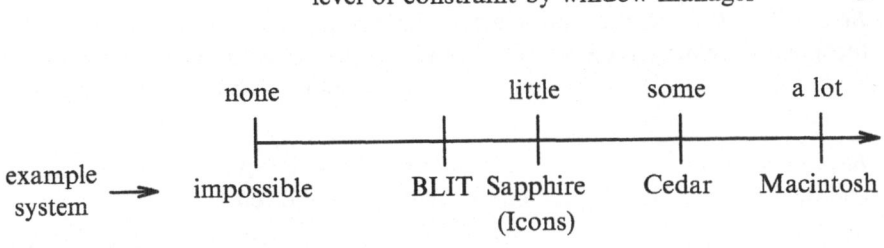

Figure 18.3

18.3 USER INTERFACE GUIDELINES

The Working Group believes that the publication of guidelines and the demonstration of systems with consistent default user interface choices is of value. Some relevant guidelines are given here, based on a list prepared by Warren Teitelman; the context is oriented to a program development environment where the user would be expected to be in control.

(1) *Be intuitive*: use icons and cursor images suggestive of the operations being performed, menu highlighting, previewing, etc.

(2) *Accommodate novices and experts*: there is a range from ease of use to power and expressibility. Techniques such as double click to override confirmation mechanisms, complex operations attached to multiple buttons, keyboard meta-shift keys, function keys, and so on can all be used as *accelerators* for expert users.

(3) *Allow customization*: default settings should be used (perhaps depending on user type such as novice, occasional user, expert). Configuration languages or files can also be provided to associate window manager operations with buttons, keys, sequences, etc. Macro mechanisms can be made available for expert customization (as in Emacs).

(4) *Provide extensibility*: again macros can be used to extend basic functionality, and languages to map user actions onto window manager functions. Use of a language such as PIT (Programmable Input Translation) should be considered (previously called TIP).

(5) *Use lots of feedback*: normal interaction with a user should not be intrusive. For example, a blinking caret may be suitable to show type-in position, but a flashing window is marginal - some users will object or get concerned - while a blinking screen is objectionable and should only indicate impending doom! Pop-up prompt or reminder boxes may be objectionable after the one thousandth use, and should be capable of being overridden. In general, taking and using a user resource should only be done in extreme circumstances; consider that a prompt or reminder in a typescript window may ruin the user's

data, and the Unix 'man' entry should perhaps use a separate window to help preserve the user's data at the current working point.

(6)   *Be predictable*: use the "principle of least astonishment". A consistent, uniform, easily remembered set of basic actions which is extended in obvious ways should be used. Use of buttons, keys, etc should be regular, and icon interpretation should be uniform.

(7)   *Be deterministic*: type ahead and mouse ahead effects should be considered, and deterministic (hence predictable) methods preferred.

(8)   *Avoid modes*: states that persist should be avoided. If modes are necessary make the feedback and paths out highly obvious. For example, guarded buttons (which fall out of a state after a time) could be used rather than confirmation boxes.

(9)   *Don't preempt the user*: users should not be forced to respond, and user resources which are expected to be used for an application should not be grabbed.

18.4 THE USER'S CONCEPTUAL MODEL OF A WINDOW MANAGER

Insufficient attention has been paid to user's models, which enable window manager concepts to be taught more easily. The model that the user has of the system is meant here, rather than the model the system has of the user or that the designer has of the user. The window manager has enriched the user's model of the system as a whole with several new concepts. These concepts need to be clear and simple in order to maintain the usability of the system. There is a danger that a window manager with a poorly conceived user's model will have an adverse effect on usability. Ways in which users would conceptualize the window manager were considered during the Working Group discussions; this is still a research area and ways of describing user's models are still being developed.

One way of representing the user's model is to describe it in terms of objects, actions, and modes. *Objects* are the entities of which the user is aware, *actions* are performed on the objects by the user, and *modes* are states in which objects exist that affect how they respond to actions. This object model is hierarchical and should be viewed at a number of levels. An initial, incomplete breakdown gives:

Objects	Actions	Modes
Window	move grow top bottom	full/icon listener/not (per device)
Application Control Task	scroll create destroy	
Menu	select	
Cursor Screen (output) resource Input resource	select	

At some level, objects that are relevant to the user's model will include window, task, icon, menu, cursor, and screen. There are others which appear to occupy a less prominent position in the user's model, for example, a window title line or an attached menu. Various user's models of icons, windows and tasks were discussed, with the following comments:

(1) The *task* is a more abstract concept that appears in some user's models of some systems.

(2) In some user's models the window is used as a means of accessing and controlling a task.

(3) An icon may be thought of as an alternative representation of a window, ie a mode of a window. Alternatively it can be considered as a separate object, such as a representation of a task, a data item or a function. In many systems the relationship between icons and windows is not very clear.

Actions on tasks can include create and kill operations, while windows can move, grow, be altered in screen priority (top/bottom in window managers which permit window overlap), and be closed to icons. Icons can be moved, or opened.

The separation of the user's model of the window manager and the user's model of the application is not clear; for example there are operations such as scroll and zoom which the user may *perceive* to be under the operation of the window manager but which are in fact an operation of the application.

Recommendations

The user's model should be considered in any attempt to define standards for window manager user interfaces.

Present ways of representing the user's model are not satisfactory - and there is no obvious route to standardization of the user interface.

More research is required, and where there is development work it should consider user's model issues. Research work could include the study of existing window manager user's models, and better ways of representing user's models.

18.5 APPLICATIONS DOMAIN AND WINDOW MANAGER DESIGN

There is a wide range of applications domains across which a window manager may be used. These include:

> Office Automation
> Computer-Aided Design
> Publishing/Printing
> Real-Time Command and Control
> Decision Support
> Program Development
> Computer-Aided Instruction
> Process Control
> Communications - Mail
> Domestic/Entertainment
> Art/Music.

There is also a wide range of applications within each domain, for example office automation includes word processing, spreadsheets, databases, electronic mail and so on. Across these domains and applications various styles of dialogue are appropriate, for example user-in-control (Office Automation), system-in-control (CAI), and mixed-initiative (Process Control). Tasks in different application domains have many variables, eg they may be continuous, interrupted or occasional.

Some window manager user interface decisions are a function of the application domain and others are reasonably independent. For example, "don't be too intrusive" is a good principle for the design of a programming or word processing system, but *not* for the design of a critical real-time process control system; whereas "be intuitive" and "use lots of feedback" seem to be application independent.

Recommendations

A configurable toolkit approach should be taken. This should provide an extensive set of defaults to provide a *house style*, encouraging consistency in future applications, plus access to lower-level facilities to enable inclusion of applications for which this style is inappropriate.

The window manager should provide generic select, cut and paste operations to be interpreted according to application semantics.

Categorization of application domains, the applications within them, and the tasks performed should be undertaken. Some axes for classification are: the distribution of control in the dialogue; the temporal nature of the task (eg continuous/occasional/interrupted); and the difficulty of the task (data entry $\longleftrightarrow$ problem solving).

An adequate abstract window manager model should be created and related to the application and task categories. The "Card, Pavel and Farrell" model [15] is a useful starting point.

User Interface Management Systems should be developed which enable the rapid tailoring of window managers to application requirements.

18.6 USER TYPES AND WINDOW MANAGER DESIGN

It is unlikely that just one window manager will be appropriate for all types of user. Users vary in many ways, having differing amounts and types of ability, motivation and experience.

These user characteristics can be further subdivided as shown below:

(1)   *Ability*: cognitive, manual.

(2)   *Motivation*: to use computers, and to complete the task.

(3)   *Experience*: of systems that could serve as metaphors; computers in general; the underlying operating system; the application program; the task; window managers in general; and the particular window manager being used.

It is not clear at present how each of these factors maps onto window manager features (if at all). However, some examples can be given where common sense suggests there will be an effect. Cognitive ability has implications for the ease of initial use of the window manager and the degree to which it supports accelerators, combined operations, customizability, etc. Poorly motivated users (such as senior executives!) place great demands on the window manager design to ensure that it does not need much effort to interact effectively with it. Users' experiences have implications for the selection of metaphors such as the desktop model, the nature of help, error messages, the complexity of facility provided, and so on.

Recommendations

A customizable/configurable/extensible window manager system is necessary to cope with the requirements of a wide range of users. If the characteristics of the target user group are known the default settings of the window manager system should be matched to their needs/preferences.

More work is needed to:

(1)   determine good ways of classifying and describing users and how far it is possible to go beyond a simple novice/expert categorization;

(2)   determine the window manager system requirements of different user groups;

(3)   develop ways of enhancing window manager system configurability, such as configuration languages.

18.7 USER INTERFACE EVALUATION

More work is needed on measurement and testing methods for assessing the user interfaces of window management systems. Some work has been done on analysing human-computer interaction using formal grammars and then applying metrics (eg counting the number of grammar rules needed to generate a command language) to estimate ease of initial use, learnability, error rate, etc. These techniques can be applied at an early stage in the design of a system and can guide the design process. This work should be encouraged and augmented in order to develop methods of analysing and predicting performance with window-based systems.

Usability assessment involving tests of representative users interacting with simulated, prototyped or real systems is currently the only way of determining how well-matched a system is to its users. The evaluation of text editors forms one focus of this work. Techniques appropriate for the assessment of window managers should be researched; for example, a collection of benchmark tasks should be developed for use in user tests with such systems.

An important related effect is to provide tools to aid in the development of user interfaces easily and quickly. These tools, often called User Interface Management Systems (UIMSs) are now progressing to the point where they can be used to generate window managers, but more work is needed.

18.8 SPECIFIC ISSUES

A series of questions of the form:

"How should the user do this?", "Is paradigm X the correct one?"

was presented to the Working Group. It was felt from the start that, given the range of possible applications and users, these were the wrong sort of questions and that it was not possible to be dogmatic about any one position in questions of this form.

Some specific issues required resolution of whether the user should be allowed to do X,Y,Z and whether the applications should be allowed to do similar things. It was felt that the window manager should allow, in principle, an application to be able to do *anything* that a user can do and *vice versa*. In an extensible system the distinction between *user* and *application* may be arbitrary.

18.8.1 Consideration of End-users

The designer of the window manager must consider who the end-users are. In the ideal case all possibilities should be catered for, but it is recognized that this will be prohibitively expensive. The design choices must therefore be based on the needs of the end-user community. As an example: a general purpose undo command may not be relevant for professional users since most window manager commands are reversible. However the ability of users to make use of accelerators may require the window manager to maintain too long a history of commands to guarantee reversibility.

If the user type is not pre-decided then the window manager must be more general and configurable, which will clearly increase the cost of providing the window manager and may be less satisfactory for any particular user group.

18.8.2 Responsibility for the User Interface

In most of today's non-adaptable systems, the responsibility for the user interface does not lie with the user. In the future, however, when the interposing of a User Interface Management System (UIMS) between user and application allows the users to customize the interface to their own requirements, consistency across applications as well as within them can be maintained. By and large the application should *not* be interested in acquiring data via the interface and passing data out in some form. For instance, an application may require the user to scroll but neither the application nor the window manager should really be concerned with where the scroll bar is placed either in or around the window. Similarly, 'selection from a list' is another operation whose accomplishment via a static or pop-up menu is unlikely to be of serious concern to an application. In general, window manipulation functions (such as the meaning of keystrokes, mouse movement and button action) should be specified separately from their user interface. This will require adaptable layers and configuration tools.

This level of customization is now being demonstrated in some window managers.

18.8.3 Control of Interaction Style

Given the range of applications and users, it is not practicable to prescribe styles of interaction - consider, for example, the different styles required by a Command and Control system and a program development environment. In the first case user control is necessarily restricted, while in the latter a high degree of customization is desirable. Questions to be considered are such as the following:

- How should conflicts between user and application be resolved, in cases such as window priority or current input destination?

- What styles of control structure should the window manager support or impose?

- Should applications be able to change window size, priority, position autonomously?

All have the same answer: *it is dependent on the application and the user*.

18.8.4 Icons

Icons are regular (small) pictograms which may be defined and changed by applications. They can serve many functions, frequently to conserve screen real estate. They can be used as an alternative to a window as in Cedar; as an alternative representation (perhaps concurrently visible) of the window (Sapphire); or as a representation of a task to be invoked or data which is to be operated on (STAR,

Macintosh). The icon can thus range from an application-prescribed static bitmap representation to an entity which has all the attributes of a window (eg can receive all types of input). Since use of icons in user interfaces is commonplace, the provision of support in the window manager for operations on them is desirable.

18.8.5 Window Size Alteration

A user in a given application may have the ability to alter the size of the window. In such circumstances, the action taken is application dependent (although it may be under user direction). For example, if a window expands, the extra area may be used to provide a larger image of the object previously there; alternatively, the new area might be required to provide annotation of, say, the previous image which is unchanged. Similarly, if a window shrinks, a previous image may be *shrunk* to fit, or clipped, while text may be clipped or reoutput so that the last part of the previously displayed text is seen. Alternatively, a new, concise, representation may be used.

19 Architecture Working Group Discussions

19.1 INTRODUCTION

The membership of the Architecture Working Group was as follows:

> George Coulouris (Chairman)
> James Gosling
> Alistair Kilgour
> David Small
> Dominic Sweetman
> Tony Williams
> Neil Wiseman

The group worked loosely from the issues list assigned to them. The issues were used to delimit the topics for discussion, though within those topics the issues were not directly debated. At the end of a session, the group would tie their discussion back to the issues list and see which had been resolved.

The group met in four sessions, the fourth of which was a joint session with the Application Program Interface Working Group.

The first three sessions covered approximately the following ground:

Session 1

      The graphics interface to window managers

      Device independence

      Models of window managers

Session 2

      Redrawing and resizing windows

      Window structure

      Terminology

Session 3

      Input and feedback

After the second session there was a plenary session at which it became clear that there were some conflicts between the Application Program Interface Working Group and the Architecture Working Group in the terminology area and in the fundamental assumptions each group was making, for example: "Can more than one process write to the same window?" Thus a joint session was held with the Application Program Interface Working Group to attempt to resolve these questions.

The remainder of this chapter summarizes the group's discussions. The final report of the Working Group is contained in Chapter 20. The structure of the next section reflects the organization of the group's sessions given above.

19.2 DISCUSSION

19.2.1 Session 1

The first issue to be addressed was: "Is the window manager responsible for all images on the screen?" The general view seemed to be, yes, it is, and that all objects on the screen must be windows. Icons caused some difficulties, is an icon a window or not? It was agreed that if icons are not windows, then certainly they are the responsibility of the window manager at least as far as rendition and handling clicks on icons are concerned.

At this very early stage it became apparent that terminology and definitions were going to be significant issues - there appeared to be as many definitions of what a window is as there were window manager systems. In the Whitechapel MG-1 window manager, for instance, a window is made up of multiple rectangles which move together but are not all necessarily owned by the same application. The Application Program Interface Working Group would think of windows more as a unit of screen resource managed by a single application. This is an issue that is addressed in Chapter 22.

The discussion then turned to the subject of the graphics interface to the window manager. There are two basic models for this: first, that the application passes a (possibly virtual) bitmap to the window manager; or second, that it passes a structured display list. The SUN and Whitechapel window managers both use the bitmap approach. The window manager provides access to a bitmap that the client process can write into.

One idea that came up was to have two levels of graphics package, one to draw lines, text etc on the screen, the second at a higher application level, for example GKS. The drawback to this approach seems to be that to take complex data structures and draw them efficiently at the lower level requires rich functionality (for example, to deal reasonably with proportional spacing, kerning etc in text), and effectively what happens is that the functionality of the lower level is pushed up a level. With bitmaps you do not have this problem. There is, however, a need for some output capability in the kernel, for example to display messages during system booting.

It was generally agreed that separating the generation of text and images into two levels was the wrong thing to do. The next question was whether bitmaps should be constructed and passed to the window manager or whether the window manager and application should be allowed to call primitives. Ideally the window manager would generate graphics from a powerful general-purpose representation fed into it from the application. At present the general representation is the bitmap!

In the SUN system the main problem with having graphics primitives in a library in the user process is that even trivial programs are then 200-300Kbytes because the library is so large. The origins of this problem lie in not knowing what the output device will be at load time. The problem is exacerbated by not having shared libraries under Unix systems. Of the three options for where to put the graphics code, application, window manager or kernel, the last is ruled out because of the undesirability of putting complex code in the kernel. To put the code in the application really requires that the operating system supports shared libraries if substantial overheads in application program size are not to be incurred.

There was no general resolution of the problem of where to put the code; at the present time the answer seems to be that it depends on local circumstances and tradeoffs.

It was felt that there should be a better way of specifying images to the window manager than as bitmaps. One of the problems with bitmaps is that they are not device independent. Very few systems actually deal with device independence. The SUN does reasonably well but there are some problems when it comes to device independence between monochrome and colour devices.

Out of this discussion grew the first window manager architecture shown in **Figure 19.1**.

The portability of graphics primitives applies between the application and the library. If the library does not reduce the image to a bitmap, it would be possible to achieve device independence by having a separate device driver for each device in the centralized window manager. The centralized manager knows about the hardware and so this is a good place to contain device dependence.

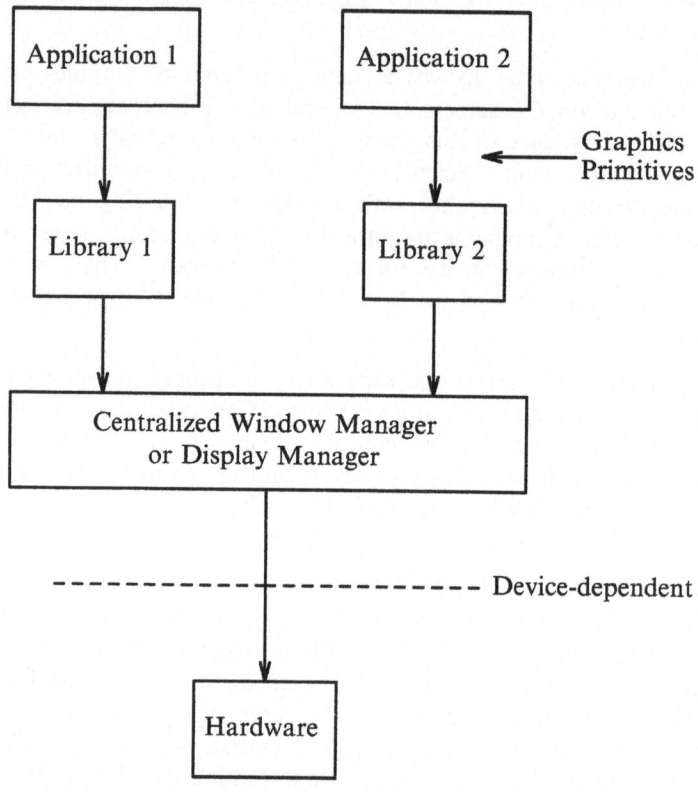

Figure 19.1

If the window manager does contain graphics primitives it is important to get the functionality right. Should the functionality include circles, ellipses, conic arcs etc? There are neat schemes available for generating such primitives, but are these at the right level? The ISO standardization work on the Computer Graphics Interface has some bearing here.

The ability to generate images in places other than on the screen (in a saved bit-map say) was thought to be important, though more doubtful if the hardware can do antialiasing. SunDew, for example, generates images on a canvas which you can make visible on the screen, say, or the image might be transferred to a laser printer by DMA.

For some applications, the ability to work in terms of painting bits was thought to be important and a natural way to work. The GKS cell array primitive was seen by some as one possible way to achieve this. Cell array is effectively a virtual bit-map in an abstract coordinate system. By setting the coordinate transformations appropriately, cell array primitives can be mapped directly onto the hardware resolution bitmaps.

19.2.2 Session 2

The first part of the discussion in this session concerned redrawing.

There was general agreement that the window manager should be able to say to an application program 'redraw the contents of this window'. The more difficult question to answer is when redrawing should be done by the window manager and when by the application. If the window manager handles redraw, then the window manager has to maintain an off-screen copy of each window. This is expensive for multiplane colour images. Some systems have the concept of a damage list which records the regions of the window which need to be redrawn when the window pops to the front. In general this facility seems to have been found hard to use by applications.

A complication for redraw is that the size of the window may have changed. Some systems do not allow window size changes, some applications do not support size changes. In some terminal emulators, changing the size results in the same information being displayed but at a different font size. Only the application program can know how to handle resize requests and it was felt to be important that an application should be able to ignore or refuse such requests.

The discussion for the remainder of this session concerned the vexed issues of structure and terminology.

The necessity for grouping windows was thought to be doubtful.

The Whitechapel window manager uses the term *panel* for an unadorned region. SunDew uses the term *canvas*, the Cambridge Rainbow display uses the term *pad*. The words *cluster* and *window* are used for adorned regions. An adorned region is a hierarchy of unadorned regions.

It was felt that panels should be clipped to the boundaries of their parents, though in some applications one might want to have children hanging off the side. There was some support for the view that adorned regions should not be restricted to rectangular shapes.

The client is given control of part of the screen, and three clipping rectangles: the physical boundary, the current clipping region and the maximum clipping region. The client cannot expand into the adorned region unless explicitly requested to do so.

19.2.3 Session 3

This session concentrated on input issues.

The first issue addressed was whether the window manager should support user-in-control, application-in-control, or both modes of operation. There was agreement that both modes should be supported; there was felt to be no danger in doing this.

The GKS input model was discussed as a basis for input in a window manager. The GKS model supports six classes of logical input devices, LOCATOR (returning a position), VALUATOR (delivering a value in some range), CHOICE (delivering a selection from a number of choices), PICK (identifying a group of primitives in a picture), STRING (delivering a text string) and STROKE (delivering a sequence of positions). Each logical input device may operate in each of three modes, REQUEST (in which the application is suspended until the operator supplies input from the specified device), SAMPLE (which gives the current status of the specified device), and EVENT (the operator may generate input asynchronously which is collected in a central queue which the application program may interrogate). The mapping of physical to logical input devices is the responsibility of the application program.

An immediate need for pointing devices, keyboards and valuators (knobs or potentiometers) could be seen. There was a view that the window manager should merely pass all input on to the application.

Feedback was seen as an important issue. To guarantee smooth feedback it seems to be necessary to do this in the window manager. It was recognized that downloading procedures to the window manager, to be executed in response to specific types of input, is an elegant way to control feedback.

The GKS input model was felt not to be rich enough in some respects. For example, there is a need to be able to treat single and multiple key clicks differently. This implies a finer grain of reporting than that provided by GKS.

In the Cambridge Rainbow terminal, an unencoded keyboard has been found to be very useful. The interface to this device is tailored so that the application can state which keys are to be encoded and which not. This is achieved through a code table.

In the GKS model, input events are entered onto the queue when some trigger device fires. The same physical trigger may control more than one logical device, though the standard does not specify how such clusters of logical input devices can be configured. Most existing implementations do not provide much, if any, control at this level. It was thought that a configuration language in the window manager, analogous to Cedar's TIP program, would be useful.

There was a general view that the GKS input model should be supported in some form. It was recognized that the GKS primitives are too restricted for some applications and lower level events should be reported, such as crossing region boundaries, depressing or releasing mouse buttons etc. It seems that a library of input tools would be a sensible way to present different input techniques.

The problem of where input is directed was addressed. The idea of input from a window being directed to a *port* was proposed and accepted. There was discussion of what should happen to input in the queue when the process connected to the port dies. There seem to be various answers to this question ranging from "destroy the input" to "forward the input to the next process listening to the port".

Examples from different contexts were put forward. Some users rely heavily on the ability to type or click ahead, though this may in part be attributable to system response time - ie impatience. In the SunDew system feedback is given immediately by a PostScript function which can do echoing if it wants to. One system built in this way actually recognized termination commands for applications and switched listeners when a termination command was encountered. This can lead to some very undesirable situations, for example if a termination command demands confirmation. In some circumstances the onus must be on the application to close down the input queue.

There was a general view that the ability to download procedures to the window manager was a good way to tailor facilities to applications, for example to filter out all mouse events for a particular application. The same effects can be obtained through table-driven systems, though downloading was felt to be more elegant. However, there is still more work to be done in this area.

It was felt that the level of abstraction on the input side should be related to the level of abstraction on the output side. For example, the coordinates in input events in a particular panel should be in the same coordinate system as the output primitives used to create the panel. This was considered an important point.

Where to put menu-handling was seen as an issue. Putting menu-handling in the window manager was felt to be too restrictive unless it were programmable. Requiring everything to be programmable was felt to be too extreme a view.

Sneak paths were discussed at some length. Sneak paths are certainly used in window managers even if they are not always recognized as such. Rubber band lines done in the window manager are a good example of a sneak path. Often sneak paths are used to buy speed. Sneak paths attempt to anticipate the application program's interpretation of an event. They should be considered harmful because they will sometimes get the interpretation wrong and may mislead the user.

It was thought that events in the input queue should be timestamped.

There was felt to be a need for the window manager to be able to interrupt the application program as a general mechanism. Some application programmers want to be able to use this control mechanism. This implies a prerequisite for operating systems supporting window managers.

The pointing device should have at least one button. The group were intrigued to hear that someone has invented a pointing keyboard - there was speculation that the next pointing device will be a chair on wheels!

The Whitechapel MG-1 system has the idea of a *listening window*. Input is directed to the listening window. The listening window can be changed by clicking on another window. The character stream does not automatically move with the mouse as happens on some systems. The Whitechapel system has the advantage that you can move the cursor outside the listening window whilst typing on the keyboard.

The group agreed to the use of the term *listener* for the port receiving input.

The major issue in this area seems to be the degree of graphics functionality below the centralized window manager. In the discussion following the presentation of the Working Group's report Peter Bono argued that the impact of distributed systems on the architecture needs to be addressed. If this is not done, it may well not be possible to take advantage of distributed systems techniques in realizing the architecture. David Rosenthal pointed out that there must be a configurable mapping of the keyboard to avoid the problem of applications wiring-in more than one mouse button.

20   Architecture Working Group Final Report

20.1 INTRODUCTION

The Working Group's discussion concentrated upon the following issues:

(1)   nomenclature for the objects displayed and manipulated;

(2)   levels of interface: especially the functionality of the *client-server interface*;

(3)   the input model;

(4)   responsibility for redrawing of portions of windows following damage or size changes;

(5)   hardware and operating system prerequisites.

20.2 NOMENCLATURE

This group came up with the following nomenclature. Later in the Workshop nomenclature was reexamined as reported in Chapter 23.

A *window* is a composite object which the user perceives as an entity and with which the user interacts.

A *panel* is a lower level object from which windows are composed and with which the application interacts. Panels are often, but need not be, rectangular.

The *window manager* groups one or more panels into a window. Such panels are usually juxtaposed but need not necessarily be.

Panels grouped into a window are related hierarchically. They may, for instance, be moved as a group.

Output to a window is clipped by the window manager to a panel within it.

Input may be associated with a window or panel, which is then referred to as the *listener*.

20.3 ARCHITECTURE OVERVIEW

Figure 20.1 summarizes the Working Group's view of a system architecture. Graphics in this context includes text. API denotes the Application Program Interface.

The following issues relate to this architecture.

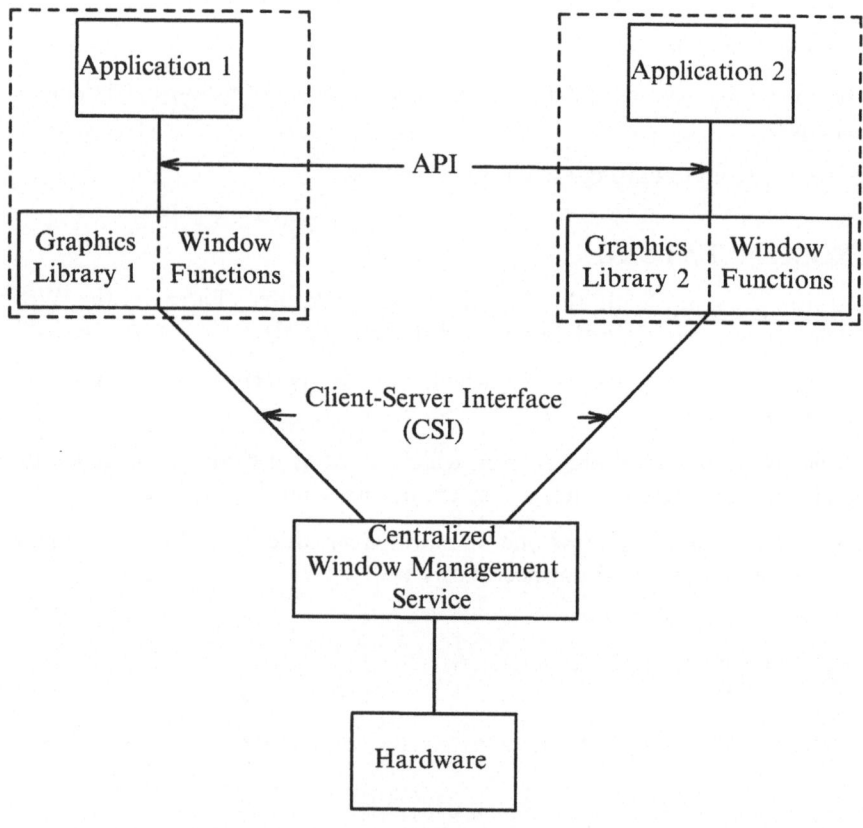

Figure 20.1

Issue: *A6 Should all screen output be via the window manager?*

Alternatives:

(1) Yes.

(2) No - applications may write directly to the screen without the window manager being aware of it.

Recommendation:
    Unanimous for Alt 1. See also A11.

Issue: *A8 and A15 What level of abstraction should be used for the graphics primitives communicated to the centralized window manager service?*

Considerations:

(1) Degree of device independence.

(2) Completeness and/or extensibility.

(3) Performance.

Alternatives:

(1) High level graphics with rich functionality - world coordinates used for output and input.

(2) Screen resolution bitmaps (logically copied) representing window contents. Note this is not entirely device dependent.

(3) Somewhere in between.

Arguments:

(a) PRO 1: This is preferred, and agreed as the goal. Achieving this with good performance is regarded as not proven and is a good topic for further investigation, especially when covering extensibility in input and output.

(b) PRO 2: This is regarded as implementable (by existence proof), and sufficiently complete to satisfy A16 following.

Recommendation:

Alt 1 for research work. Alt 2 for short term implementation.

Issue: *A11 Should the window manager always clip output to the window boundary?*

Alternatives:

(1)   Yes.

(2)   No - the application may perform its own clipping, and suppress the window manager clipping.

Recommendation:
Unanimous for Alt 1. It is recommended that the window manager provide clipping to an application-specified subregion, and implement a single clip to the intersection of the two regions.

Issue: *A16 Should the window manager support multiple graphics packages?*

Alternatives:

(1)   Yes.

(2)   No - a defined package will be supported (eg GKS - subissue!).

Recommendation:
Unanimous for Alt 1.

Considerations:
Each application has its own library implementing the graphics package. This library communicates with the centralized window manager service. Issue A8 covers the primitives communicated at that interface (CSI). The size and complexity of the library varies according to the similarity between the two sets of graphics primitives.

20.4 INPUT AND LOCUS OF CONTROL

The record of input events returned to the application should be at the same level as the output primitives accepted by the window manager. In particular, coordinate values should be relative to the panel in which the event occurred, and in the same *world* system used by the application to define the contents of the panel.

However, it was felt that the client (application) process should be able to control both the level of detail of reported events, and the method of reporting. Things which should be eligible to be reported as input events should include:

> movement of mouse;
> crossing region boundaries (by mouse/cursor);
> depressing or releasing mouse button;
> depressing or releasing key on keyboard.

The last two imply the availability of an unencoded keyboard, which should be capable of being coded by the client process via a code table. (The difficulty of doing this in a device independent manner was recognized.)

The possibility of allowing the client process to download a procedure to be executed in response to a specific class of input events was discussed, and felt to be desirable in principle. However, more work was needed to establish the practicality in general of programmable window managers. The success of Jim Gosling's Sun-Dew project would be an indicator, but it was felt that it would be fruitful to initiate a UK investigation into this issue. John Butler pointed out in discussion that in the Microsoft MS-Windows system an input event received by a client process could be sent back to the window manager for interpretation by one of a set of translation routines.

Although not strictly required by the GKS input model it was felt essential that the client process should be able to request notification by signal (as well as by an event record) of the arrival of a particular class of event. It was also felt essential that events should be timestamped, so that the client process could recognize such composite events as a double click on the mouse button.

Event records should contain identification of the panel in which they occurred. Events in title panels, scroll bars, etc would normally be interpreted by the window manager, which by default has control of these panels, but could be passed back to the client if the window manager is requested to do so.

The group felt it was essential that the window manager should make no assumptions about the locus of control, and should be capable of supporting reactive (user-in-control), active (application-in-control), and mixed initiative modes of operation.

20.5 WINDOW REDRAW

The division of responsibilities between the window manager and application program should be such as to minimize their mutual awareness. With presently available hardware, the rearrangement of the screen may require that data already output by an application program to its window be repeated either wholly or in part. The application program may have had no part in causing the screen rearrangement and have no obvious incentive therefore to redraw anything. If it is to retain unawareness of what the window manager has just done then a redrawing ought to be undertaken by the window manager. There are some special cases however:

(1)   The volume of data which the window manager needs to keep for obscured areas may be very large (as when a many-plane image is being held) and in that event regeneration could be preferred to copying - only the application program can of course then act.

(2)   The screen rearrangement may have induced a size or scale change for the particular window. The window manager may then not have the data needed to do the redraw. This is best treated as a request to the application program for a size or scale change which then results in redraw, rather than a redraw request. The application program is entitled to refuse or ignore a size change or scale change request.

As hardware costs diminish and display processor designs evolve, the need to tolerate the compromise of special cases reduces and the ideas of no redraw by the application program as a response to screen rearrangement will be achieved.

20.6 HARDWARE AND OPERATING SYSTEM PREREQUISITES

20.6.1 Inter Process Communication

The input model calls for separately identified input channels associated with each window. These are most easily mapped into the operating system's input-output structure as named inter process communication channels or *ports*. If the window manager is to be portable or extensible, a similar method will also be required for communication of output and control messages from the application programs.

20.6.2 Shared Library Facilities

The division of responsibility for the graphical processing required to generate the contents of a panel is difficult. The range of options is widened if the operating system enables application programs to share procedural information, since then at least the memory and swapping overheads associated with locating the majority of graphical processing in the application process is minimized. (The current SunWindows system requires 200-300Kbytes of library code to be loaded into *each* application process because sharing of libraries is impossible in BSD 4.2.)

20.6.3 Input Devices

There is assumed to be at least one pointing device, with at least one button on it. Other interactive devices may be needed, eg potentiometers, multiple pointing devices, 3D input. All interactive input should be routed by the window manager to applications (via the communication ports associated with panels). The integration of such devices into Unix operating systems normally requires the installation of new driver code. It should be possible to control the driver in all of the ways implied by the *input model*, and preferably, to load dynamically that part of the driver that transforms mouse and keyboard input to event sequences.

20.6.4 Direct Frame Buffer Addressing

Portability of the Window Manager is much enhanced if the hardware places the frame buffer directly in the address space of the main memory, since the window manager can then be a user-level process.

21   Application Program Interface Task Group

21.1 INTRODUCTION

This group was formed during the final plenary session on the second day of the Workshop and was charged with producing a set of conclusions about the application program interface. The group met for one two-hour session on the morning of the third day and then reported its findings to a plenary session. Membership of the Task Group was:

James Gosling
Paul ten Hagen
Harold Thimbleby

Previously these people had been in different Working Groups at the Workshop and were effectively asked to bring the insights of their previous groups to this new task.

The group had a wide ranging discussion which is summarized below. The group report as presented to the plenary session is then given along with the ensuing discussion.

21.2 GROUP DISCUSSION

The group decided their task was two-fold; first to come up with a list of principles for the application program interface and second to say something about taxonomy.

The first principle discussed was that the API should be able to do everything the window manager can do and that the user interface can do. There should be symmetry between what the client can do and what the window manager can do. It was recognized that some of the possibilities might not be terribly sensible, for example if the user decides to give an area of the screen to an application, the application should not tell the window manager to move the space elsewhere. It was also recognized that if both the user and the application can perform a given action, then some discipline must be imposed to avoid constant conflicts.

An interesting idea that came up at this stage was to have predicates in the API to allow the application to determine anything the user can determine. For example, one could inquire through the API whether window X was to the left of window Y or not. It was thought that it would also be useful to be able to say to the window manager "I like this screen layout, please use it again".

The discussion then moved on to considering whether the API should be synchronous or asynchronous, ie can the window manager send signals to the application when nominated events happen. It was generally agreed that an asynchronous interface is much harder to handle than a synchronous interface. It was generally thought desirable that asynchrony should be kept to a minimum.

Hierarchical structuring of windows was discussed. The general view was that no one has yet found a use for hierarchical structuring, but that there is a need for some kind of structuring. Constructions like pop-up menus in windows can be handled by subwindow-level structuring. If the window manager is capability-based, there is a need to inherit capabilities and this leads to some form of structuring. It was also generally thought that windows needed to have attributes which define the relationships between windows. It was clear that there is a need for more work in this area.

The object-oriented programming approach was felt to be particularly appropriate for window managers. While the window manager may be object-based, this does not imply that applications using the window manager have also to be written in an object-oriented language.

There was a strong feeling that, at this stage in their development, window managers need to be very flexible. The *downloading-of-procedures* idea in James Gosling's work was seen as a nice way to achieve this. In this context protection issues were seen to be important. There need to be some limits on loading arbitrary code, especially since the window manager has in some sense the status of an operating system in that it must be reliable and not crash. One idea for achieving protection was through the use of applicative languages which are by their nature side-effect free.

An important aspect of the CMU window manager is that it takes hints rather than demands. For example, if the application program asks that some text be displayed in 10 point Times Roman, and this is not available, then the system will do the best it can to satisfy the requirement. Clearly it is application dependent what the strategy here should be, whether, say, to provide 10 point text in some other font, or the nearest available size in the specified font or something else. Strategies in this sense need to be programmable. Applicative languages again support one way to achieve this - through the use of higher order functions to define the strategy. However, there is no existence proof that such a system could be made to perform well.

The redraw and size change problems were again discussed. At CMU a standard module is provided which handles these problems. Most applications use it. It seems that it is not too difficult a task to write such a general purpose module and also provide hooks so that applications can add new objects. The toolkit approach was thought to be a good paradigm. Tools need to be extensible by the application. Toolkits are also a useful aid to consistency across applications.

The need for a layered approach to structuring was identified, though there was no agreement on what the layers should be, nor precisely what should be provided in the window manager layer and what is provided by a toolkit on top. The taxonomy discussion did not advance very far.

There was agreement that the interface to the window manager should be procedural rather than through shared data structures.

There was some support for the idea of providing a number of fixed window types from which richer systems can be built. A design based on fixed window types which are parameterized through a state list whose entries may be set and inquired is being pursued at Centrum voor Wiskunde en Informatica (CWI), Amsterdam.

21.3 FINAL REPORT

The following report was presented at a plenary session on the Wednesday morning.

The Task Group produced the following list of principles to be obeyed when designing window managers.

(1) *Symmetry*: the application should be able to do anything and enquire anything that the window manager can. Clients as well as the window manager should be able to move windows about, move them to the top, enquire about size etc. A number of these are deemed to be in *bad taste* but are not prohibited. For example, surfacing a window is not reasonable; but it could be used, especially if an application uses two windows, if the user surfaces one, the application should be allowed to surface the other.

(2) *Synchrony*: clients should be able to run as a single thread of control. Asynchrony is hard to handle, though a small degree of asynchrony (for example, asynchronous notification via Unix signals) is reasonable. The bulk of the application program should be synchronous.

(3) *Hints*: applications make requests to the window manager which may not be satisfiable. Graceful mechanisms must exist for coping with such situations. This makes applications more robust. There should be a graceful mechanism for clients to interrogate whether their request was satisfied, and to provide some sensible recovery if it was not (for example, if a particular text font is not available).

(4) *Redraw requests*: redraw requests should be hidden where possible. The redraw mechanism should be kept simple. However it must be recognized that redraw requests are an inescapable fact of life, for example when there is insufficient memory to hold off-screen copies of windows.

(5) *Procedural interface*: the interface to the window manager should be procedural, rather than through exposed data structures. Exposed data structures are often obstacles to evolution.

(6) *High level libraries*: applications probably never need to talk directly to the window manager, but instead should talk through libraries such as GKS and a window manager toolkit. Exceptions should also be handled in libraries, for example to handle situations such as non-availability of the requested font. If libraries are embedded in the window manager, then the number and types of libraries available are fixed.

(7) *Strategy specification*: it should be possible to specify strategies, for example for font matching or colour matching.

(8) *Generality*: this is hard to achieve. Compromise is likely.

21.4 DISCUSSION

Teitelman: Referring to point (3) in your list, can you characterize the conditions under which a window manager would refuse requests from a client? It feels so soft that the user might feel uneasy. Is the window manager surly? Is it the intention that requests are honoured most of the time, and that failure is rare?

Gosling: Yes, but failure should be handled gracefully.

Bono: I think that there are two situations which arise from the same mechanism. The first is occasional failure such as a disk crash. The program environment should be robust enough to deal with it. The other situation is where device independence is written into the system. What happens if a colour device is used to run the program today, where a black and white device was used yesterday? This may show up in the same mechanism, so you cannot say that it is rare.

Gosling: When an application makes a request, it should nearly always be satisfied. The application program can inspect the result to see if it is satisfied exactly. If it asks for pink and it doesn't get it, it should be able to find out what it did get. Only then should the application deal with the complex recovery strategy that it may need. We need some sort of strategy specification. What sort of strategy should we use to select a font or colour if there is no exact match? What feature is more important in matching a 10 point Roman font, its size or its typeface? At CMU, if you point at a thing and want 14 point Roman you may get 14 point Cyrillic, which is not very useful.

Williams: On point (7), are you implying a dynamic strategy, or one determined at system configuration?

Gosling: Harold (Thimbleby) is all for downline loading this. In reality this is not usually very easy. GKS adopts a compromise - an integer is used to select a predefined procedure. As you may only have 32 bits, this does not give you many Turing machines. Something of that flavour would not be a bad idea.

Cook: Justify synchrony in point (2).

Gosling: This is mostly a matter of complexity of program. Not many languages handle asynchrony very well. If we have Cedar or Mesa then this is possible.

Teitelman: How we do it in Cedar is that the application is given the opportunity to take action. In Mesa we require that the application catches the signal and takes any action. In the absence of the application program intervening, something sensible should be done, but it may impose a little bit more of a burden on the implementor.

Gosling: In Unix software there is no synchronization around data objects. In Cedar/Mesa there are monitors which continue while the mainline code is running; there are no notions of interrupt routines.

Teitelman: This is a single address space system. We are unlikely to see this in Unix systems.

Newman: How realistic is it to design an interface using your criteria?

Gosling: Bits and pieces already appear all over the place. The CMU system deals with most of this OK, but is poor on symmetry. The SUN system is good for symmetry, but not for synchrony. It is terrible on hints, and has problems with redraw requests. There is no intrinsic reason why we can't deal with all of these though. The problem is dealing with them all at the same time.

Williams: A point that I read in the SunWindows manual was that once a client has done a 'create window' then the process will probably get a signal to redraw its windows for the first time.

Gosling: Right, but it's a case of maybe rather than will. Some programs may redraw and redraw again if multiple events aren't handled very well, and give screen flicker.

Hopgood: Do you have a view on the level of interface to the window manager?

Gosling: Clients don't want to talk to the window manager at all, but should talk to something fairly abstract. Do you want to talk about this as the window manager as well? The window manager shouldn't implement scroll bars, or buttons or dialogues, we need another name for the thing which handles the higher level operations.

22 Structures Task Group

22.1 REPORT

The Task Group membership was:

Colin Prosser
Dominic Sweetman
Warren Teitelman

This Task Group arose mainly from the Architecture Working Group discussion and the joint session with the Application Program Interface Working Group. We thought it was a good idea to look below windows to see if there are more fundamental objects. We attempted to characterize the common structure properties among all the window systems of which we were aware. We will dodge the issue of overlapping versus tiling. There seem to be good reasons for both styles of use. We will concentrate on what is common between them.

We have to be careful with our terminology here: a *conventional window* is a Byte reader's idea of a window and is a box on the screen with a name stripe, a border, etc. that you can move about on the screen, change the size of, and so on. A conventional window is shown in **Figure 22.1**. Windows can also be *unconventional* as shown in **Figure 22.2**.

We will not insist on the bits of a window being enclosed in a rectangular border. Fast non-rectangular operations will permit windows with non-rectangular shapes. We want to find a primitive subcomponent of windows to divide the architecture into manageable lumps. We have been through several names for these parts: pads, panes, canvases etc and Colin Prosser has convinced us that we should use a word

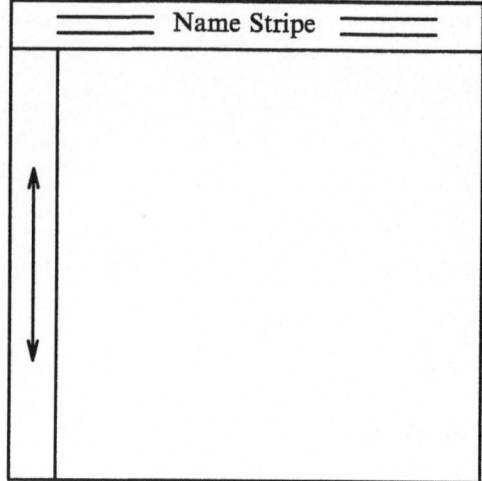

Figure 22.1 Conventional Window

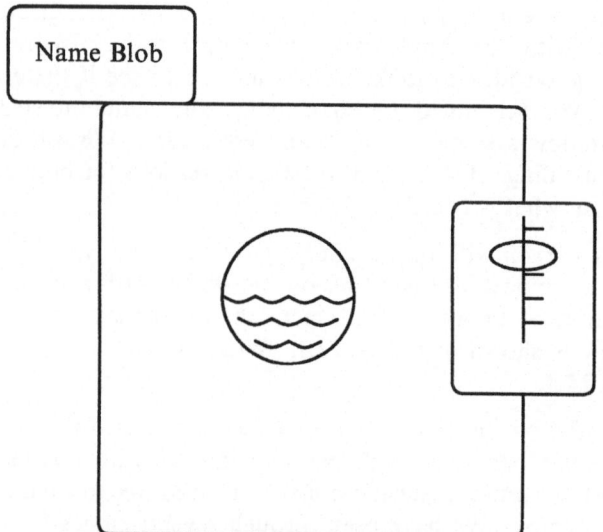

Figure 22.2 Unconventional Window

which is appropriate in graphics terms, namely *viewport*. A viewport is an area of transparency on the display through which something can be seen.

So the conventional window example is made up of three visible viewports: the name stripe, the scroll bar and the main interaction area, as shown in **Figure 22.3**. The more complex unconventional window example consists of four viewports, as shown in **Figure 22.4**.

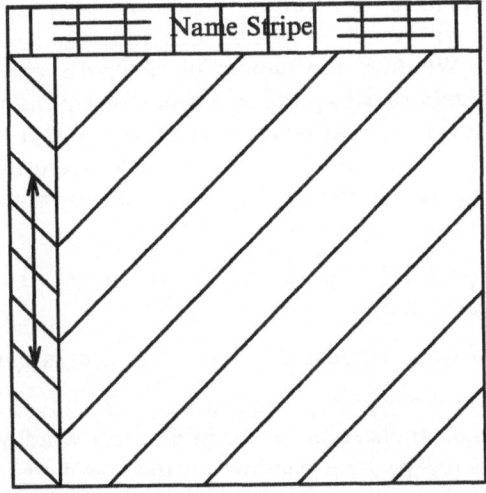

Figure 22.3 Viewports of a Conventional Window

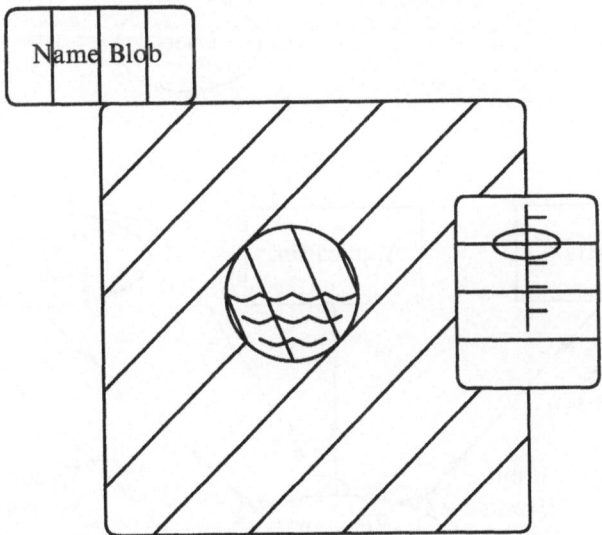

Figure 22.4 Viewports of an Unconventional Window

Viewports are not necessarily limited to being rectangular either. RasterOp leads to rectangular images, ultimately there might be *BlobOp* graphics primitives leading to *blobs*. You may have viewports hanging outside a window although the user interface people might say this is bad taste.

Viewports are defined hierarchically with the positions of child viewports being defined relative to the parent viewport. Clipping of the child viewport is independent of the parent.

A *window* then consists of a *family of viewports* organized as a subtree. The viewports of a window will usually be contiguous and non-overlapping although this need not be the case. Windows can consist of viewports only in one family. The intention is that the family of viewports in a window are all at Z coordinate levels such that they are either all behind or all in front of another window. Interleaving of viewports from different windows is not allowed. Algorithms determine where input goes according to the viewports. Input control attributes are associated with viewports (echo, ignore mouse hits etc).

When you look through a viewport, you see an image, (the sea!) and we do not really have a satisfactory name for that.

A tentative model of what happens in a window system is shown in **Figure 22.5**.

Applications draw into viewports. Applications can draw into several viewports, and viewports for a single application can be in different windows. This enables support for icons either as independent windows in their own right, or as elements of a group (the family of windows concept) within a window, in the style of Sapphire. As the substructuring notion is recursive, icons (of either variety) might themselves be

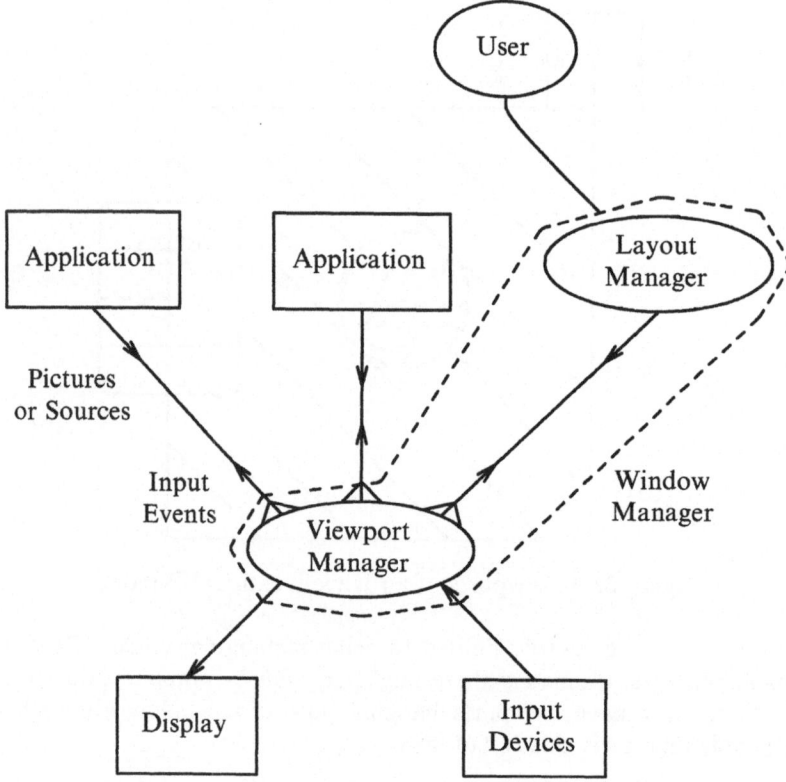

Figure 22.5

composed of subfamilies of viewports. Extending this idea, and recalling that viewports are not necessarily rectangular or constrained to lie within some boundary, it should become apparent that the structuring concept presented also covers items like *rubber borders* which dynamically echo the new position a window would take were it to be moved or have its size changed.

These ideas were discussed and it was felt that they provided the basis for a sound model for substructuring. However, we did not have time to consider in any depth how well the model would stand up to close analysis, and consequently, this presentation aims to propose the model in overview only. Substantially more work would need to be undertaken before we could be sure that we do indeed have a useful model of substructuring.

A layout manager (which is one component of the window manager) constructs windows out of viewports, moves windows around and constrains them to behave properly.

The viewport manager clips the images and handles overlapping. It also handles input devices, for example, mouse events are directed to whichever viewport the cursor is over.

We looked at the interface between the bottom of the application and the viewport manager. The application passes things we have called *pictures* or *sources* to the viewport manager. We are not entirely happy with what we have called them and need a name. These pictures may be bitmaps, display lists or PostScript programs, for example. The viewport manager clips pictures and presents them on the display. This level ought to be device independent but this will usually be too difficult to achieve - although it would be nice if it were.

22.2 DISCUSSION

Cook: Where does the association of viewports into windows happen?

Sweetman: It's mostly about holding their inputs together, so associations are set up by the layout manager. It builds a window out of its Lego bricks which are viewports and returns a handle to the application to permit it to write on the window. The dashed lines in the diagram of a window system show how the application talks to the layout manager.

Myers: This is very much like the Sapphire implementation. However, there are problems with it as an application now has two separate things to talk to: the viewport manager and the layout manager. It's not obvious which one of them to call and some calls may have to be repeated to both of them. For example, displaying something in the title line requires a call to the layout manager. It is very difficult handling input, for example, changing the listener.

Sweetman: The viewport manager decides where the input goes.

Myers: We did that and it is difficult to handle. The layout manager also needs to know who the listener is so that it can draw borders, annotate titles etc.

Teitelman: These are really problems still to be solved, rather than being insuperable.

Sweetman: But we need to consider whether the problems are so bad that we want to coalesce the viewport and layout managers.

Teitelman: The separate managers are a way of discussing things. Most applications will have a fixed relationship but we do not want to be restrictive unnecessarily.

Thimbleby: As soon as there's an argument for two there exists an argument for n managers, for example, a font manager, a colour manager etc.

Sweetman: That's possible. The layout manager is not privileged. It's just an application.

Coulouris: I don't see anything wrong with having other managers. If there is a resource, there should be a manager of it.

Sweetman: The architecture is not committed to this setup, there is no reason why managers cannot proliferate.

Teitelman: The viewport and layout managers need not be separate bits of software. The only reason for their separation is because of their different functions. Whether or not they are implemented as one module is in the category of implementation details.

Sweetman: It's the same as sharing the application interface. The layout manager will make calls on the viewport manager that applications don't do.

Myers: It works fine for output, but is a mess for input.

Sweetman: That's probably true for anything.

Bono: Does the viewport manager have a single coordinate space?

Sweetman: There is some kind of unified coordinate space.

Bono: This is different from yesterday where we decided that there were multiple coordinate spaces.

Sweetman: The display lists passed to the viewport manager need to have a notion of size in the viewport. There is nothing to stop scaling first.

Bono: There is an issue as to whether the viewport manager has to maintain multiple transformations.

Sweetman: The viewport manager must have a consistent mapping of the panels on the display. The location of a viewport on a screen is determined recursively by following from parent to parent until the root is reached which is in a fixed position on the screen.

Hopgood: Do viewports have special attributes not in windows or are they all the same?

Teitelman: From a practical standpoint, name stripes might not be fully-fledged viewports.

Hopgood: Do they have attributes?

Sweetman: Yes, we don't want separate classes of viewport.

Prosser: For example, you would turn off input in name stripes.

Bono: The hierarchy is for positioning of viewports. Does it also imply some inheritance of attributes?

Sweetman: That's for further study. There are other implications of the hierarchy, for example, deleting a parent deletes the children, unwanted input is passed on up the hierarchy etc.

Prosser: You should also mention soft events.

Sweetman: Yes. The interface allows you to inject events to the viewport manager as if they came from a soft device.

Part IV

23   Future Work

23.1 INTRODUCTION

This section summarizes the results achieved at the Final Session where the Working Group Reports were submitted. Each Group made comments about possible areas for future work and these were discussed and relative priorities established.

23.2 EXPERIENCE

Window managers are not yet in widespread use and few people have experience of using window managers and developing applications in a window manager environment. There was a clear consensus that the UK needs to gain experience in these areas.

Recommendation: Make window managers more widely available and put effort into developing expertise in writing applications for a window manager environment.

23.3 APPLICATION PROGRAM INTERFACE

There was general agreement that the Application Program Interface was better understood than the Operator Interface. Existing systems had large differences both superficially and architecturally. However, many had similar interfaces to the application particularly if it is assumed that the application interfaces to the window manager via a graphical toolkit.

There was a view that an application interface could be agreed even if many other parts of the window manager system required fuller study. This would give applications the ability to move from one environment to another without extensive change. The experience with existing window managers is that it is difficult to port applications from one to another if the facilities provided by the window manager are used in anything but a trivial manner.

Recommendation - Short Term: Define an Application Program Interface (possibly at more than one level) that can be used by the second generation window managers currently under development.

A major research area is discovering how graceful interaction can be achieved by an application running under a window manager. Portability and device independence are difficult to achieve without sacrificing the ability of the application to use the facilities provided by a particular hardware configuration. The meeting was impressed by the work of Gosling in downloading procedures to the window manager from an application in a device independent language to allow a more intimate connection between the application and hardware. While not believing that all the problems had been solved, there was a strong feeling that research should be conducted in this area to establish the viability of this approach.

Recommendation: Define and implement a window manager using downloading of procedures to achieve both a higher level interface between the application and window manager and a closer control of input by the application.

23.4 PORTABILITY

The work of Rosenthal and Gosling has indicated that it might be feasible to achieve a portable window manager that could run efficiently across a range of hardware if constraints were applied to the level of functionality provided. The idea of producing a *Level 0 portable window manager* received some support. It could be used as a vehicle for testing the application program interface defined above. A major advantage would be that it would provide an environment in which comparative studies of applications on different hardware could be achieved.

There was general agreement that we needed more effort in producing applications that ran under window managers so that experience could be built up into their use. Doing this on First Generation Window Managers tended to waste significant time getting round the problems arising due to the early design.

Recommendation - Short Term: A Level 0 portable window manager should be defined using the "standard" API and implemented on a range of hardware.

23.5 ARCHITECTURE

A major topic of the Workshop was establishing a model of substructuring for windows which included window boundaries, pop-up menus and icons as specific examples of a more general facility. An attempt was made to put a preliminary proposal forward. In the time available it was recognized that the model was incomplete and did not address all the problems.

Recommendation - Short Term: Establish a consistent model of substructuring which encompasses icons, window borders, pop-up menus etc.

23.6 USER INTERFACE

The User Interface was the area where more problems were raised than solutions proposed. It was demonstrated that window managers had many of the usual problems of the human-computer interface. The user needed to be able to understand the model of the window manager. Experience needed to be gained in assessing different styles of user interface. The balance of control between the user and the system needed to be analysed. Consistency of style in the interactions to the window manager and application must be provided.

There was a strong desire that any window manager should be customizable, configurable and extensible at the user interface to cope with the requirements of a wide range of users. Tools needed to be provided so that prototype systems can be produced and tested quickly. It was clear that the requirements for a User Interface Management System differed when interaction was being performed in a window manager environment.

Recommendation: Much more hands on experience needs to be gained and prototype systems for experimentation need to be developed.

23.7 INPUT

Many issues were raised in this area. While believing that the GKS input model had provided a basis for future discussion, it was not clear that it was applicable in the window management environment. Sneak paths were needed between the device input and the associated echo. How should this be fitted into an overall model? How should ordering of events be handled to ensure correct ordering while allowing mouse-ahead etc? What issues arose due to the use of a Unix operating system?

Recommendation: A better model of input in this environment needs to be defined.

23.8 STANDARDS

While believing that it was too early to standardize a window manager, there was some hope that agreement at the Application Program Interface might be possible.

The activities by the ANSI graphics community in putting forward proposals needed to be tracked and similar activities in the UK should ensure an input into this arena. The long time needed to establish standards probably means that it is time to start the process as a method of exploring the methodology.

Recommendation: The UK should track the ANSI standards activities.

23.9 CUT AND PASTE

The ability to move information between one application's window and another window associated with a different application was a useful and desirable facility. There were clearly problems in establishing the sensible functionality.

There was a view that cut and paste facilities could be bolted onto existing window managers to establish the functionality required even though the implementation would be far from optimal. It would give valuable insight into the required functionality.

Recommendation: Cut and paste facilities should be implemented on existing systems as research prototypes to assess their relative merits.

23.10 DISTRIBUTED SYSTEMS

Distributed systems raised a number of new issues, accentuated particular problems and provided criteria for assessing two different approaches. It was felt that the impact of moving to more distributed systems would be significant and more effort needed to be put into seeing the particular problems of distribution in a window management environment.

23.11 CONCLUSION

Window managers are still in their infancy. The second generation of window managers should provide answers to many of the more pressing problems. However, significant research and experience is still needed before the area can mature.

As a caveat, the general view is that the window manager is not that important long term, being servant to both the application and operator. While it is an important area of activity for research now, it is hoped that a methodology can be established that does not require a large on-going activity in this area. The urgency now is due to the recent explosion of bitmap displays which make this area one of timeliness and promise at the moment.

24 Bibliography

1. Adobe, *PostScript Language Manual*, Adobe Systems Inc., 1870 Embarcadero Road, Suite 100, Palo Alto, CA94303.

2. Alvey Directorate, *Alvey Man-Machine Interface Strategy*, Alvey Directorate (August 1984).

3. Alvey Directorate, *Alvey Programme Annual Report*, Alvey Directorate (November 1984).

4. Alvey Committee, *A Programme for Advanced Information Technology*, HMSO (1982).

5. ANSI, "Graphical Kernel System," X3H3/83-25r3, ANSI Committee X3H3 (February 1984).

6. ANSI, "Programmer's Hierarchical Interactive Graphics System (PHIGS)," X3H3/85-21, ANSI (February 1985).

7. Apperley, M. D. and Spence, R., "Hierarchical Dialogue Structures in Interactive Computer Systems," *Software - Practice and Experience* **13**, pp.777-790 (1983).

8. Apple, *LisaWrite*, Apple Computer Inc, Cupertino, CA (1983).

9. Ball, J. E., "Canvas: the Spice Graphics Package," S108, Computer Science Dept, Carnegie-Mellon University, Pittsburgh, PA (1981).

10. Bechtolsheim, A., Baskett, F., and Pratt, V., "The SUN Workstation Architecture," Tech Report 299, Computer Systems Laboratory, Stanford University, Stanford, CA (1982).

11. Bolt, R. A., "Spatial Data Management," DARPA Report, MIT Architecture Machine Group, Cambridge MA (March 1979).

12. Burton, R. R., Kaplan, R. M., Masinter, L. M., Sheil, B. A., Bell, A., Bobrow, D. G., Deutsch, L. P., and Haugeland, W. S., "Papers on Interlisp-D," Report SSL-80-4, Xerox PARC (1980).

13. Buxton, W., "Lexical and Pragmatic Considerations of Input Structures," *Computer Graphics* 17(1), pp.31-37 (January 1983).

14. Cahn, D. U. and Yen, A. C., "A Device-Independent Network Graphics System," *Computer Graphics* 17(3), pp.167-174 (July 1983).

15. Card, S. K., Pavel, M., and Farrell, J. E., "Window-based Computer Dialogues," *Proceedings of Interact 84, 1st IFIP Conference on Human-Computer Interaction* 1, p.355, London UK (September 1984).

16. Cargill, T. A., "The Blit Debugger," *The Journal of Systems and Software* 3, pp.277-284 (1983).

17. Cook, S., "Playing Cards on the Perq: An Algorithm for Overlapping Rectangles," *Software - Practice and Experience* 13(11) (November 1983).

18. Espinosa, C. and Rose, C., *QuickDraw: A Programmer's Guide*, Apple Computer Inc., Cupertino, CA.

19. Foley, J. D., Wallace, V. L., and Chan, P., "The Human Factors of Computer Graphics Interaction Techniques," *IEEE Computer Graphics and Applications* 4(11), pp.13-48 (November 1984).

20. Goldberg, A. and Robson, D., *A Metaphor for User Interface Design*, Xerox PARC.

21. Goldberg, A., *Smalltalk-80: The Interactive Programming Environment*, Addison-Wesley, Reading, MA (1984).

22. Gosling, J. A., "A Redisplay Algorithm," *SIGPLAN Notices* 16(6), pp.123-129 (June 1981).

23. Gosling, J. A., "A User Interface Toolkit," *Proceedings of Protext I* (October 1984).

24. Graphic Standards Planning Committee, "Status Report of the Graphic Standards Planning Committee," *Computer Graphics* 13(3) (1979).

25. Guedj, R. A. and Tucker, H. A., *Methodology of Computer Graphics*, North Holland, Amsterdam (1979).

26. Guedj, R. A., Hopgood, F. R. A., ten Hagen, P. J. W., Tucker, H. A., and Duce, D. A., *Methodology of Interaction,* North Holland, Amsterdam (1980).

27. Ingalls, D. H., "The Smalltalk-76 Programming System: Design and Implementation," *Proceedings of the 5th Annual ACM Symposium on Principles of Programming Languages* (1978).

28. ISO, "Information processing systems - Computer graphics - Graphical Kernel System (GKS) functional description," ISO 7942, ISO Central Secretariat, Geneva (1985).

29. ISO, "Information processing systems - Computer graphics - Graphical Kernel System for Three Dimensions (GKS-3D) functional description," ISO/TC97/SC21/WG5-2 N277, ISO (January 1985).

30. ISO, "Information processing systems - Computer graphics - Interfacing techniques for dialogues with graphical devices," ISO/TC97/SC21/N597, ISO (March 1985).

31. Joy, W. N., Cooper, E., Fabry, R., Leffler, S., and McKusik, K., *4.2BSD System Manual,* Computer Systems Research Group, Dept EECS, University of California, Berkeley, CA (September 1982).

32. Kay, A. C., "The Reactive Engine," Ph.D. Thesis, University of Utah (1970).

33. Kilgour, A. C., "Graphical Input Study," Report 83R1, Dept of Computing Science, University of Glasgow (July 1983).

34. Lamb, M. and Buckley, V., "New Techniques for Gesture-based Dialogue," *Proceedings of Interact 84, 1st IFIP Conference on Human-Computer Interaction* **2,** p.145, London UK (September 1984).

35. Lampson, B. W., "Bravo Manual," in *Alto User's Handbook,* Xerox PARC (1978).

36. Lantz, K. A. and Nowicki, W. I., "Structured Graphics for Distributed Systems," *ACM Transactions on Graphics* **3**(1) (January 1984).

37. Lemmons, P., "Easy Software," *Byte Magazine* (December 1983).

38. Lipkie, D. E., Evans, S. R., Newlin, J. K., and Weissman, R. L., "Star Graphics: An Object-Oriented Implementation," *Computer Graphics* **16**(3), pp.115-124 (1982).

39. Marcus, A., "Corporate Identity for Iconic Interface Design: The Graphic Design Perspective," *IEEE Computer Graphics and Applications* **4**(12), pp.24-32 (December 1984).

40. McGregor, S., "The Viewers Window Package," in *The Cedar System: An Anthology of Documentation,* ed. J. H. Horning, Xerox PARC CSL-83-14.

41. Mitchell, J. G., Maybury, W., and Sweet, R., "Mesa Language Manual," Report CSL-79-3 Xerox PARC (1979).

42. Myer, T. H. and Sutherland, I. E., "On The Design of Display Processors," *Communications of the ACM* **11**(6), pp.410-414 (June 1968).

43. Myers, B. A., "The Importance of Percent-Done Indicators for Computer Human Interfaces," *Proceedings of the ACM CHI '85 Conference on Human Factors in Computing Systems* (April 1985).

44. Myers, B. A., "The User Interface for Sapphire," *IEEE Computer Graphics and Applications* **4**(12), pp.13-23 (December 1984).

45. Negroponte, N., "The Media Room," Report for ONR and DARPA, MIT Architecture Machine Group, Cambridge MA (December 1978).

46. Newman, W. M. and Mott, T., "Officetalk-Zero: An Experimental Integrated Office System," pp. 315-331 in *Integrated Interactive Computer Systems*, ed. P. Degano and E. Sandewall, North Holland, Amsterdam (1983).

47. Pfaff, G. and ten Hagen, P. J. W. , "Seeheim Workshop on User Interface Management Systems," *Computer Graphics Forum* **3**, pp.169-179 (1984).

48. Pfaff, G. and ten Hagen, P. J. W. , *Seeheim Workshop on User Interface Management Systems,* Springer Verlag, Berlin (1985).

49. Pike, R., Guibas, L., and Ingalls, D., "Bitmap Graphics," SIGGRAPH 84 Course Notes, AT&T Bell Laboratories, NJ (1984).

50. Pike, R., *The Blit: A Multiplexed Graphics Terminal,* AT&T Bell Laboratories, NJ (July 1983).

51. Pike, R., "Graphics in Overlapping Bitmap Layers," *ACM Transactions on Graphics* **2**(2), pp.135-160 (1983).

52. Pike, R., Locanthi, B., and Reiser, J., "Hardware/Software Tradeoffs for Bitmap Graphics on the Blit," *Software - Practice and Experience* **15**(2), pp.131-151 (February 1985).

53. Pratt, V., "Techniques for Conic Splines," *Computer Graphics* **19**(3), pp.151-159 (1985).

54. Reid, B. K., "Scribe: A High-Level Approach to Document Formatting," *7th Symposium on the Principles of Programming Languages*, Las Vegas, NV (January 1980).

55. Reid, L. G., Wallace, S., and Karlton, P. L., *Don't Call Us, We'll Call You: The Structure of Tools in Tajo,* Xerox Office Systems Division, Xerox PARC.

56. Roberts, T. L. and Moran, T. P., "The Evaluation of Text Editors: Methodology and Empirical Results," *Communications of the ACM* **26**(4), pp.265-283 (1983).

57. Rosenthal, D. S. H., "Managing Graphical Resources," *Computer Graphics* **17**(1) (1983).

58. Sheil, B., *Power Tools for Programmers,* Datamation (1983).

59. Smith, D. C., et al., "Designing the Star User Interface," pp. 297-313 in *Integrated Interactive Computer Systems*, ed. P. Degano and E. Sandewall, North Holland, Amsterdam (1983).

60. Sproull, R. F., "Raster Graphics for Interactive Programming Environments," *Computer Graphics* **13**(2), p.83 (1979).

61. SUN Microsystems Inc., *Programmer's Reference Manual for the SUN Window System,* SUN Microsystems Inc., 2550 Garcia Avenue, Mountain View, CA94043.

62. SUN Microsystems Inc., *User's Manual for the SUN Unix System,* SUN Microsystems Inc., 2550 Garcia Avenue, Mountain View, CA94043.

63. Taylor, C. and Pratt, V., *A Technique for Representing Layered Images,* SUN Microsystems Inc., 2550 Garcia Avenue, Mountain View, CA94043.

64. Teitelman, W., "A Display Oriented Programmer's Assistant," *Languages and Systems* **1**, pp.905-915 (1981).

65. Teitelman, W., "A Tour Through Cedar," *IEEE Software* **1**(2), pp.44-73 (April 1984). Also in Proceedings 7th International Conference on Software Engineering, Orlando, FL, March 1984.

66. Test, J. A., "The NUnix Window System," MIT Report.

67. Thimbleby, H., "Dialogue Determination," *International Journal of Man-Machine Studies* **13**, pp.295-304 (1980).

68. Wallace, S., Karlton, P. L., and Reid, L. G., *Tajo: Integrated Interactive Programming Environment,* Xerox Office Systems Division, Xerox PARC.

69. Warnock, J. and Wyatt, D. K., "A Device Independent Graphics Imaging Model for use with Raster Devices," *Computer Graphics* **16**(3) (1982).

70. Williams, G., "Software Frameworks," *Byte Magazine,* p.124 (December 1984).

25 Acronyms and Glossary

The following acronyms are used in this book.

ACM	Association for Computing Machinery
ANSI	American National Standards Institute
API	Application Program Interface
CGI	Computer Graphics Interface
CMU	Carnegie-Mellon University
CWI	Centrum voor Wiskunde en Informatica
FMS	Frame Management System
GINO	Graphical Input/Output (graphics package)
GKS	Graphical Kernel System
GSPC	Graphic Standards Planning Committee of SIGGRAPH
ICL	International Computers Limited
IPC	Inter Process Communication
ISO	International Organization for Standardization
IT	Information Technology
ITC	Information Technology Centre (Carnegie-Mellon University)
MIT	Massachusetts Institute of Technology
MMI	Man-Machine Interface or Interaction
NDC	Normalized Device Coordinates
NFS	Network File Server
OI	Operator Interface
PARC	Palo Alto Research Centre of Xerox Corporation
PHIGS	Programmer's Hierarchical Interactive Graphics System
PIT	Programmable Input Translation
RAL	Rutherford Appleton Laboratory

RPC	Remote Procedure Call
SIGGRAPH	ACM Special Interest Group on Computer Graphics
TIP	Terminal Interface Package
UI	User Interface
VDI	Virtual Device Interface
VGTS	Virtual Graphics Terminal Service
WMS	Window Management System
WYSIWYG	What You See Is What You Get

Accelerator:

an alternative interaction technique (eg for command invocation) which is faster to use, but may be harder to learn or remember; for example, use of a reserved mouse-button instead of selection from a menu. Accelerators are typically provided for frequently used commands.

Accent:

a message-based distributed operating system kernel, originally developed on PERQ workstations by Carnegie-Mellon University's Spice project.

Adobe imaging model:

the imaging model provided with the PostScript language [1] from Adobe Systems, described in [69].

Application Program Interface (API):

the software interface between an application program and the window manager.

Asynchronous:

(of events, notifications etc): occurring at times unpredictable by the recipient. For example, in relation to input, the term is typically used to describe systems in which the window manager notifies an application by a software interrupt that input has been received from the operator.

BitBlt:

bit boundary block transfer; see RasterOp and [49].

Bitmap:

an image composed of an array of pixels, and in a machine-related sense, an area of memory where such an array is stored.

Bravo:

a display-based WYSIWYG document editor developed at Xerox PARC for the Alto workstation.

Canvas:

the abstract object on which an application can draw in the SunDew system.

Caret:

the "∧" symbol used to mark the point of insertion in some text editors.

Cedar:
an integrated program development environment developed at Xerox PARC.

Cedar graphics model:
forerunner of the Adobe imaging model [69].

Child window:
a window directly subordinate to another (its parent), in a hierarchical window system.

Click:
the action of pressing and quickly releasing a button within some time interval to cause an input event. For example on a mouse a button click is distinct from dragging or drawing actions while a button is held down.

Client:
an application program which requests services from the window manager.

Cluster:
a group of *pads* corresponding to a window on the Rainbow terminal.

Computer Graphics Interface (CGI):
a proposed ISO standard defining the functionality required between a graphics system and a device.

CORE:
a graphics system developed by the Graphic Standards Planning Committee of ACM SIGGRAPH [24].

Courteous windows:
windows which save and restore the images of any windows or their parts that they obscure.

Covered window paradigm:
windows may overlap on the display, one window thus (partially) obscuring the contents of another.

Cursor:
a visible representation on a display of the position of a graphical input device, which follows the movement of the device.

Cut and paste:
the ability to select output from an application running in one window and to supply it as input to an application running in another window. In editors, the inter- or intra-document movement of text.

Damage repair:
restoring a window to its current appearance when it becomes (partially or totally) uncovered.

Desktop metaphor:

likening windows to pieces of paper on a desk. A window may be on top of another window just as one piece of paper may be on top of another. Windows can be moved around the screen and shuffled, just as pieces of paper can on a desktop.

Display list, display file:

a set of commands, for example line drawing and character drawing commands, generating a picture. The term is normally associated with vector displays, in which a picture is maintained on a screen by repeated regeneration by a display processor, from a stored display list.

Double click:

two consecutive clicks (q.v.) occurring within a certain time interval. In some systems, single and double clicks have different (possibly related) meanings.

Events:

input data normally generated by input actions, for example depressing a mouse button.

Fixup:

the process of recreating the image of an obscured portion of a window. A common example is scrolling a partially obscured window by moving the image. This could be achieved by moving the unobscured part of the window and *fixing up* the portion which was previously obscured.

Geometry pipeline:

a sequence of geometric transformations (including clipping) to which coordinate data are subjected.

Gino: GINO-F:

a graphics package developed by the CAD Centre which became a *de facto* standard in the UK. It encompasses input and 3D graphical output.

GKS:

the Graphical Kernel System. An ISO International Standard (ISO 7942) for computer graphics, providing 2D graphical output and input [28].

GKS-3D:

an extension of GKS to include 3D graphics. This standard is currently under development [29].

Grouping:

a collection of objects which can be manipulated as a single entity.

Guarded button:

a protected button. Before the button can be activated, the guard must be removed by a click. If a second click does not activate the button within some time interval, the button returns to the guarded state. The Cedar system used this concept.

Icon:
a small pictogram capable variously of representing windows, operations, operands, processes or process status.

Imaging model:
a set of graphics primitives, and the protocol for their display.

Input model:
a set of input primitives and modes, and associated protocol.

Inter Process Communication (IPC):
a communications mechanism and protocol between separate processes, possibly on different processors, usually implemented by message-passing.

Lightweight processes:
processes which have only small overheads for context switching; commonly a group of lightweight processes share a single address space.

Listener:
the window which currently receives input.

Mode:
a state of the system, sometimes invisible to the user, and usually lasting for a period of time, which causes input actions to be interpreted in a particular way. Commonly the same input action has different effects in different modes.

Mouse ahead:
generating input from the mouse buttons in advance of the application being ready to process such input.

Name stripe:
see title bar.

Object-oriented language:
a programming language consisting of a collection of *objects* (containing data) that receive *messages* identifying functions to be performed and any further operands required. Each object has a set of messages it can understand, called *methods*. Objects are grouped into classes, which themselves may be a subset of other classes. Smalltalk [21] embodies an object-oriented language.

Operator:
see user.

Operator interface:
the interface between the operator and the window manager.

Overlapping window paradigm:
see covered window paradigm.

Parent window:
that window which is the next level up from a given (child) window, in a hierarchical windowing system.

PHIGS:
> Programmer's Hierarchical Interactive Graphics System, a standard under development within ISO [6].

Pointing device:
> an input device, such as the mouse. Input from the pointing device is frequently guided by feedback from the display.

Pop-up menu:
> a menu that appears on demand, at or near the current cursor position, and disappears when an item has been selected.

Port:
> an inter process communication channel.

PostScript:
> a Forth-like page description programming language [1], developed by Adobe Systems Inc., to describe the appearance of text, images and graphics material on a printed page efficiently.

Pull-down menu:
> a variant of pop-up menu which appears when a mouse button is pressed over a fixed menu item. The pull-down menu appears to hang downwards, like a roller blind, from the fixed item.

RasterOp:
> an operation for merging rectangular source and destination bitmaps. Each pixel in the final destination bitmap is a logical combination (eg *and, or*) of the corresponding pixels in the source and the initial destination bitmaps. The source and destination bitmaps may overlap.

Retained (cached) windows:
> windows whose contents are remembered by the window manager for purposes such as damage repair.

Remote Procedure Call (RPC):
> a mechanism enabling a client process to call a procedure in a server process, where client and server are not in the same address space and, indeed, may be located on physically separate systems connected by a network.

Rubber band:
> a technique used to give feedback to an operator. A rubber band object is an object whose geometry at any time varies to reflect the state of the input devices controlling it.

Scroll bar:
> a region of a window used to control scrolling of the window's contents.

Smalltalk:
> an early example of a window-based environment developed at Xerox PARC [21, 27].

Sneak path:
   a feedback path which short-circuits the normal user→application→user path. For example, echoing of the currently selected menu item by the window manager would be a sneak path.

SunTools:
   a layer in the SunWindows window manager [61].

Synchronous:
   (of events, notifications etc): occurring in response to requests from the recipient.

Tiled window paradigm:
   individual windows do not overlap on the display.

Title bar:
   the area at the top of a window provided by many systems where the system or application can put information that identifies the window.

Trigger:
   a physical input device that an operator can use to indicate significant moments in time. Firing a trigger typically generates input events.

TTY emulator:
   a software subsystem which emulates a teletype in a window.

Type ahead:
   generating input from the keyboard in advance of the application being ready to process such input.

Typescript:
   a complete transcript of a TTY session.

User:
   user or **operator** is used to specify the person who uses an already-defined application by sitting at a workstation and interacting with it.

User Interface Management System (UIMS):
   a system which allows the user interface to an application to be defined separately from the application itself. Such systems often allow rapid prototyping of user interfaces.

Viewport:
   in a *conventional graphics system*, that area of the display screen onto which output is mapped. In a *window management system*, a panel or pane of a window into which an application maps output.

Virtual Device Interface (VDI):
   now called Computer Graphics Interface (CGI).

Window:

> in a *conventional graphics system*, that portion of the user coordinate space that is mapped onto the viewport. In a *window management system*, a virtual area associated with an application which is mapped to the display screen under the control of the window manager.

Window descriptor:

> information associated with a window giving the window's size and attributes.

Wireframe:

> a method of representing objects where only the edges are drawn.

Index

EurographicSeminars
Tutorials and Perspectives
in Computer Graphics

Editors: **G. Enderle, D. Duce**

User Interface Management Systems

Proceedings of the Workshop on User Interface Management Systems held in Seeheim, FRG, November 1–3, 1983

Editor: **G. E. Pfaff**

1985. 69 figures. XII, 224 pages.
ISBN 3-540-13803-X

Contents: Subgroup Reports. – Role, Model, Structure and Construction of a UIMS. – Dialogue Specification Tools. – Interfaces and Implementations of UIMS. – User's Conceptual Model.

Eurographics Tutorials '83

Editor: **P. J. W. ten Hagen**
1984. 164 figures. XI, 425 pages.
ISBN 3-540-13644-4

Contents: Introduction to Computer Graphics (Part I). – Introduction to Computer Graphics (Part II). – Introduction to Computer Graphics (Part III). – Interactive Techniques. – Specification Tools and Implementation Techniques. – The Graphical Kernel System. – Case Study of GKS Development. – Surface Design Foundations. – Geometric Modelling. – Fundamentals – Solid Modeling: Theory and Applications.

Springer-Verlag
Berlin Heidelberg
New York Tokyo

Springer

G. Enderle, K. Kansy, G. Pfaff

Computer Graphics Programming

GKS – The Graphics Standard

1984. 93 figures, some in color.
XVI, 542 pages. (Symbolic Computation, Subseries Computer Graphics). ISBN 3-540-11525-0

The book covers computer graphics programming on the base of the Graphical Kernel System GKS.
GKS is the first international standard for the functions of a computer graphics sytem. It offers capabilities for creation and representation of two-dimensional pictures, handling input from graphical workstations, structuring and manipulating pictures, and for storing and retrieving them. It presents a methodological framework for the concepts of computer graphics and establishes a common understanding for computer graphics systems, methods and applications. This book gives an overview over the GKS concepts, the history of the GKS design and the various system interfaces. A significant part of the book is devoted to a detailed description of the application of GKS functions both in a PASCAL and a FORTRAN-language environment.

Springer-Verlag
Berlin Heidelberg
New York Tokyo

From the reviews
"A thorough introduction... Very well written, with excellent figures..."   *Choice*

Springer